D
545
.S66
J64
1999

Johnson, Douglas V.

Soissons, 1918.

28185

$29.95

DATE			

Soissons, 1918

C. A. Brannen Series

Soissons
1918

DOUGLAS V. JOHNSON II
AND ROLFE L. HILLMAN, JR.

Texas A&M University Press
COLLEGE STATION, TEXAS

All maps adapted by Dan B. Barnett; all diagrams created by Douglas V. Johnson II,
drawn by Dan B. Barnett

The paper used in this book meets the minimum requirements
of the American National Standard for Permanence
of Paper for Printed Library Materials, z39.48-1984.
Binding materials have been chosen for durability.
(∞)

Library of Congress Cataloging-in-Publication Data

Johnson, Douglas V.

Soissons, 1918 / Douglas V. Johnson II and Rolfe L. Hillman, Jr.

p.   cm. —(C. A. Brannen series ; no. 3)

Includes bibliographical references and index.

ISBN 0-89096-893-4 (alk. paper)

1. World War, 1914–1918—Campaigns—France—Soissons.   2. World
War, 1914–1918—United States.   3. Soissons (France)—History,
Military.   I. Hillman, Rolfe L.   II. Title.   III. Series.

D545.S66J64   1999

940.4'34—dc21   99-22548

CIP

Passant

In the Forêt de Retz, the point of assembly for the troops counterattacking southwest of Soissons, the French erected a monument depicting a lady veiled in mourning. In one hand she holds a sword, in the other a laurel extended as though to crown a victor. The inscription, "Passant, arrête-toi," can be translated as "Passing Stranger, Pause Here."

In Memorium

Colonel Rolfe L. Hillman, Jr., U.S. Army (Retired), began research on the Battle of Soissons with the intent to produce an article for *Military History Quarterly*. His research produced a great more material than he anticipated, and then his health failed. When I first met him to consider taking over, he gave me full authority to modify whatever I saw fit and insisted I be listed as coauthor (even though editor might better fit what I was contracting to do). As I was bringing the draft to a state I was somewhat more satisfied with, he called to ask me to be certain to acknowledge his son Rolfe's extensive contribution to the research, and to advise me of a new article and a book that might have some pertinence. Before I could bring him the revised drafts of the introduction and conclusion, which I had completely rewritten, he died quietly in his sleep. This work is, therefore, dedicated to its primary author:

COLONEL ROLFE L. HILLMAN, JR.
Infantry, U.S. Army—Husband, Father, Leader, Author.

Contents

Illustrations

Maps and Figures

Maps

Figures

Preface

Leading men in battle is serious business—there is nothing in the human experience more serious except for one's relationship with God Almighty. Successful command in combat is, therefore, the ultimate measure of merit for higher command. However, if the so-called Peter Principle is operative at all—and there is ample evidence to support its claims—promotion between levels of command needs to be considered most carefully. War is the most unforgiving arena. As Elliot Jacques and others have established, there are distinctly different forms of competence required at different organizational levels. This suggests there is room for the Peter Principle to be operative in military operations. Good division and lower-level commanders do not necessarily make good corps or army commanders—positions where managerial skills are of much greater importance. Nevertheless, it is important that higher-level commanders have experienced the horrors of close combat in order that they will be sensitive to that horror and manage their campaigns with that grim reality ever in view.

This book is written first to tell the tale of an often forgotten battle. It is a battle absent from many lists of engagements in which the American Expeditionary Forces (AEF) fought, absent from most British accounts, and, ironically, from the plentitude of accounts of World War I armored warfare. Other American divisions participated in the Aisne-Marne campaign, but the 1st and 2d Divisions were essentially the main attack and their story deserves special attention.

Second, it is written to examine the AEF's first major offensive operation. This battle was the first true measure of the AEF's ability to fight at the basic organizational level, the division. Everything up to this battle consisted of battalion or regimental fights, with the exception of the 2d Division fight at Château-Thierry. That battle involved the division in offensive operations, but it began as a meeting engagement—an emergency stopgap operation. Soissons was supposed to be a carefully planned, deliberate attack. It's genesis lay in a message from Field Marshal Ferdinand Foch to Maj. Gen. Pierre Emile Berdoulat on June 14, 1918. At that stage of the war, a month's planning time was plenty.

Third, this book is written to examine the manner in which the AEF was commanded in battle. Combat leadership experience was thin in the American army prior to World War I. Most of the men who became the senior officers of the AEF had seen some combat either in Cuba, the Philippines, or in Mexico. Those with combat experience in Cuba had seen operations approximating what was taught in the service schools and described in textbooks. Those with Philippines experience participated in a different version of Indian fighting in a totally foreign environment. Some few had been fortunate enough to observe the end of the Russo-Japanese War, a war whose lessons tended to be overlooked because the combatants were so different from the observers. Then there was the Punitive Expedition to Mexico. But it, too, was little more than a replay of frontier Indian fighting with a rather different political twist. In short, no one in the American army in 1917 had anything like the experience of European combat. They had to learn fast, and from foreigners.

In telling the story of this battle, the authors have tried to keep before the reader a mixture of accurate history and a personal feel for the battle. Soldiers' observations are valid for their small piece of the action but they rarely have any appreciation of what is happening for the unit as a whole, and certainly not for the next higher level. As the reader will see, even senior commanders seldom had a very good picture of what was happening in their sectors. Today the U.S. Army is moving toward a revolutionary new force based upon the incredible developments in computer technology. Nevertheless, the first requirement continues to be "Comprehensive Situational Awareness," or knowing the truth in battle. The much-publicized efforts to create a "digitized" force are an attempt to permit commanders to know exactly where their units are and what state they are in simply by calling up the correct display on their computers. If this system works, battlefield communications can be cut some 60 percent. But knowing where units are and what condition they and their soldiers are in is only part of the challenge of command. Ultimately, even if all the electronics work, command in combat is still going to require commanders to go out on the ground and see and be seen by those who do the killing and suffer the most casualties. Some things cannot be done by remote control.

The authors, both combat veterans, hope this mixture of motives and methods will convey a reasonably well-rounded picture of what actually took place (as best they can reconstruct it). Records for the two American divisions involved in this battle are spotty. Some units, like the 28th Infantry, have substantial records, whereas other units have almost none. We have relied on German records to fill in some of the gaps, accepting the fact that those records have distortions and gaps as well. The German records are especially instructive because the defender has the luxury of knowing the ground being defended, and he has time to establish communications nets and observation posts that together allow him a better feel for most of the action. Then there are the personal accounts. If these seem ugly and gruesome, please keep in mind that combat is exactly so.

Rolfe would have thanked all of the following for their contributions of time, imagination, research assistance, reproduction efforts, letter writing, critiques, and advice: National Archives—Tim Nenninger; Cantigny/1st Division Museum—John Votaw; U.S. Army Military History Institute—Dick Sommers, Dave Keough, and John Sloanaker; U.S. Marine Corps Historical Center—Brig. Gen. Edwin Simmons (Ret.); Professors Allan R. Millett, Douglas Porch, and Edward "Mac" Coffman, whose efforts brought Rolfe and me together; Mrs. Ned Beard for sharing her brother's (L. T. Janda) papers and the Thomason monograph; Tom Gudmestad; George MacGillivray; Patrice Demanais; Captain Bazerque, French Ministry of Defense Archives; Maj. Gen. John R. D. Cleland; Mrs. Beverly McMasters, U.S. Army Infantry School; and Mrs. Karla Norman, Combined Arms Research Library, U.S. Army Command and General Staff College. Particular thanks are due his son, Rolfe III, for an immense effort in all kinds of support to his Dad and encouragement to me. We both owe a special vote of thanks to Texas A&M University Press for having faith in the two of us through considerable uncertainty.

There are doubtless dozens of others who deserve thanks but whose names are buried in Rolfe's notes. To them, my apologies. All the errors, omissions, and problems of interpretation are mine.

Douglas V. Johnson II, Ph.D.
Lieutenant Colonel, Field Artillery
U.S. Army (Retired)

Soissons, 1918

Introduction
The War to Date

In 1914 all Europe was expecting war. But not quite yet, and certainly not from the assassination of some poorly regarded Austrian archduke. The event was so minor that European royalty went about their late-summer vacations without significant concern. Unfortunately, the delicate balance of power and prestige that had kept the peace to that point could not be so casually neglected, and all Europe fell into war.

Austrian demands upon Slavic Serbia raised ethnic anger in Slavic Russia. Russian mobilization plans did not allow for partial mobilization against Austria only; Russia felt compelled to mobilize against both Austria and Germany. Russian mobilization was therefore a threat to Germany but German war plans called for an initial thrust against France. Great Britain refused to be forthright about its semiformal commitments to France and ultimately waited until the wheels of war were already grinding inexorably forward before making its position clear, using the pretext of German violation of Belgian neutrality. France, burning to avenge its defeat in the Franco-Prussian War of 1870–71 and to recover the lost provinces of Alsace and Lorraine, was tied to Russia for their mutual protection. War came because no one in a position of authority could muster the courage to act decisively in time to stop the first troop movement, after which everything unfolded according its own logic.

The German invasion of France, following the scheme set forth in the vaunted Schlieffen Plan, was halted at the Marne River north of Paris by a combination of desperate French battle management and German exhaustion. On the eastern front, the Russian steamroller came apart under inept Russian battle management and adept German hammering in the classic Battle of Tannenberg.[1] There followed a succession of desperate but very effective German maneuvers that nullified the Russian threat for a time. Austria invaded Serbia only to be humiliated and driven back. The Battle of the Frontiers along the western front ended and the trenches were dug from the English Channel to the Alps, setting the stage for all that followed.

The first year of war, 1914, was mercifully brief but stupefying. After the Battle of the Frontiers, finding themselves too weak to move decisively and—by late in the year—very low on ammunition, the opposing armies sat through the winter, fraternized across the newly created no-man's-land, and awaited the decisions of the high commands.

Italy stood on the sidelines in 1914, invoking Germany's initial aggression as the reason for not honoring its treaty with its former Allies Austria and Germany. But Allied pressure and tempting offers in terms of postwar settlements sufficed to bring Italy to the Allied side in 1915. The consequences were disastrous for the Italians. Beginning in 1915, the Italian army bled itself almost white in a constant succession of battles along the Isonzo River. These battles netted Italy nothing but a steadily growing casualty list—and material for an obscure American writer, Ernest Hemingway, to make his literary mark on the world.

The Germans continued their successes on the Russian front, but these were not quite enough to bring the war there to closure. Part of the reason was that the French and British both fielded hugely expanded armies that attacked clumsily, but with great weight, several times in 1915. The force of those attacks was sufficient to bring German forces from the eastern front to the west, thus weakening the Germans' eastern effort. But neither side fully understood the transformation that had taken place in the nature of war and their preparations thus continued to be inadequate. By the end of 1915, however, the reality of the war was becoming clearer to all belligerents.

The basic problem for the Allies was that German forces stood on French and Belgian soil—a lot of it, and some of it extremely valuable from the point of view of its industrial value, all honor aside. Consequently, Allied forces in France and Belgium felt obliged to attack to drive the invader out. Germany needed a clear decision on the eastern front so as to be able to deal with the principal threat to its heartland: the French and British armies. Austria, who had started it all, was performing so poorly that German forces had to be diverted to keep the Austrians in the fight even against the Italians. Meanwhile, the British, loath to commit all their forces to the meat grinder in France, sought to strike indirectly at the Austro-German entente through Iraq, Turkey, and Palestine. Efforts in the Iraqi theater failed miserably, with one British Army falling into the none-too-gentle hands of the Turks and Iraqis. In Palestine, however, the British under Gen. Edmund H. H. Allenby showed promise, making some headway. In an effort to neutralize Germany's ally Turkey, the British launched an attack toward Constantinople, up the Dardenelles, and onto the Gallipoli Peninsula with British and Australian and New Zealand (ANZAC) forces, only to become mired in a brutal, if mutual, slaughter.

By 1916, most of the belligerents understood that the war was going to be a bloodbath. Peripheral strategies had proven to be costly failures, so—in the absence of a miracle weapon that no one seemed able to produce—waging attrition warfare appeared to be the only way out. But that meant one had to have favorable exchange ratios. The Germans tried first at Verdun but failed to do better than about one-to-one at a cost of five hundred thousand casualties on each side—give or take a few tens of thousands. The British, partly to relieve pressure on the French, then launched the first of two memorable attacks—memorable primarily because of their seemingly suicidal nature. The opening day of the Somme offensive cost the British Army more than fifty thousand casualties. Although the Germans got off relatively easy on day one, in the end the exchange ratio was again almost even. On the eastern front, the Russians enjoyed their one success of the war, Gen. Aleksei A. Brusilov's offensive. This too was launched to help take German pressure off the beleaguered French. It succeeded brilliantly but, like most battles of the war, was pushed too long. German counterattacks eventually recovered all that had been lost at enormous cost to the Russians. The Alps forestalled any significant developments on that front, but Gen. August von Mackensen ran wild in the Balkans, destroying the Serbians and the Rumanians—who had incautiously entered the war on the Allied side just as the Allied efforts for the year were failing. The year ended with everyone having a clear-eyed view that focused combat power was the only solution to the stalemate in the trenches and that focusing was best achieved by massing artillery above all.

By 1917, all of the armies in Europe had built their artillery establishments to monstrous size, and they had mobilized their economies to produce guns and shells in huge numbers. French confidence in 1917 rode on the shoulders of Gen. Robert Nivelle, who enthusiastically threw French armies against fully alerted and well-prepared German positions in the Chemin des Dames sector. The slaughter of French soldiery was so great that the *poilus* refused to attack again.

The Nivelle offensive conditioned the French Army for the remainder of the war and bears some explanation. With most of their offensives stymied and having suffered enormous losses in defense of Verdun, the French high command cast about for someone who could plan and execute a truly successful attack. Robert Nivelle wormed his way to the forefront and was given massive resources with which to work. He would have played well on CNN but his planning skills were much less than the situation required, and his sense for security was miserable. The Germans easily discovered everything about the offensive and ruined it in a matter of days. Despite his promise to pursue his objectives only if success was attained easily and early, Nivelle continued the offensive long after it should have been aborted. General Charles M. E. Mangin, one of his subordinates, continued his attacks relentlessly with only mounting French casualties to show for it. Following that failure, Mangin was sent into limbo in Paris. General Henri Philippe Pétain was called in to replace Nivelle after disastrous losses brought the *poilus* to a state of "collective indiscipline." Pétain quelled the mutiny and worked hard to restore morale. He also promised no more such offensives. If the *poilus* were going to be asked to attack again, it would only be with massive artillery support and for strictly limited objectives.

In the second most infamous battle of modern military history, Gen. Sir Douglas Haig threw the British Army into the Passchendaele campaign, only to see it too die in the mud. German efforts finally bore fruit on the eastern front as the combination of military defeat of the Russian armies and the insurgent political activity of Vladimir Lenin brought the Russian house of cards down in a heap.[2]

In April, 1917, Germany launched an unrestricted submarine campaign hoping to bring the Allies to their knees by sinking much-needed supplies. It seemed a safe bet at the time. German calculations of America's inability to intervene effectively were sound. The bulk of the tiny U.S. Army was deployed in Mexico and the Philippine Islands. It's strength was a joke when compared to the huge European armies, amounting to a pitiful 250,000. It's training was laughable compared to that of European armies, and its organization was that of a constabulary force fit only to chase *insurrectos* and *bandidos*. Besides, German submarines had demonstrated singular efficiency in interdicting commerce between the United States and Great Britain. That last problem would soon be solved by the intervention of an American admiral who convinced the British and Americans both that convoying was the only possible way to deal effectively with German submarines. His judgment proved correct, but what no one took into consideration was the paucity of available troop shipping. Of course with a mere 250,000 soldiers to transport, what did it matter? Nobody anywhere imagined that the United States was capable of raising an army of more than four million men in less than eighteen months. So what if they were not all well trained? Numbers were what mattered. After all, not every soldier actually fights. Who could have rationally calculated that the United States would ship more than two million of those soldiers to France and not lose a single one in transit to German submarines? Who could have predicted that such an amateur army would hurl its weight into the lines against the vaunted, if tired, German Army and eventually learn how to drive it from the battlefield? In April, 1917, the answer was "nobody."

The Americans began to arrive in June, 1917, and immediately paraded proudly down the Champs-Elysées to the cheers and tears of the Paris crowd. The American's numbers grew slowly at first, and they needed a great deal of training. By December, 1917, Frenchmen were wondering when the American Expeditionary Forces were going to join the actual fighting.

Strategic Overview, 1918

Immediately following the Russian armistice in December, 1917, the German high command began a race against time. The collapse of Russian forces in the east permitted the Germans to transfer major combat forces to the decisive western front. At the same time, there was famine and political upheaval on the German home front, and the Americans were accumulating strength with an accelerating speed that would make their inevitable impact felt. German strategy, shaped by mounting desperation but with a clear window of opportunity, was to end the war with a series of hammer-like offensives. These offensives were based on a new tactical doctrine that was developed in part from a treatise by a French officer on a new tactical system of concentrated artillery fire and decentralized movement—infiltration tactics. These were improved upon by the Germans with the brilliant orchestration of masses of supporting artillery, the brainchild of a reserve colonel of field artillery, Georg Bruchmueller. Beginning in March with Operation Michael, the German "Freedom Offensives" rocked the Allied armies, nearly splitting them apart physically and relationally, consuming Allied political confidence and carefully hoarded reserves of men and supplies. The German drives threatened both Paris and the Channel ports, but these tactical successes were purchased at the expense of the irreplaceable German reserves.[3]

The Allies profited unintentionally from the German offensives. So severe was the threat of defeat in March, 1918, that the Allies were finally driven to appoint and acknowledge the authority of a single commander for the western front: Marshal Ferdinand Foch. This was a wise, if political, choice, for it was Marshal Foch who sensed the culmination of the last German offensive, refused to be drawn in by the Germans's final lunge toward Paris, and ordered Allied forces to counterattack even before the collapse of the German attack was certain.

Operational Overview

In all, the Germans launched five offensives that spring. Their next to last offensive aimed at Paris, launched in May, 1918, penetrated deeply into the French lines and rushed forward to the Marne. They were slowed and eventually

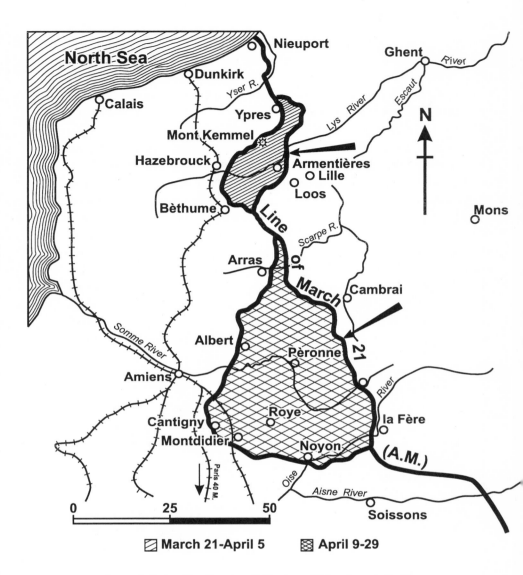

map 1. Ground Gained by German Offensives of March and April, 1918

stopped by a combination of actions that included their own logistical insufficiencies, the solid blocking action of American units near Château-Thierry, and the attacks of newly formed French tank units. The story of the "Rock of the Marne" is well known and needs no retelling here. Likewise, the certainty that combat units would outrun their logistics and stall as they forced the enemy back upon his own is, in important ways, the true story of the entire war.

The action of the French tank units is another story that must be told in detail elsewhere also, but is important here for two reasons. First, these units were significant contributors to the strength of the Allied shoulders of the penetration. As an example of their effectiveness, five Renault light tanks were launched into action south of Soissons in support of the Moroccans, who were desperately defending the Villers-Cotterêts forest. Although three fell victim to uncertain causes, two tanks pushed ahead and broke through the German lines. After blasting their way through the German 3d Battalion, 111th Infantry Regiment, which broke under their attack and rapidly withdrew, the two tanks passed on to attack the 2d Battalion, 111th Infantry Regiment and "encircled" it. "It required five battalions to pool their combat troops in order to dispose of these steel boxes," as quoted in the German after-action report.[4] Second, their performance in May paved the way for their much more numerous employment in July in support of the Soissons operation.

Tank attacks elsewhere along the flanks stymied the Germans and contributed significantly to their loss of momentum. The French use of tanks is seldom discussed in the English-language history of this period, but the Aisne-Marne campaign and the battle we know as Soissons saw the largest use

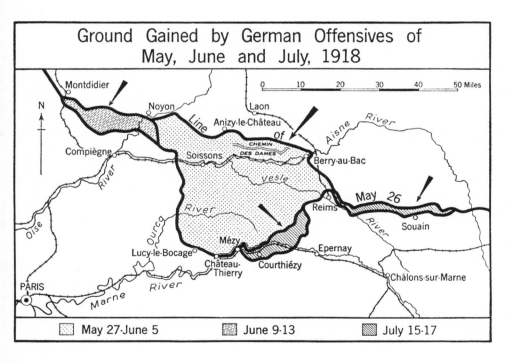

map 2. Ground Gained by German Offensives of May, June, and July, 1918

of French tanks in the war. The bulk of those tank forces were employed in the XX Corps sector, principally in support of the two American divisions, and therefore figure significantly in this story. The initial distribution of tanks was fairly even but the reserves were to be committed in support of the greatest success, which meant they should have gone to the American division sectors. However, the final distribution and strength remains a point of further research in French archives. Tank Groupement 11, for example, was reported delayed in its assembly area and a Renault battalion substituted in its place. However, the 2d Brigade, 1st Division, AEF, sent a message commending Groupement 11's assistance in the battle.[5] This is only one of a number of still unanswered questions surrounding this battle.

Once the May attack stalled, the German command found its forces positioned tantalizingly close to Paris but for the moment stuffed into a rather narrow salient whose shoulders had little give. As a matter of doctrine, the shoulders of a penetration are always the critical point. Even if the attacking force is able to penetrate the final enemy position, if it is unable to break the shoulders, it is in danger of being cut off. In this case, the German divisions in the tip of the salient were utterly dependent upon a supply line or line of communications whose central hub was Soissons, precariously close to the unyielding western shoulder. It took little in the way of basic staff analysis to see the vulnerability of the situation. Ludendorff noted in his memoirs, "In the attack on Rheims we reckoned on an enemy counteroffensive between the Aisne and the Marne, with Soissons as its principal objective." Although Ludendorff may be suspected of postwar revisionism on many points, other German sources confirm him on this one. Thus, it was hardly a surprise when a spy or traitor passed the word to the Germans that the French had decided to attack both sides of the salient with the particular purpose of severing that lifeline to the south. The information passed suggested that the attack might take place on July 14, France's Independence Day. This became a date of major concern for the Germans as their plans called for a resumption of their own offensive, code-named Strassenbau (Road Building), on July 15.[6]

Planning the Allied Counterattack

Foch aimed to attack the Germans as soon as their momentum was spent on his newly developed elastic defense, which had been adapted from the Germans. Seeing the obvious vulnerability of the salient, he pushed development of a converging attack employing the Group of Armies of the Reserve and the

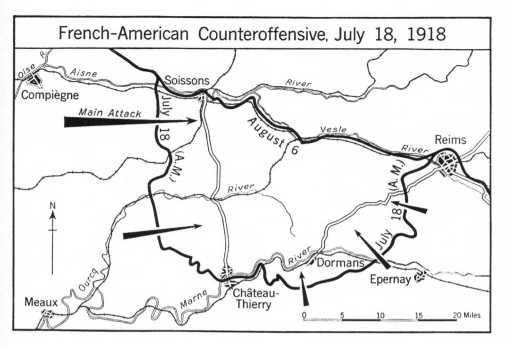

map 3. *French-American Counteroffensive, July 18, 1918*

Group of Armies of the Center. Tenth Army fell within the Group of the Armies of the Reserve and was chosen to make the main attack. Foch canvassed the Allied commanders for additional resources and gained the services of two American divisions and a brand new American corps headquarters for this huge counterattack. The 1st Division was available, rested, and supposedly the best-trained unit in the AEF. The 2d Division had learned most of its trade at Belleau Wood and Vaux and, when the planning began, was still in the line. The III Corps headquarters was too new to entrust with the management of a major operation, so it would serve only as the administrative manager for the two AEF divisions.[7]

In mid-July, General Mangin, nicknamed "The Butcher" for his heartless expenditure of men in relentless pursuit of his objectives, was ordered to deliver a counterstroke against the Germans pushing south toward Paris. His instrument was the Tenth Army. However, Tenth Army would not attack alone. All of the armies along the face of the Marne salient were to go over to the attack on the same day, although not at the same time. Tenth Army would aim for the jugular vein while the others would pummel the body.[8]

The French Tenth Army issued Operations Order No. 227, on July 16, 1918. The overall aim of the Allied attack was to rupture the German front between the Aisne and the Ourcq Rivers, pressing without hesitation toward Fère-en-Tardenois, the German logistical hub within the salient. Tenth Army's initial objective was a general line running through Chaudun, Hartennes, the plateaus north of Fère-en-Tardenois, Arcis-le-Ponsart, and Rosnay.[9] The primary objective for XX Corps, one of Tenth Army's five corps, was the line Saconin-et-Breuil–Chaudun–Vierzy, and the secondary objective was the plateau between Charcrise and Oulchy-le-Château. If the Allies could seize the first objective, they would break the German initial defensive line and be able to place long-range artillery fires on the German line of communications. If they could seize the second, they would have their hands around the Germans's throat. The three divisions in XX Corps's first line, two American and one Moroccan, would be followed by two French divisions in reserve.

Mangin's Tenth Army would attack eastward from positions southwest of Soissons with the purpose of threatening or severing the line of communications to the forty German divisions stuffed into the Marne salient. Supply of those forces required twenty-two trains per day, all of which had to pass through Soissons. If the German divisions could not be trapped by such a maneuver, they would at least be forced into morale-shattering retreat. The German spring offensives were touted to the German soldiery as the final necessary sacrifices that would bring the war to an end on favorable terms. A major reversal could only signal impending defeat or an unbearable prolongation of the agony.[10]

TERRAIN

From ground level, the view to the east showed only a rolling plateau, almost bare of trees, with many fields of waist-high wheat. There was no apparent complex of trenches, certainly nothing similar to those lines that had remained fixed for months or years and created a major barrier to forward movement. The final objective, six miles to the east—the road and rail network running south from Soissons in the valley of the Crise River—was hidden by the gently sloping terrain.

From the railroad and highway center at Soissons, the railroad to Paris ran south, then veered to the southwest across Tenth Army's front. The road from Soissons to Château-Thierry, the city located at the tip of the German salient, continued straight south. Another road of prime importance was the

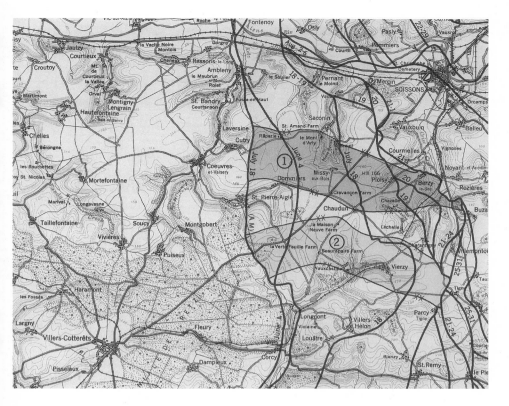

map 4. XX Corps Attack Zone showing daily advances

Soissons–Paris road. That road ran directly southwest, crossing Mangin's Tenth Army front in Maj. Gen. Pierre Emile Berdoulat's XX Corps zone from top right to bottom left—far from the jump-off line of the American 1st Division but crossing the American 2d Division's zone right at the jump-off line. Only an overhead view would show the true military difficulty of traversing that plateau.

A series of formidable ravines containing villages with solid masonry buildings, woods, marshlands, large chalk caves, and steep, rocky slopes cut across the plateau. Disposed transversely to the advance of the three divisions scheduled to conduct Berdoulat's attack, there was no feasible way to avoid the ravines. There were four major ravines, one each at Missy, Ploisy, Chazelle, and Vierzy. General Mangin, fully understanding the difficulty posed by these ravines, dispatched special instructions to I Corps, located north of XX Corps, and to the 153d Division, the right flank division covering XX Corps's northern flank, telling them, "It is important that the attack of the . . .153d . . . progress at the same rate as the divisions advancing on Chaudun . . . attack across open country . . . [and] avoid the deep ravines. Any other maneuver requires too much time."[11]

Tactical Overview — German Preparations

German planning for Operation Strassenbau called for a thrust toward Paris, with the intermediate aim being the capture of Reims, the anchor of the eastern shoulder of the salient. The Germans hoped the attack would consume remaining French reserves, which would in turn destroy or finally cripple the French army. Then, once those objectives had been achieved, the guns and reserves would turn back to Flanders and the British and destroy them in turn.[12]

Curiously, the Germans paid no attention to the western shoulder of the penetration. Short of practically everything, they had to bank on the force of their attack being so strong that the French would have to pull forces from their flank positions to block the road to Paris. The Germans were conscious of their weaknesses and were struggling to manage their dwindling resources. On July 17, for example, the 94th Reserve Brigade, in position on the western face of the salient, reported, "Our troops are no longer in possession of their full combat power. They need replacements and rest—about 6 weeks." Replacements would be few and in six weeks German plans would be wrecked beyond recovery. But the German high command had begun to substitute wishful thinking for clear-headed analysis.[13]

More than that, the Germans had been careless—and this time the French were more than ready for them. Second Lt. Herbert Sulzbach, a German artillery officer with the crack 9th Infantry Division wrote, "15 July At 1:10 am on the dot . . . in just the same way as the three and a half years of static warfare up to 21 March 1918, became commonplace, these offensives have lost all their novelty. . . . The first thousand French who have been taken prisoner . . . I talk to some of them and find it strange to hear that our plans for an offensive are supposed to have been accurately known for the last ten days."[14]

Although the Germans ultimately crossed the Marne for a short distance, it was obvious any further movement toward Paris was simply going to place those forces into a smaller and increasingly vulnerable sack. Schulzbach's division was an assault division and had always dashed forward but, "Strangely enough, we have thus far received no orders to move forward. . . . [I]f a giant attack like this does not succeed straight off, it is all over." The shoulder at Reims proved to be quite solid. The successful French defense stymied the German attack and for the moment the entire German strategy lay trembling in the balance. Should they renew their attempt to push on toward Paris? Should they simply hold in place and then shift the weight of their remaining artillery and few reserves to one final attack against the British as planned? Or . . . ? Before they could decide, Foch struck.[15]

As previously noted, the Germans were alerted to an impending Allied attack by a possible traitor who was close to the French general staff. Shortly before the attack, they were warned again by deserters from frontline units. The German Ninth Army headquarters received a telephone message from Army Group Crown Prince at 7:05 P.M., July 11, 1918, noting that deserters reported that an attack was scheduled to take place about July 15. This Army Group message directed subordinate commands to take detailed countermeasures, specifically including antitank measures. Specific divisions were designated for counterattack and were allocated to the defending corps' rear areas. But all of this took place while the principal German focus was on preparations for their own offensive, and little preparation was actually undertaken. Although heavy activity was noted along the western shoulder of the salient, German air reconnaissance was unable to gain any useful information indicating the normal massing of forces for an attack from the Villers-Cotterêts forest.[16]

Tactical Overview—Allied Preparations

While the Germans were generally aware of French intentions, perceptive German field commanders near the Soissons shoulder noted that vigorous French activity was clearly directed at securing favorable attack positions—and so it was. On June 20, Mangin developed his "Plan of Action," which identified its First Phase as the seizure of a bridgehead "on the far side of the COEUVRES Brook." This would in turn "provide an easy and rapid take-off point . . . and will insure the best means for employment of tanks." A brief look at any map or terrain sketch will make clear why this was done. Coeuvres Brook (shown on American Battle Monuments Commission maps as the Retz Creek) lay between steep valley slopes and it was thus a substantial barrier to eastward movement, especially for tanks. Mangin reported to his immediate superior, Gen. Marie Emile Fayolle, commander of the Group of Armies of the Reserve, on July 13, "we have progressed beyond the SAVIERES stream . . . assuring a bridgehead as favorable as possible." Actually, Savieres Creek flowed out of the 2d Division sector and through that of the neighboring French 38th Division. One of its minor branches did, in fact, obstruct passage through the 2d Division rear area. However, the movement beyond Coeuvres Brook permitted the tanks to pass uphill through the town of Cutry and deploy immediately behind the 1st Division on the nearly flat part of the plateau that runs from there to the edge of the Crise River valley.[17]

A July 13 entry in the German Seventh Army War Diary sounded a worrisome note. It stated that forty attacks had taken place along the army's front during the period June 6 to July 13. The entry noted that these ranged in size from battalion to multidivision efforts, and were supported by tanks and airplanes in addition to vigorous artillery employment. They had exacted a terrible toll from the defenders, who, it must be remembered, were simply holding the flank in preparation for what turned out to be the final major German offensive of the war. This flank-protection mission was supposed to be handled by units needing rest and recuperation. Holding its troops fighting qualities in very high regard, the German high command tried to spare them unnecessary burdens, clearly sensing the decay of talent and morale. Instead, those units "were materially shaken in strength and morale by these incessant and in part most intense and sanguine engagements, a fact . . . frequently pointed out by Army HQ." Indicative of the rapid decay of these units, the 115th Division, positioned astride the French XX Corps's southern boundary, reported on July 11 that it was "fully able to conduct the defense." However, the division's combat power deteriorated so rapidly that it was in the process of being relieved the night of the attack, July 17–18, having been found "incapable of repelling even the weakest enemy efforts." Indeed, Mangin's July 13 report noted that the German units replacing some of the worn-out frontline units were "not yet rested or replaced and their effective strength is feeble (40 to 50 men per company)."[18] Nevertheless, on July 15, the opening day of the Strassenbau offensive, the intelligence and operations officers of the German Crown Prince's staff reported: "On (July 15) the Soissons–Chateau-Thierry front, no change had occurred. The enemy had in line, or in reserve, 13 divisions, against which the Ninth Army had 14 divisions, and that part of the Seventh Army on this front, 6 divisions. The front seemed to be well guarded."[19]

Mangin's Deception

General Mangin was determined to spring a surprise upon the Germans but he had actually been practicing his new techniques for some time. He experimented with sharp local attacks as he nudged his Tenth Army gradually forward to secure the attack positions it required. Heavy artillery preparations had become standard practice since the failure of the Nivelle offensive. In his moves to restore French morale in 1917, General Pétain assured the mutinous French soldiery that they would not be asked to attack any position if adequate artillery support could not be provided. Consequently, French attacks for some time thereafter were preceded by massive local artillery preparations. Contrariwise, Mangin began local experiments with no artillery preparation at all—only a rolling barrage, with no registration of the barrage beforehand. Registering the guns meant actually firing each and every battery on aiming points close to the ultimate target so as to be certain of accurate fire. The practice was standard throughout all armies and was easily detected. Mangin's practice would necessarily sacrifice accuracy, but it was a price he was willing to pay. Under Mangin's scheme of maneuver, the first indication of an attack was a barrage landing on the enemy's first-line positions, where it would hold for perhaps five minutes or whatever length of time was thought necessary for the attacking infantry to close upon the enemy front line. Then the barrage would move forward at a normal rate of one hundred meters every two minutes if the ground was of average difficulty, every three or four minutes on difficult ground. Even if local German commanders understood this was a new style of attack, none expected the French to attempt it with an entire field army. Furthermore, in order to enhance the shock effect, Mangin directed that all units move into position at night and stay under cover during daylight hours. If one of the attacking divisions arrived late the last day and attacked from the march, so much the better.[20] Both American divisions arrived undetected by the Germans. But what did those divisions look like and how ready were they for the ordeal facing them?

German reports stressed the location and activity of the Allied field artillery as a key indicator of enemy intentions. When the guns moved forward, an attack was imminent. This activity had become a prime intelligence and warning indicator. But the French knew it as well. Mangin chose to reap a double reward from his new attack technique: By keeping the guns to the rear all available artillery fire would fall on the forward area (since that was all the farther much of it could range), and this stupefying barrage—fired without deep interdicting fires or registration—would multiply the shock effect upon the Germans. As the German XIII Royal Wurtemburg Army Corps (also known as Corps Watter after its commander) reported: "Up to about July 10 the French artillery kept within its normal strength. At this period a noteworthy increase in strength appeared . . . [h]owever, the impression of a defensive concentration on the enemy side remained unchanged. All of his artillery, especially the heavy and flat trajectory batteries were located far back."[21]

Just to emphasize the point, on July 14 General Fayolle issued a memorandum to the entire Group of Armies of the Reserve detailing extraordinary secrecy measures akin to those Hitler directed in his preparations for the 1944 Ardennes offensive. In essence, the entire army group was enjoined not to trust anyone not personally known to be reliable, to move only at night, to light no fires, and to report anything and anyone suspicious. It also meant that the guns would have to be moved forward rapidly once the attack got underway, a tactical maneuver almost certain to weaken the momentum of the attack if the enemy maintained coherent resistance. Also, deep interdiction fires would not be available to slow the arrival of enemy reinforcements.[22] Mangin was willing to take these risks but his need for surprise went further.

German reports for July 16 noted some successful French attacks in the area of the Villers-Cotterêts forest as well as some difficulty in flying reconnaissance over the Retz forest, which almost completely surrounded the town. On July 17 great French air strength was again noted in this area, precluding deep observation, but no particular traffic was noted around the railhead. The Germans noted that "There was no special sign pointing to a major attack . . . there was so much to argue against it," and cited the constant local attacks and artillery concentrations well to the rear as evidence. As part of the deception planning, Mangin made certain that this front continued to be moderately active—not enough to draw undue attention to French activity but enough to make movement and momentary strength changes more or less normal. The deception was working.[23]

CHAPTER I

The American Army in 1918

The First World War is so distant and so little written about from the American perspective that some review of the American Army that fought in that war is required. In 1918 there were really two American armies, one in the United States and one in France. The former was the training and replacement army, and the AEF in France constituted the deployed army. However, the distinction went further than just names. In France, officers wore the Sam Browne belt as a required part of their uniform, whereas it was frowned upon in the Continental United States (CONUS—a term that came into vogue after World War II but which serves here to help the reader distinguish between the two). As forward-deployed armies always do, the AEF considered itself the more important force, the cutting edge of American military power. Its distant successor in the 1960–89 period was often referred to as the "Imperial Seventh Army Europe." The AEF published its own regulations, established its own schools, promulgated its own policies, and became furious whenever the War Department acted in any way that was perceived to be less than 100 percent supportive. The CONUS army, on the other hand, struggled to be the replacement and training base and meet all the rapidly changing and expanding AEF requirements until Peyton C. March became the army chief of staff in March, 1918. Thereafter, and because it was desperately necessary, March imposed a new management system upon the CONUS army and the War Department to enable them better to perform their legitimate supporting functions while taking cognizance of the realities they faced.[1]

Training the Army

To understand the 1918 AEF, it is necessary to drop back to about 1910. Armies change after every war and it took until 1910 for the U.S. Army to recover from the Spanish-American War and the following suppression of the Philippine Insurrection. Because of legislation restricting the size of the Regular Army, volunteer regiments were a significant factor in that conflict and had to be relied upon after the war as well, particularly in the Philippines. The peculiarities of that war resulted in many National Guard units converting to volunteer organizations, with all the evils attendant therewith. In 1910 the Regular Army—the standing force of long-service professionals—which included the remnants of the force that subdued the Spanish Army in Cuba and that had mostly pacified the Philippine Islanders, held its first important summer maneuvers with several state National Guard organizations. New legislation had not only made this arrangement possible, it demanded that the Regulars make a commitment to training the National Guard. The maneuvers were extremely useful in revealing how poorly prepared the National Guard forces were for modern combat.[2]

Some things had been learned from the 1905 Russo-Japanese War, but not many. That war strongly suggested that machine guns were going to be a problem and that barbed wire was difficult to overcome. The combination of the two made the defense appear to be the stronger form of warfare, a message echoing all the way back to the American Civil War. But Japanese aggressiveness was the message most strongly reported, for that was what eventually brought them victory. Few counted the enormous cost in casualties or bothered to examine deeply alternative interpretations. When the success of Japanese aggressiveness was coupled with the universally admired French Army's school of the attack, the strength of the defense was quietly ignored in most armies. American officers, who felt a close kinship with the French, came to believe that an aggressive offensive philosophy was most congenial to American soldiers. The first *Field Service Regulations,* published in 1905, hinted strongly at this in the chief of staff's opening endorsement: "Every individual, from the highest commander to the lowest private, must always remember that inaction and neglect of opportunities will warrant more severe censure than an error in the choice of the means."[3]

Furthermore, Article V, "Combat," begins: "Combat is divided into two general classes, the offensive and the defensive. The defensive is divided into the purely passive defense and the temporary defense, which has for its object the assumption of the offensive at the first opportunity. Decisive results are obtained only by the offensive."[4]

But the offensive was difficult to control and made strenuous demands upon the leadership. Learning to control offensive operations takes practice—lots of it. Because the National Guard (which grew out of the militia) was and is only a part-time force with tightly limited training funds, it is seldom able to schedule all the practice time it needs, especially with larger formations. It is always criticized by the Regular Army for this inadequacy but when provided sufficient training funds and time, it usually does a quite good job. In 1910 the Regulars felt the National Guard was not up to the job. Gen. John J. Pershing's experiences in the Mexican theater did little to alter this prejudice. He held this prejudice so strongly, that when the AEF was forming, he insisted that each corps-sized unit be composed of two Regular Army divisions and two National Army divisions. (National Army divisions were created during the war and had no prior Regular Army or National Guard affiliation.) He felt National Guard divisions were so corrupted by hometown favoritism and bad training habits that they were barely worth the effort to train. There was some substance to his prejudice as suggested by the Inspector General reports on the 35th Division and its subsequent poor performance in battle. However, it was an insupportable position and was more off the mark than on it.[5]

The year 1910 is important because it was the first time the Regular Army made a concerted effort to train National Guard units to something approaching its own standards. Large numbers of National Guard soldiers had volunteered for the Spanish-American War, and their tactical deficiencies were as glaring as the managerial deficiencies manifested by the War Department. Some National Guard units were mobilized in 1916 to help secure the border with Mexico. The apparent lack of progress in training the National Guard was manifest and should have sent up a warning signal. But even if the nation's "strategic reserve" proved to be still ill-trained after six years of "attention" by the Regular Army, did it really matter? The war in Europe was several years old and showed only signs of the continued corruptness of Old Europe. A thoughtful staff officer might have asked this question, "If it takes two years to make a good soldier under the present system, then how long would America need to raise an army capable of meeting a European army? The calculus of the time would likely have produced an answer of "Two years for the soldiers, one year for the larger units, one year for the staff officers—About four years."

Throughout the nineteenth century, with the exception of the Civil War, the U.S. Army was little more than a rather small constabulary force whose primary tasks, after manning the nation's coastal defense batteries, were pacifying Indian tribes, quieting striking miners, providing earthquake relief, and other domestic activities. Largely because there was no external threat, training funds were sparse and training requirements for the Regular Army far exceeded those funds—leaving precious little for National Guard formations.

Every expansion found the War Department with an inadequate staff in terms of numbers and experience. Although the army had a fledgling general staff in 1917, the declaration of war on Germany found the War Department grossly unprepared. Although the general staff had an outline plan for training the army for a large-scale war, it scarcely envisioned training a force of the size needed for the impending endeavor.[6]

Historically, training in the American Army had been managed primarily in the unit, on the job, by the unit's noncommissioned officers (NCOs). The governing tactical doctrine was the infantry, cavalry, and artillery drill regulations, of which the infantry's were by far the most important. The first edition of the army's *Field Service Regulations* was an attempt to synthesize all the branch regulations in a way that provided senior officers—commanders and staff officers above brigade level—with general guidance for the employment of larger units in action. This regulation became the basis for the army's principal twentieth century doctrinal manual, Field Manual 100–5, *Operations*.

Once in France, General Pershing quickly developed the idea that every unit would pass through a three-stage training cycle. After arrival, everyone would be trained to standard in basic and specialist skills, which had proliferated with the changes in weaponry. Infantry companies in 1910 were concerned almost exclusively with M1903 Springfield rifles, bayonets, and pistols. By 1917 in France, the infantry had discovered the intricacies of several kinds of hand grenades, rifle grenades, trench mortars, heavy and light machine guns, flare pistols, telephone communications, wireless telegraph (TBS) and ground wireless telegraph (TFS), blinker, and buzzer systems—not to mention pigeons and tanks. Infantrymen knew a little about coordinating indirect fire by supporting field artillery but nothing approaching the highly complicated, carefully detailed manner in which they would need to orchestrate their movements on the modern battlefield. And there were airplanes, balloons, and poison gas to use or defend against. This meant careful use of camouflage, carefully planned deceptions, and personal protective measures. All in all, the Americans entered a completely different world when they arrived in France and rapid training in the basics alone was a formidable challenge.

The change in equipment brought concurrent changes in tactics and organization. It also meant that even the most experienced Regular soldier had to be retrained before he could train the new men. Some of that training was accomplished in CONUS, and Allied instructors were sent over to help. However, once units arrived in France, they still had to be brought up to Pershing's standards in individual and specialist training, then small-unit training. Once they were deemed ready, units would then be rotated into the trenches a battalion at a time, preferably in a quiet sector. After the entire division had experienced the trenches, division-sized maneuvers would be held and then . . . ?[7]

The training programs belonged to the division commanders and, except for some general guidance from the War Department, everyone assumed that the *Infantry Drill Regulations* and the *Field Service Regulations* were adequate for teaching the basics. Despite the translation and publication of Allied documents "for information," no other guidance existed. If all that was required of those regulations providing instruction in the basic "School of the Soldier"— that is, how to dress, march, and salute—they would have been fine. However, the sections on combat were very much out of date, although Pershing himself pronounced them adequate.[8]

Every division commander or officer scheduled to become one was sent to Europe for an orientation. During that visit they observed the staff procedures and tactical performance of Allied units. Pershing or his agents closely observed the visiting officers. Those found to be lacking the required vigor or the intellectual ability to comprehend the changes in warfare were quietly shuffled off to staff positions. Even so, training continued to be idiosyncratic, with each division commander in CONUS developing his own program. Once in France, however, the AEF imposed a standard training regime which, had time been available, would have proved valuable to soldiers and units alike.[9]

Manning the Army

Until March implemented a new training program in CONUS in March, 1918, when he became the new chief of staff, there was no design for a replacement system either. This lack of a functional replacement system has plagued the U.S. Army since its inception. It would only be solved briefly in this war, but the problems would continue into the Second World War, Korea, and Vietnam. In order to send full-strength units overseas, most units required "fillers" to make up for soldiers on details, in schools, sick—and a huge number became sick with mumps, flu, and a host of other diseases—or who were otherwise not available for overseas shipment. Since there was no replacement pool, the fillers were drawn from existing units in training, consequently disrupting those units' training cycles. The magnitude of this problem is best illustrated by the experience of the 86th Division, which trained more than eighty-seven thousand soldiers—almost four times the division's authorized strength—before it deployed to France. In World War II, the 106th Infantry Division blew apart in December, 1944, when hit by the Germans in the opening attacks of the Battle of the Bulge. That division, like many of its World War I counterparts, was levied three times for most of its trained infantrymen. Consequently, when it arrived in Europe it was anything but a trained division, even though it had been in the training cycle long enough to have been fully trained under normal circumstances. That this pernicious personnel policy lasted from the First

World War through the Second and into the latter part of the twentieth century is an indictment of the U.S. Army's attention to the lesson-learning process. It may be that memories of the Civil War died harder than we know—memories of entire units made up of men from the same region being decimated, and the accompanying trauma that shook the towns from which they had come. That is exactly what happened to the British Expeditionary Force in 1916 on the Somme. In any event, the army's personnel replacement policy changed only briefly when March established centralized replacement training centers. Unfortunately, the 1918 German spring offensives overwhelmed this efficient process and soon trained, partly trained, and eventually untrained soldiers were being shipped to France willy-nilly to meet the demand for replacements. They were even sent when sick with the flu. March calculated that most would survive and that losses en route would not compare with the possible consequences of larger shortages of infantry in fighting divisions in the field. Those were truly hard times.[10]

Equipping the Army

The basic equipment used by the U.S. Army was very good. The M1903 Springfield rifle was beloved by American soldiers and was at least the equal of any weapon on the European battlefield. The 1902 model 3-inch field gun was likewise the equivalent of the vaunted French 75-mm and German 77-mm field guns. But American production capacity, even though growing in response to Allied production demands, was incapable of producing the quantities necessary to equip the American Army while simultaneously sustaining the Allied armies. The consequence is clearly visible in photograph after photograph of American soldiers training with stick rifles, log cannons, and sawhorses. It is a testament to the men who went willingly into mortal combat with only the most rudimentary knowledge of the weapons upon which their lives depended. How much more effective might they have been had they been properly trained and equipped?[11]

For many American soldiers the full panoply of weaponry remained a partial mystery until they arrived in France. There they found themselves training with British Enfield rifles and Lewis or Vickers machine guns, French Hotchkiss or Chauchat machine guns, and either British or French artillery pieces. Those who attended the British schools learned their weapons well, although they hated British rations. Those attending the French schools enjoyed better cuisine.

Uniforms presented another irritant. War was declared in April and the draft began delivering men in September. But the winter of 1917 was one of the most bitter on record. Many soldiers trained in civilian clothing until their summer uniforms were issued in the fall. Many more did not receive winter uniforms until winter was well along or almost over. Clothing stocks were equally slim in France, where the supply requirements were significantly higher both from the demands of rigorous training and combat and the need to delouse after every trip into the trenches. The consequence was that poorly clad soldiers sickened and some died from a lack of proper clothing.[12]

Military Management

The rush to raise army strength for the Spanish-American War had resulted in a near catastrophe from a management perspective. The reforms initiated by Secretary of War Elihu Root after the Spanish-American War brought improvements in the training of senior officers and produced a small general staff structure to plan for major contingencies. But the American people and their representatives in Congress saw no need for a large military establishment and continued in their somewhat irrational fear of a large standing army. The result, beyond keeping the numbers quite small, was a severe restriction on general staff officers serving in the Washington area at any one time. The law mandated two-year breaks in service in that arena so as to preclude officers from developing any kind of constituency that might prejudice civil-military relationships. The ultimate result was that very few army officers, even though a growing number graduated from the newly established Army War College, had practical experience in planning for large organizations.

The story of the breakdown of the logistics system in December, 1917, is better told elsewhere. Suffice to say that management was so poor that civilian experts had to be called in to reestablish the flow of railroad traffic on the East Coast. In late 1917, scenes first observed in 1898 in Tampa, Florida, and painfully repeated in Saudi Arabia ninety-two years later, confronted army quartermaster officers. Box cars (in 1990 it was overseas shipping [CONEX] containers) clogged eastern railheads. What was in the cars no one knew; where they were supposed to be going, none could say; how they were to get from one point to another was beyond imagining. Scale had overwhelmed talent.[13]

In the 1898 and 1917 cases, the expansion was beyond the management structure and intellectual abilities of most of the army's staff officers. A successful businessman will readily acknowledge that things operate very differently at the corporate level than they do on the shop floor. Timelines are different. Planning must be longer-range, and one must cope with greater uncertainty. Personnel management practices are different because competence is measured differently. Finally, costs are calculated with lesser precision and different motive forces in mind. So it is with any large organization—and armies are no exception. A great deal of study has gone into determining just how greatly cultures change at different levels and what types of people are more likely to succeed at one level than another. One of the fundamental purposes of the War Colleges is to introduce officers to those realities. Constabulary armies do not expand to handle world wars without very great difficulties.

General Pershing, who had a mandate from the secretary of war to create an independent American field army to fight as a full-fledged partner with the Allies, turned to creating the necessary infrastructure to support the American Expeditionary Forces. The magnitude of that undertaking overwhelmed him. It would have taken a man of much different background and training to be able to manage the task he confronted.

As an example at the micro level, before 1917 infantry company strength hovered at about fifty men, with one to three officers assigned. The officers included a captain company commander (who was 30 percent more likely to be detailed to duty somewhere else), and several lieutenant platoon leaders if the unit was fortunate. When the U.S. Army expanded from 125,000 to about four million men, there were precious few officers who had the capacity to understand what this meant in management terms. Cognitive theory suggests that many people function well at levels where ambiguity is minimal—where routine governs their activities. Others function well at higher levels of ambiguity and complexity. A major problem arises when an organization becomes routinized and innovation and imagination are often frowned upon. When it is then forced to break out of its routine to operate on a totally different scale, it often cannot do so. When the basic fighting unit of the 1917 army, the company, expanded from its authorized peacetime strength of 58 to its wartime strength of 150, and then saw its Table of Organization and Equipment (TO&E) change unexpectedly to 250, chaos was induced from the bottom up.

The army first attempted to come to grips with this very basic issue on July 8, 1917, shortly after Pershing's headquarters arrived in France and almost three months after war was declared. In the process of developing what came to be called the "General Organizational Project" (a detailed structure for the AEF) it was agreed to adopt the British infantry company structure of 250 men. This change was brought about by General Pershing's observations of British organizational structure, which was based on experience gained in three years of war. The larger number was necessary because of the proliferation of weapons systems at company level and—although no one advertised it very loudly—to ensure there was a core around which to rebuild the unit should it suffer massive casualties in any single action. One might well ask why it took until 1917 to discover this rather critical fact.

It is a relatively small but illustrative point but, as the War Department rushed to build cantonments for the army in 1917, its plans were temporarily knocked askew by the requirement for two more fifty-man barracks per company. To the army's credit, it managed its construction program well and, for the most part, made the necessary changes and had suitable cantonments available for the draftees before they reported for duty. This was a significant improvement over the Spanish-American War experience, but it was one of relatively few.[14]

On the larger scale, as American officers arrived in France and began attending French and British staff schools, both of the Allies noted that an absence of competent staffs was going to hamper American performance more than mere battlefield technique. The company-level problem could be managed if the company commander had several years of service and was supported by several experienced NCOs. But neither existed in anything like the required numbers. Magnify this situation for the division commander who was confronted with the task of training a completely new, twenty-eight-thousand-man organization while simultaneously having to train his officers and senior NCOs in their basic duties and establish and operate specialist schools for the new, unfamiliar weapons systems. Now move to the corporate level—the War Department or Headquarters, AEF—which was responsible for feeding, equipping, and moving this behemoth. When it was but a stripling of 125,000 men spread between the Philippine Islands, Cuba, and the Atlantic coastal defenses, the army could be managed in penny packets. Following the first draft call, its numbers grew until some four million men were in some form of uniform and two million of them ultimately made it to France. It was possible to move a thousand-man regiment by road, rail, or steamship with ease, but a single new division demanded twenty-eight times that effort—and General Pershing was asking for a hundred divisions!

The above discussion addresses only the combat portion of the force. It does not include the supply, training, maintenance, and administrative infrastructure—the absence of which had so long delayed the fielding of combat-ready units in the first place. If the requests for everyday items like food do not have a channel to flow through to some point that has food stocks available and a means to transport them to the troops, the troops don't eat. Until very recently the commonly accepted ratio of combat to support troops was roughly one to three. If accountants claim it is less now, their figures should be very closely examined.

It was all too complex. Thinking at the corporate level must focus on the big picture, not on minute details. Resources must be called forth weeks and months in advance of their anticipated need, not simply fetched from the nearest bin. Subordinate managers must be grown over years, not coached one-on-one for a few days. More importantly, in war, the total resources of a nation must be surveyed and apportioned among the claimants. Not even total war may have total claim on the totality of resources.[15] This is a phenomenon Carl von Clausewitz noted when he differentiated between theoretical absolute war and real war, which he said would always be less than its theoretical absolute.

The inestimable value of a Leavenworth education during those years is attested to by every commentator of the period. The dramatic changes wrought at Leavenworth focused upon the practical application of the accepted principles of war in the field. Had this been extended to more of the newly commissioned officers flooding into the army, the quality of the AEF's tactical performance would have been greatly enhanced. As to the quality of a War College education, there were too few graduates to have much effect. Those who did well there were sought for command and staff positions at division and lower level and thus were lost to the War Department, which desperately needed their talents.

Doctrine, Tactics, Techniques, and Procedures of the Attack

One of the most contentious subjects when World War I is discussed is doctrine and the tactics, techniques, and procedures of the attack. Throughout the war both sides implemented new offensive tactics, culminating with the Germans' stunning successes in the spring, 1918, offensives. When America entered the war, its army was a pitifully small and poorly trained organization by European standards. Its training was not suited to the war in France, although it was well prepared for what had previously been required of it. The U.S. Army's tactical doctrine rested on the 1911 *Infantry Drill Regulations*. This regulation established a reasonably solid base for training the individual soldier to be a member of a larger unit. It also grounded junior leaders in rather rigid small-unit tactics. It also left a great deal to the imagination of the senior leaders. The consensus was that it took two years to make a good soldier, an opinion based in large measure on the fact that there was no systematic training structure as we know it today. Prior to the First World War, recruits were provided clothing, a health inspection, and some rudimentary drill instruction before being sent to their units of assignment, where the real training took place. As a result, when the army began to rapidly expand in 1917, very few of its officers or NCOs were prepared to teach anything beyond close-order drill and rifle marksmanship.[16]

American doctrine was in fact superior to earlier French doctrine in that it recognized that firepower was essential to the success of an attack. The *Infantry Drill Regulations* emphasized that as the infantry moved forward, their intermediate purpose was progressively to thicken the firing line so as to establish fire superiority. Once that was achieved the assault could begin, but not before—save as a desperate measure.

Fire superiority was central to infantry training. Every American soldier was expected to be an excellent shot, and Pershing eventually insisted that all AEF soldiers be trained to fire accurately at ranges of five hundred to six hundred yards. This was a practical reaction to the realities of the trenches but very few men ever trained at those ranges. Not only was the American soldier expected to be a capable individual marksman, he was supposed to be trained in "musketry." Musketry is a form of firing carried over from the days when individual weapons were so notoriously inaccurate that to insure a target was hit the fire of the entire unit was concentrated on that target. That could be a salutary practice even in trench warfare if the fire could be controlled. The acme of marksmanship training and musketry occurred at the battle of Mons, Belgium, in 1914 when rapid and accurate British rifle fire temporarily stymied the German advance.

Pershing evidently thought musketry still had a place on the modern battlefield. After berating the War Department for sending poor marksmen to France, he then lambasted it for sending officers who were ignorant of musketry concepts. In these exchanges it is evident that Pershing had a firm grasp of at least some of the realities of modern war. Neither he nor the War Department completely accepted the British and French prewar devotion to the spiritual force of the attack over the material strength of firepower. One of Pershing's earliest messages to the War Department noted that marksmanship had so decayed in the French Army that soldiers hardly knew how to use a rifle at all. Grenades, yes; knives, yes; trench mortars, yes; aimed rifle fire, no.

Pershing found a sympathetic ear when he visited British Field Marshal Sir Douglas Haig. As old professionals, the two men were remarkably alike in attitude. Pershing reported that he had convinced Haig to restore rifle marksmanship to the British soldier's training program. Whether that is so or not is not relevant here. What is important is that the British and French fully understood the necessity of *massive* firepower—a fact that illustrates the essential difference between the neophyte Americans and the battle-hardened Allies. The Allies had been driven to deeply appreciate the value of massive indirect artillery firepower in support of an infantry advance, a doctrinal concept very different from that with which they entered the war. In the aftermath of the French mutinies, for example, General Pétain promised the *poilus* that massive fire support would precede all of their future operations or else they would not be asked to attack. On the other hand, the Americans, who never departed from a practical appreciation of the value of firepower, took almost a year to learn what fire superiority really meant. In modern war it was not just rifle fire. In fact, historians Robin Pryor and Trevor Wilson suggest that Haig and his senior officers had not yet fully learned the lesson themselves as late as the Passchendaele operation in the summer of 1917. They continued to place their guns more or less evenly across the zone of attack. German artillery genius Colonel Bruchmueller, on the other hand, had learned to concentrate firepower in overwhelming quantities at the point of attack, leaving other sectors lightly covered. The American successes at Cantigny and Saint-Mihiel were partly the product of massive fire, air, and tank support. The AEF's qualified success in the Meuse-Argonne campaign is somewhat attributable to the absence of those tools. American combat doctrine was properly oriented but failed utterly to comprehend the complexities and realities of modern warfare. The depth and breadth of the changes were simply too great to be absorbed within the relatively short time available.[17]

At least until the German 1918 spring offensives, trench warfare had imposed its requirements upon all armies. Attacking enemy trenches required that all movements conform to the activity of the artillery. Preparatory fires increased in volume until they lasted for weeks for major offensives and at least several hours for local actions. The enemy trenches had to be pulverized and the defender's barbed-wire entanglements blown away before the attacking infantry could hope for success. Then, at the appointed minute, the attacking infantry would climb out of their trenches and move forward, more or less on line, behind a barrage of artillery fire that would advance at some predetermined rate—a hundred yards every two minutes for example. The infantry had to stay as close to that barrage as possible, close enough that some men became casualties of "friendly" fire, in order to be able to make their way safely across the intervening no-man's-land to the enemy trenches. The basic idea was that as long as the barrage was falling, enemy machine gunners would have to keep their heads down or stay in their protective bunkers. Once the barrage passed, they would be free to leap up and begin their deadly firing upon the attackers. If the infantry followed the barrage properly, they would be at bayonet distance from the machine gunners as they emerged from shelter.

The practice further developed that the rolling barrage would halt just beyond the first objective and the guns would lay down a protective barrier of fire in order to protect the attackers against a counterattack. It is an inexorable law of war that the attacker will become disorganized in the process of the assault. Leaders will be hit but their absence may not be noticed until the assault stops, and then replacements must be appointed and oriented. Units will suffer losses and will have to be reorganized and amalgamated in some cases. Supporting weapons will be lost and new support arrangements must be made. In short, while the assault is a deadly affair, if the leaders have done their job properly, everyone will have a pretty good idea of where to go and what to do in the first phase. The most difficult problem, however, is reorganizing on the objective in preparation to continue the attack. All the exertions of the attack will sap the psychological reserves of men and leaders at a time when utterly heroic efforts are required to move forward a second time—unless the attack has been a walk-over, which it seldom is. Utterly heroic because each man has just seen the horror of combat afresh and is being asked to engage in it a second time when everything in him shouts, "Stop, stop, this is madness!"

In trench warfare, the barrage only stopped for a while and then moved on, not according to what actually happened on the ground but according to a timetable. Communication between the infantry and artillery was largely beyond the technical capability of the communications systems of the day. Once the barrage was "lost," which is to say that the distance between it and the following infantry had widened, the infantry became increasingly vulnerable to enemy machine-gun fire. A well-established enemy would place his machine guns in mutually supporting positions so that their fires would crisscross. In this manner, an attack on one position could be overwhelmed by fire from the others. The artillery therefore had to smother these mutually supporting positions and the infantry had to stay close behind the barrage in order to achieve a breakthrough.

Tanks had begun to show that they could assist in this process, but they in turn had to be protected from direct-firing artillery pieces, which at this stage of the war the Germans had begun to position near the front line for just such a purpose. These artillery pieces were in turn vulnerable to attack from the air as well as from other artillery if they could be spotted and reported. It all amounted to an elaborate dance and resulted in operations orders that prescribed movements of men and material down to the yard and the minute.[18]

General Pershing observed this after his arrival in France and found it appalling. This practice, he concluded, was destructive of initiative and maneuver, the hallmarks of the American way of war. American soldiers, innately possessed of imagination and initiative, would not be trained for the stultifying form of trench warfare, they would be trained for what Pershing called "open warfare." Doctrinally, open warfare called for scouts to advance ahead of the attack formations. They would find the enemy and, using prearranged signals, orient the attacking infantry so that they could bring accurate rifle fire to bear on each enemy position until other troops could close within bayonet attack distance.

"Innocent" is the most charitable way to describe this thinking. However, it was founded on the idea of fire and maneuver, which was an essential element of trench warfare. But trench warfare involved a good deal more than the infantryman with his rifle and bayonet. Infantrymen in France were equipped with mortars, small (37-mm) guns, hand and rifle grenades, and light and heavy machine guns, all which were foreign to the American Army. How these weapons interacted with each other and with supporting guns, be they artillery pieces or tanks, and possibly airplanes and balloons, was something new and startlingly complex to the Americans. The reality that faced the AEF was that trench warfare continued to predominate and open warfare simply could not take place until the trenches were overcome.

Command Philosophy

The first mention of leadership in combat in the *Field Service Regulations* is found under the heading "Post of the Leader":

> During action, in forces no larger than a brigade, the leader places himself far enough to the front to personally direct the movements of his command. In divisions, it will, at times, be possible to find a point of observation from which the division commander can personally supervise the course of the action. . . . In forces larger than a division, the post of the leader during combat is usually near the position of the reserve . . . and . . . where the terrain does not permit of personal observation, it is best for the leader . . . to be well to the rear, removed as far as possible from the sights and sounds of the battlefield in order that his decisions may not be unduly influenced by the local conditions. In this case, communication with all parts of the battlefield must be direct, rapid, and continuous.[19]

How idealistic those words seem today, how innocent. When further describing "Combat Orders," the *Field Service Regulations* direct that: "The following factors must be considered in arriving at the decision: The mission, relative numerical strength of the opposing force, relative efficiency of the troops on both sides, the terrain, and probable results of victory or defeat. In doubtful cases aggressiveness and initiative will usually win."[20]

Then, among the most important directives for this study, there is the following: "Combat orders are the expression of a fixed decision and must definitely state the end in view. . . . Troops have a right to be told, in terms that are direct and unmistakable, exactly what it is their leader wants them to do. If the subordinate commander knows what the general plan—the end in view—is, lack of initiative on his part is inexcusable."[21]

These two directives have not changed except in form of expression to this day. Communicating the "Commander's Intent" constitutes the essential basis of instruction to leaders at all levels of command.

Command and Control Practices

The 1917 edition of the *Infantry Drill Regulations* reflected the constabulary conditions of much of the U.S. Army's history. Immediately after the war, *Infantry Drill Regulations (Provisional) 1919*, reflecting the AEF's interpretation of the war's lessons, was published in France, and later adopted by the entire army. The "General Principles of Offensive Combat" in this postwar regulation read: "The primary duties of infantry commanders in combat are to maintain direction on their objectives, establish and maintain contact with the units on their flanks, and keep the higher command informed as to the situation. The post of the commanders and their message centers should be chosen with reference to these requirements."[22]

That army was very much a learn-by-doing organization that expected leaders at all levels to lead by personal example. At the same time, as the above quotation indicates, it was recognized that there was a difference in requirements between the brigade and division level. That was as far as the regulations went. Army corps and larger organizations were not relevant to that army.

Recent work on battle command breaks "command" into two subcomponents: command and control. Command is what the commander does in defining the mission, developing the plan, prioritizing the resources, and then sensing the development of the action and ordering adjustments as appropriate. It is a mixture of art and science and, in the U.S. Army, has traditionally been viewed as acceptably idiosyncratic. The "art of command" cannot be hemmed in with too many rules lest it cease to be an art in which informed intuition plays a large role. When the great German philosopher of war Carl von Clausewitz writes of the quality of genius, he is addressing this function, where the creative spirit is free to roam. Control, on the other hand, is the more mechanistic staff process. The staff's function is to provide as much certainty as possible by overseeing the proper execution of the plan. Effective control requires regular, accurate reports so as to keep the commander properly informed and keep resources moving forward. The synergy between the commander and his staff is a product of staff training and personalities. Staffs in

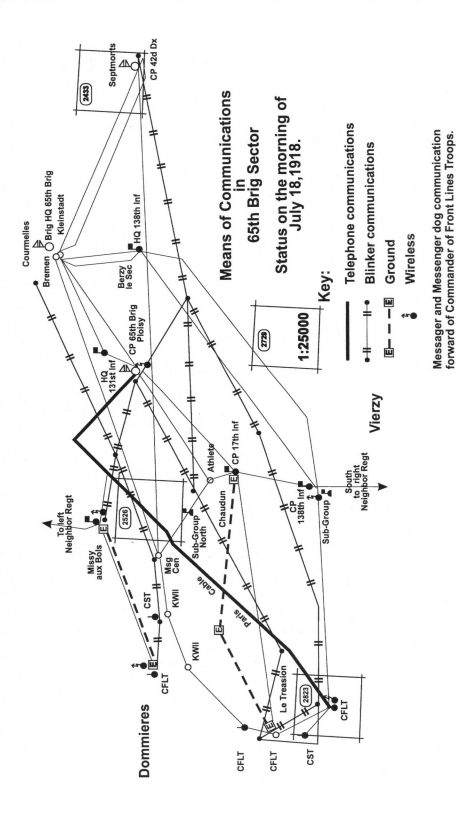

map 5. Means of Communications in 65th Brigade Sector

World War I were still small and relatively personal bodies below corps level. Above that level they grew in size as their functions changed somewhat and they became more bureaucratized.

In order to ensure continuous communications, it had become standard in the Allied armies for the commander to remain at his post of command (PC) or command post (CP) as we call it today. This was new to American commanders, whose previous training, as directed by the previously cited regulations, emphasized moving forward with the troops or to positions from which they could oversee and maintain control of the action. But American doctrine was developed before the days of massed artillery fires and the machine gun. Furthermore, the fields of France offered few points from which to observe since much of the higher ground was in German hands. And what was there to be seen but pounded earth and barbed wire? No man showed his head above ground in daylight for fear of being shot by a sniper. In order to maintain control, higher commanders had to maintain contact with front-line leaders. The British soon discovered that contact with the forward line of troops could not be maintained in the face of German defensive fire. They ordered commanders down to regiment, and sometimes even battalion, to remain in their PCs and maintain telephone contact. Major Gen. John F. C. Fuller, a British tank enthusiast wrote: " In the World War nothing was more dreadful to witness than a chain of men starting with a battalion commander and ending with an army commander sitting in telephone boxes, improvised or actual, talking, talking, talking in place of leading, leading, leading."[23]

This was especially galling to American leaders, who frequently disregarded this practice and moved forward anyway. However, when they did they abrogated a certain amount of control and broke contact with higher headquarters in the rear. Some did so with the latter purpose in mind. This was in contrast to the German practice, which pushed command forward and relied upon a wider variety of methods to maintain communications with the rear. A German PC might have blinker, telephone, wireless, pigeon, dog, and motorized messengers available, providing multiple means and routings for message traffic. The Americans were eventually equipped with telephones and some radios, but in the attack they, like everyone else, had to rely ultimately on runners. No one will ever know how many soldiers died trying to get a message through.[24]

Consequences

So it was that the AEF entered combat for the first time in strength: partly trained, dubiously led, questionably administered and managed, reasonably well equipped thanks to the Allies, and operating under a mixture of doctrines understood by only a few. Most soldiers knew how to fire the weapons they were carrying though some did not. Most knew they were to follow their leaders wherever they led, although not all could figure out what to do if the leaders went down. Senior officers knew that objectives had to be taken but the finer points of *how* had to be learned on the job. Keeping large organizations focused on the deadly task of slaughter was a daunting challenge for all concerned.

CHAPTER 2

Promise

July 18 — 1st Division and 1st Moroccan Division

Advance units of the 1st Division sailed for France in June, 1917, at approximately full wartime strength according to War Department TO&Es of about 1914 vintage. The division was constituted from a skeleton force of four Regular Army regiments heavily leavened with volunteers—there were no draftees as the first draft call did not require reporting until after the training camps were completed later that summer. They sailed with M1903 Springfield rifles, bayonets, and soft campaign hats. Immediately after they paraded down the Champs-Elysées to the frantic cheers of the beleaguered French citizenry, they were dispatched to training camps to learn the rudiments of soldiering in a totally new environment. The carefully crafted training program devised by General Pershing's staff fell apart under the incessant demands of infrastructure requirements and the need to get American soldiers into combat. For a while the French despaired that the Americans would ever enter the fray and even sought Pershing's relief. The hammer blows of the German spring offensives in 1918 changed all that. Faced with the real possibility of defeat, the Allies set aside their differences—Americans would enter the battle regardless of their level of proficiency. Their numbers and enthusiasm were expected to make up for their other failings, even if at considerable cost.[1]

The XX Corps Attack Plan

The French XX Corps's attack order emphasized that "vigorous, rapid and orderly movement is essential to the success of the attack." Likewise the order placed special emphasis on artillery-infantry liaison, movement of the reserves, and the timeliness and accuracy of reports.

Had the XX Corps commander, Major General Berdoulat, ascended in an observation balloon about five thousand feet above the northern edge of the

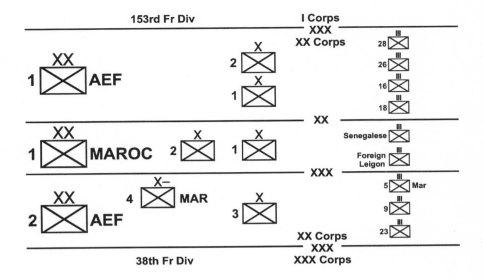

1. XX Corps Attack Formation, July 18, 1918

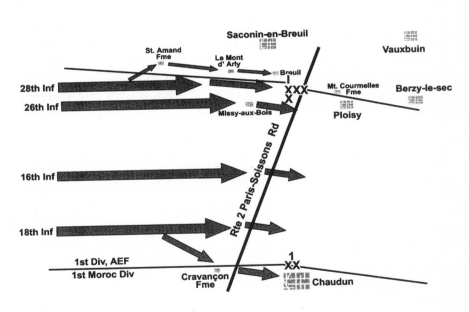

2. 1st Divison Attack, July 18, 1918

Forêt de Retz he would have surveyed, on a frontage of about five miles, a tableau very different from that seen by most observers in the Great War. Gone were the trenches and masses of barbed wire. Perhaps he might have noticed the liberal sprinkling of machine-gun positions about the terrain, but most likely not. The wheat was up and the scene was bucolic except that here and there one could observe the blackened ruins of a tank or a ruined farmhouse. The ground had been viciously fought over less than two months before and thus presented an odd mixture of pastoral peace and ruinous war. But it was nothing like the trench systems that had so long locked the combatants together. The great strength of XX Corps was the composition of its subordinate units, two-thirds of which were carefully hidden in the great Forêt de Retz. The corps consisted of two huge American divisions and one of the best attack divisions in the entire French Army, the 1st Moroccan. It also had two French divisions in reserve. The three divisions assigned to the attack echelon were numerically equivalent to between five and six normal French divisions. Did it cross Berdoulat's mind that because of the massive structure of the American divisions, four-fifths of his corps' attacking strength came from the AEF, or that none of the soldiers, save possibly the Foreign Legion's officers and NCOs, were even native Frenchmen?

Augmenting his power, Berdoulat had 156 of the 324 tanks assigned to Tenth Army. With the 154 assigned to Sixth Army, the tank force totaled 478—more than the French had ever pulled together before and, as far as the Americans were concerned, "more tanks than we knew were in the world." It was the second largest employment of Schneider tanks (123), the largest use of Saint-Chamonds (100), and the second largest employment of Renault light tanks (255) of the war. At least that was the initial design, but several changes had to be made and the number actually crossing the jump-off line was most likely less. By way of comparison, the British committed 474 tanks at Cambrai on November 20, 1917. Of that number, only 378 saw action. The remaining tanks were employed as command and supply vehicles.[2]

In addition, the French II Cavalry Corps was being held in Tenth Army reserve, possibly to exploit XX Corps's anticipated initial success. Forty squadrons from the newly organized French 1st Air Division were allocated to provide air support to Tenth Army. The aviators' orders strongly indicate a principally reconnaissance mission.[3]

Four regiments from the American 1st Division would attack abreast in columns of battalions along the northern axis of advance. The 1st Moroccan Division would attack in the middle with its 1st Brigade—a mix of Foreign Legion and Senegalese battalions—in front, and the 2d Brigade, consisting of two regiments (the 8th Zouaves and 7th Tirailleurs) with three battalions each, following. The American 2d Division, made up of an army and a marine brigade, would advance along the southern axis with three regiments abreast. The Marine Brigade would have only one regiment in line, the 5th Marines. The 6th Marine Regiment would remain in corps reserve.

Particular emphasis was placed on liaison between the 1st Moroccan and the 2d American Divisions. Their boundary extended through deep woods for about a kilometer before reaching open ground. In addition, their movements needed close coordination to overcome the strongly defended Bois de Quesnoy and the Fond d'Argent.[4]

Terrain

While one must always keep the enemy in mind, the ground itself is an important consideration. The terrain over which some sixty thousand XX Corps soldiers would fight was a plateau traversed north and south, across the direction of attack, by deep ravines. Within and near the edges of these ravines were typical French villages with sturdy stone masonry buildings. There were a number of caves, some of them substantial in size, carved out when quarrying the stone for the buildings in the area. The roadways in the valley beyond the plateau were the Germans's principal lines of communication—the lifelines of the troops in the Marne salient. The initial focus of the attack was aimed at interdicting those arteries. In fact, Foch's initial concept sought only to place them under long-range heavy artillery fire.[5]

The ground in the 1st Division's attack sector determined how its attack was likely to progress. The first major obstacle, the Missy Ravine, would be encountered early by the 2d Brigade. That obstacle was likely to slow that brigade's attack and allow the more southern 1st Brigade to make faster progress until it encountered the Chazelle Ravine, some forty-three hundred yards farther east. Then the 2d Brigade would have to contend with the Ploisy Ravine, roughly three thousand yards beyond the Missy Ravine. It would be rough going for the 2d Brigade. The Moroccan Division would not have to deal with any ravines until after both American divisions had hit at least one each, but the Chazelle-Lechelle Ravine, which the Moroccans would first encounter, opened like the side of an X with Charantigny and the Bois Gerard marking the western extremities. The 2d Division would have to deal with the two arms of the Vierzy Ravine, one of which cut completely across the division sector.

Other than the usual admonition to maintain flank liaison, the XX Corps order gave no special notice of these obstacles. In fact, no terrain features other than the objective were noted, even though they were of special interest to General Mangin. The order also made no mention of the enemy.

It is perhaps worth observing here that the standard five-paragraph U.S. Army field order has remained essentially unchanged since the First World War. Paragraph one lists both the friendly and enemy forces likely to be committed to an operation. Paragraph two describes the mission in general enough terms to convey the focus of the operation—the commander's intent—but specific enough to avoid confusion. Paragraph three assigns specific responsibilities to each unit involved in the planned operation. Paragraphs four and five detail administrative, logistical, and command and signal considerations respectively. The XX Corps order omitted mention of both the terrain and the enemy, factors that together would wreak havoc with the execution of the attack plan.

1st Division

Major Gen. Charles Pelot Summerall commanded the 1st Division. He assumed command only three days before the XX Corps attack, when Maj. Gen. Robert Lee Bullard moved up to command the newly formed III Corps.[6]

Summerall was given top marks for his performance as commander of the division's artillery brigade since December, 1917. His acknowledged leadership ability and demonstrated fearlessness underlay gale-force self-confidence and a sense of self-importance. Perhaps deliberately, he sought to make himself fit a description set down for another soldier in an earlier war: "a fine brave fellow, a hollerer and a hero, a leader of men." Summerall certainly was a hollerer. He developed a habit of exhorting his officers and men with dramatic rhetoric evidently intended to inspire or motivate them, as seen in this example: "You will take that crossing. Get into action and get across. I don't expect to see any of you again. But that doesn't matter. You have the honor of a definite success—give yourselves to that." On at least one occasion a cynical "Hogwash!" was heard from the rear ranks. In this and subsequent command positions, he found it efficacious to threaten officers with relief from command and the ignominy of the reclassification depot at Blois. He set one battalion commander straight by admonishing: "You may have paused for reorganization. If you ever send another message with the word stopped in it, you'll be sent to the rear for reclassification!" It was not a idle threat. If he felt the occasion merited it, he sent them there. He often spoke in showy, meaningless blather: "Sir, when the 1st Division has only two men left they will be echeloned in depth and attacking toward Berlin!" He would have been a wonderful "talking head" on CNN.

Despite his imperious nature, Summerall developed a reputation for being in a class by himself, the epitome of a military leader—"daring and careful, ruthless and inspiring."[7]

Thursday Morning, July 18
1ST DIVISION

At 3 o'clock in the afternoon on July 17, 1918 the 1st Division received the XX Corps attack order in the Forêt de Retz, ten miles behind the front. Within a matter of hours the division began moving forward along one of three roads leading to the front. A total of sixty-seven thousand men, five thousand animals, and three thousand vehicles, each with a separate mission to reach a certain point before a certain hour, were moving in the same direction in the XX Corps zone. Artillery vehicles held the center of the road while infantry trudged along through the muddy ditches. Several battalions of big French tanks came wallowing down the highway and, as they took the center of the road, everything had to give way toward the fields. Then came five-ton trucks, staff cars, and motorcycles. Everything became unutterably mixed in the awful congestion.[8]

As H hour (4:35 A.M.) approached, the Germans in the 1st Division's 2d Brigade sector and that of the French 153d Division to its immediate north, fired a weak counterpreparation. Soldiers either deserting or captured from the 153d Division had warned the opposing 11th Bavarian Division of the impending attack. The 11th Bavarian Division was alerted, manned the forward trenches, and fired the defensive artillery fire plan, paying particular attention to the crossroads at Cutry, close behind the Allied lines. The German corps commander had complained of a paucity of artillery in the corps as his assets were weakened by the diversion of most nondivisional artillery to support the Strassenbau attack. Although weak, these protective fires were sufficient to inflict 25 percent casualties on the 28th Infantry's support battalion, the 3d Battalion, which was second in the order of advance.[9]

It was clear the Germans did not expect this size or style of attack. The delayed concentration of troops, the chaotic movement to battle positions at night in a storm, and the absence of artillery preparatory fires had given Mangin the surprise he sought. The late-arriving 2d Division would pay the lion's share of the butcher's bill. The 1st Division, although it had been moved up to assembly areas near the jump-off line two days before the attack, still had some difficulty getting forward to its attack positions on the night of July 17–18. Both the 26th and 28th Infantry Regiments reported going into the attack without

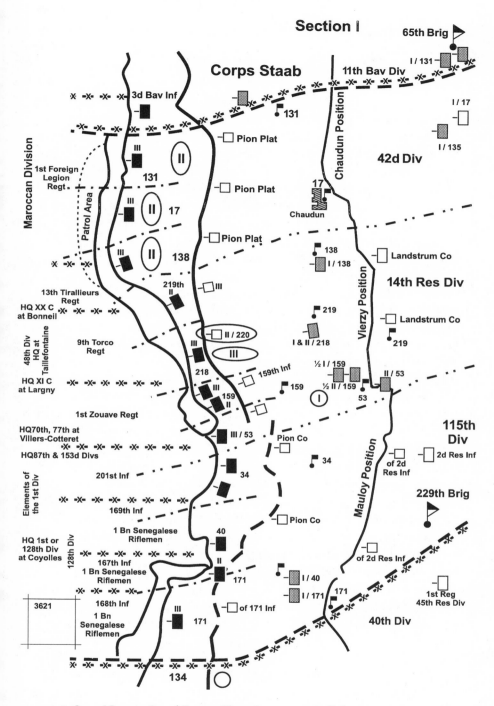

map 6. Own [German] and Enemy Situation, 5:00 A.M., July 18, 1918

grenades of any kind and with their ammunition carriers out of contact to the rear.

2D BRIGADE

The northern sector of the 1st Division zone was assigned to the 2d Brigade, which consisted of the 28th and 26th Infantry Regiments and was commanded by Brig. Gen. Beaumont B. Buck. Buck, who was known as a hard-driving infantryman and a strict disciplinarian, was seen by some as "a short, dogmatic, inflexible, and not very bright officer." He had been in command of the brigade during the 28th Infantry's minutely supervised attack at Cantigny on May 28, but that occasion was no true test of his leadership ability.[10]

28TH INFANTRY REGIMENT

Colonel Conrad Stanton Babcock was commander of the 28th Infantry Regiment. A trim, handsome forty-two-year-old, he assumed command the day before the attack, as was all too often the case in the First World War. He replaced Hanson Ely, who was promoted to brigadier general and given command of the 2d Division's 3d Brigade as a reward for his brilliant performance at Cantigny. Babcock, a cavalryman with no infantry command experience, had been in three assignments since coming to France in September, 1917, including service as Inspector General of the 1st Division and Commandant of the AEF headquarters at Chaumont. Most recently he had been commander of the fledgling AEF Tank Corps's training center at Bovington Camp near Wool, England. He seemed to have been a very thorough, thoughtful, professional officer.[11]

On Babcock's left, operating in the I Corps zone, was the French 153d Division, another colonial division composed principally of North African soldiers. To his immediate front was the Missy Ravine, the most difficult piece of terrain in the corps sector short of the final objective, and one of the obstacles the 153d had been specifically enjoined by the army commander to avoid. Conrad Babcock was in for a challenging, epic ordeal.[12]

American regiments generally attacked in column of battalions in the following order: assault, support, and reserve. The 2d Battalion was designated to serve as the 28th Infantry's assault battalion, and the 3d would follow in support. The 1st Battalion was held in division reserve. This was the first flaw in the plan stemming from ignorance of the ground: The worst terrain in the corps sector was going to be attacked by only two-thirds of a regiment's strength. Staff officers working in near vacuums are dangerous to the health of infantry soldiers.

When the attack began, 2d Battalion easily passed through the first German lines then worked with the tanks to eliminate machine guns in the wheat fields. Such a simple sentence, and how easily the eye follows it on the page! Keeping in mind that H hour was 4:35 A.M., here is what the message traffic recorded:

From C.O. 28th Inf. To: Brig Adj. 2d Brig.   Time 4:23 A.M.
Only one rifle company of Support Battalion has arrived. Have officers out looking for it.
Conrad S. Babcock

Time: 4:50 A.M.
Companies of support battalion have been found. . . . Babcock

From: C.O. 2d Bn. 26th Inf. To: C.O. 26th Inf. Time: 5:15 A.M.
Right front line company 28th Inf. has just arrived at my P.C. *It is lost.* Company Commander has made no reconnaissance . . . and his guides do not know where to take him. . . . McCloud

From: 2d Bde [Evidently from an operations journal or log—does not specify] Time: 4:22 A.M.
Lt. Graham with 3 platoons of L Co., 26th [Regiment] Lost around Brigade P.C.

Time: 5:50 A.M.
Lt. Brouston reports with 1 platoon of D Co. 28th Inf. Claims Major Roxell ordered him to go towards artillery firing. No further orders. (Brigade commander is of the opinion that this officer is scared)

Time: 5:30 A.M.
Lt. Sorenson D Co. 28th with his company outside of Brigade P.C. absolutely lost. Had no maps.

Time: 5:30 A.M.
Adjutant reported whole 1st Bn. 28th [Division Reserve] lost in woods LA FOSSE TRUE. They do not know what to do or where to go.[13]

As stray elements of two regiments swirled about it in a welter of confusion, the coherence of the attack was already beginning to break down and ought to have caused the 2d Brigade command element to become very active in its supervision. This state of confusion undoubtedly was not unique to any one unit, but in this case the somewhat more complete records of the 26th and 28th Infantry make them look the worst at this point. And this division had been close enough to do a commander's reconnaissance the day before.

Suddenly, a portion of the 2d Battalion that should have maintained a heading just south of due east veered sharply northeast, cutting across the XX Corps's northern boundary and into the 153d Division's zone. Part of the attack had shifted because heavy fire was being received from Saint Amand Farm. The farm was a veritable strong point from which heavy fire was directed at the attacking battalion's flanks. In order to deal with this problem, a platoon commanded by Lt. Jim Quinn moved to silence the tormenter. By 7 A.M., the 2d Battalion had taken the heavily defended farm, which was nearly nine hundred yards north of the division boundary. This movement pulled the 2d Battalion northward directly in front of the heavily defended Missy Ravine. Gone were the treeless plateau and wheat fields. Atop the western edge of the ravine directly before the 2d Battalion lay the village of le Mont d'Arly. There was a larger village—Saconin-et-Breuil—in the bottom of the ravine to the north, in the 153d Division sector, which the Germans had turned into a strong point. This village was located in the midst of an older line of fortifications whose existence was exploited by the Germans. A third village, Breuil, sat on the eastern lip of the ravine directly across from le Mont d'Arly. Yet a fourth village, Missy-aux-Bois, was located in the adjacent 26th Infantry Regiment's sector on the ravine's southeastern lip. All these villages contained sturdy stone buildings easily adaptable for tenacious defense.[14]

The dictionary defines a ravine as "a small narrow steep-sided valley that is larger than a gully and smaller than a canyon and that is usually worn by running water." This one, however, is half a mile wide and has heavily vegetated banks sloping at a 60-degree angle. At the bottom there was a marshy swamp that measured six hundred yards across. The area was covered by artillery emplaced throughout the ravine and on the eastern bank, in particular; it likewise bristled with machine guns and infantry emplacements, although little infantry was actually in position. The ravine extended south across the 26th Infantry's sector and slightly beyond the 2d Brigade boundary. To the north it extended far beyond the 153d Division's zone. "Avoid the ravines!" Mangin had told the 153d. And what was the 1st Division supposed to do? Had Mangin's directions been followed literally, the French would have swung wide to the north and left the 1st Division to fend for itself until it reached "favorable terrain." The ravines simply could not be avoided.

Major Clarence Huebner had commanded the 2d Battalion, 28th Infantry, since Cantigny when, his predecessor killed, he took command and earned his first Distinguished Service Cross. The citation reads in part: "For 3 days . . .

[Major Huebner] withstood German assaults under intense bombardment, heroically exposing himself to fire constantly in order to command his battalion effectively."[15] Now he had the unenviable task of leading his men eastward, through the Missy Ravine and its formidable defenses. He sent two companies to the bottom of the ravine but they made no more than a hundred yards' progress before enfilading machine-gun fire from Saconin-et-Breuil and direct artillery fire from the over-watching village of Breuil halted them. There was no assistance from the 153d Division on the left, for they had not been able to deal with Saconin-et-Breuil at all. The battalion made another try, advancing another three hundred yards at terrible cost. Five French tanks ventured down the slopes of the ravine to support the Americans. The two not blasted by artillery fire sank into the swamp. The battalion had been reduced to about half its fighting strength.[16]

Hearing the din of firing, the 3d (Support) Battalion commander, Maj. Willis Tack, had the foresight to come forward ahead of his companies and confer with Huebner. In accord with 2d Brigade Field Order no. 34, the 3d Battalion was to pass through the 2d as soon as the 2d reached the eastern edge of the Missy Ravine, the brigade's second objective. The 3d Battalion had already suffered 25 percent casualties from the German defensive barrage, which, coming down late, had missed the 2d Battalion completely. Tack and Huebner agreed they had to join forces to get out of this deadly slough and seize Breuil. There were footbridges across the swamp but, being obvious routes of attack, they were all covered by heavy artillery and machine-gun fire. So the infantrymen of the now-combined battalions waded across elsewhere, sometimes waist deep. A probably apocryphal passage from the regimental history notes: "On one occasion a German officer buried himself in the mud and water until his head and arms were exposed and continued firing upon the slowly advancing men until he was killed and trampled into the mud by the infuriated soldiers."[17]

The men somehow made it up the far bank of Missy Ravine and by 9:30 A.M. had captured all the guns. Then, still under heavy machine-gun fire, they formed a consolidated line east of Breuil.[18]

As the action waned, the 2d Battalion was reorganized into five small platoons, each commanded by a sergeant; all of the company officers had been killed or wounded. The battalion was holding ground several hundred yards north of the division boundary.[19]

In the midst of this welter of confusion and blood was Company M, 3d Battalion. The company had been placed in reserve near le Mont d'Arly. A large group of Germans emerged from a cave near the company's position with the evident intent to attack the 2d and 3d Battalions from the rear. The cave had somehow been missed in the initial advance. Huebner reports that two platoons from his reserve took care of the group. "Took care" meant that he had Americans fire upon the Germans as they were assembling and drove them back into the cave. There they held out until about 4 P.M. After the war, in a letter to the American Battle Monuments Commission, Huebner asked that Captain Manning, the Company M commander, be cited as responsible for the capture of a German battalion complete with its colonel, twenty officers, and roughly five hundred soldiers, plus trench mortars and numerous machine guns. In Huebner's words, Captain Manning "literally saved the day." Caves and quarries were plentiful in the region and served the Germans well on several occasions. However, at least twice they served as traps. Later in the day, another large contingent of Germans was discovered in the same cave but, being medical personnel, all were put to work in a common aid station treating friend and foe alike.[20]

Babcock sent several messages relating to this capture. The first, sent at 7:55 A.M., read: "Am sending . . . 25 officers and some 200 men just captured." He later forwarded a message from Tack indicating more captives had been taken, including a "Commandant."[21]

The 1st Battalion, commanded by Maj. George Rozelle, was in division reserve and could not be employed without General Summerall's permission. Standard practice in the 1st Division placed the reserve battalion of the flank regiments in division reserve and the reserve battalion of the interior regiments in brigade reserve. Standard operating procedures such as this make management of units easier and simplify orders. Given the difficulties the 28th had to face, assuming those difficulties were known to the division staff, some alteration of the standard operating procedure could easily have been made. However, it was not—for reasons we may never know.[22]

What did the 28th Regiment's commander know about these furious actions involving his leading battalions? The report he sent back to 2d Brigade at 7 A.M., two-and-a-half hours after the action started, leaps out of the musty records to shed light on command practices and the physical means of command and control of that day:

> From: C.O. 28th To: C.G. 2d Brig. Time: 7:00 A.M.
> Progress appears good. Very few of our dead seen up to this point. Wounded report support battalion near BREUIL and need of reinforcements. Division reserve (1st Bn. 28th) 1000 yds. east of here. Not much shelling at present request ambulances come up here for wounded. About 100 prisoners so far. Artillery should come forward.   Babcock

Although Babcock was not directly involved forward, it is clear he had a reasonably accurate appreciation of the situation. His next several messages address the state of the unit and make detailed requests for very specific artillery support. Anyone reading them can begin to sense that these reports have something of a remote quality about them. Messages sent during the first few hours lack the vitality of personal observation save for the comment about the dead and the need for specific artillery support. But at least he was receiving some information.[23]

Conrad Babcock was in his PC well to the rear because that was the AEF practice. As noted earlier, regimental and higher commanders were instructed to stay near their communications, meaning radio or buzzer, if any, and the telephone. Most important, they needed to be in a known location where messengers (runners on foot primarily) could easily find them.[24]

However, by 11 A.M., Babcock had made his way to the front and conferred with the French on his north flank about pulling elements of his 2d Battalion back into its own zone. He then directed Major Tack, the 3d Battalion commander, to move up front, and Major Huebner, the 2d Battalion commander, to move to Tack's immediate rear and organize his men in depth. Babcock the cavalryman was learning his infantry job quickly, making the vital lateral liaison with the French work, and then sorting out the forward situation. Unfortunately, this adjustment of battalion positions, when reported to division headquarters, gave rise to a conclusion that the 28th was retreating, committing the unpardonable sin of giving up ground already won. The journal of Summerall's aide, Lt. Alban Butler, records the situation as follows: "Liaison with the 2d Inf. Brigade was poor. . . . All kinds of reports come in. That we are retreating, that we have gone farther than we are. etc. etc. The 153d D.I. has not done so well. They are holding back our 2d Brigade."[25]

But Babcock was actually doing his dead-level best to get the regiment forward. At 8:30 A.M. he requested: "A heavy barrage beginning not over 100 yards from the east side of the Paris–Soissons Road . . . should advance not faster than 100 meters in 5 minutes. Hold it on the East side of the road . . . for not more than 3 minutes."[26]

All of this suggests two problems that require particular attention. One is the quality of Beaumont Buck's leadership as reflected in Butler's journal and Babcock's messages. The other more immediate and contentious problem is whether the adjacent French troops were putting forth their best effort or were willing, to one degree or another, to let the late-arriving Americans take over the hard work. In considering this latter issue, the attitude of the French high command, General Pétain in particular, was in full agreement: Wait for the Americans. A ground-level view provides other answers.[27]

The French 153d Division's zone encompassed a former French frontline sector that contained significant entrenchments. These obstacles notwithstanding, Tenth Army headquarters made clear in its operations orders that the 153d Division had a special task "to progress with the same speed as the adjacent divisions" and to be certain to clear the plateaus and ravines around Saconin. Mangin admonished I Corps not to dissipate its strength in any other undertakings. But those entrenchments ran exactly parallel to and along the center of the 153d Division's axis of advance.[28]

The entrenchments followed favorable terrain and the Germans could, and evidently did, turn them into hastily prepared defensive positions that would have slowed any troops. For the 153d it was like attacking up the long axis of a roll of concertina wire. The *poilus* did not have the luxury of following Mangin's orders—they had to fight with what was before them in reality. The southward-facing defensive positions also provided the Germans positions from which they could fire with almost perfect impunity into the open flank of the more rapidly advancing Americans. This was a major cause of casualties in the 28th Infantry.

In effect, the 1st Division soldiers attacking to the east were attacking across the front of an established defensive position. Furthermore, and evidently unknown to the Americans, they were attacking across the front of the position the Germans believed to be the key to the defense of Soissons: the Vauxbuin Position, which lay just north of the 1st Division boundary within the 153d's zone. The Germans considered this position so important that it was the first to be reinforced as soon as the German XIII Corps was informed of the attack. One additional brigade was alerted immediately, and then three more brigades from two reserve divisions were dispatched toward that position. Operations maps drawn up after the battle show a series of strong points constructed so as to dominate the open plateau running southwest from the town of Vauxbuin, over which the 28th Infantry in particular struggled to advance. Given the critical shortage of German field artillery, this strong point was generously provided with heavy Maxim machine guns positioned to pour enfilading fire upon the hapless 28th Infantry.[29]

The French 153d Division eventually overcame the resistance in Saconin-et-Breuil and sent a battalion to relieve the 2d Battalion, 28th Infantry, on the 153d's southern boundary. The 2d Battalion elements were back within their zone by 2 P.M. The regiment, with its 1st Battalion still held in division reserve, was alerted for another attack at 5:30 P.M. but the orders were canceled.[30]

26TH INFANTRY REGIMENT

To the south, Buck's other regiment, the 26th Infantry, had advanced in proper orientation until it hit the western edge of Missy Ravine. By 5:30 A.M. its 2d

Battalion had taken the first objective, halting halfway to Missy-aux-Bois. Then the battalion continued on to Missy-aux-Bois on the southern lip of the ravine, taking it by 9 A.M. The regiment made no appreciable advance for the remainder of the day, faced as it was with heavy machine gun fire from the eastern side of the hotly defended Soissons–Paris road. That evening, the regiment reported withdrawing to a more favorable defensive position. Evidently division headquarters was not informed (the record is unclear on this) or nothing came of it, contrary to the wrath that descended upon the 28th for a report that was misinterpreted as notification of the regiment's intent to withdraw. Was there some prejudice toward the 28th?[31]

1ST BRIGADE

Next in order to the south was the 1st Brigade, commanded by Brig. Gen. John Leonard Hines, who served as one of General Pershing's aides during the Mexican Punitive Expedition and also as the expedition's adjutant. He was starting a remarkable career of successive combat commands. Hines commanded the 16th Infantry during its formative period in France and had done a thorough job of training the regiment. He ultimately rose through division to corps-level command in the AEF, at the time a distinction shared with only one other American military figure, Confederate Lt. Gen. Thomas "Stonewall" Jackson. Hines was a remarkable, though taciturn, officer. Evidently his taciturnity extended to writing reports and to his staff, as almost no records of the brigade's actions can be found.[32]

The 1st Brigade—with the 16th Infantry under Col. Frank Bamford and the 18th Infantry under Col. Frank Parker—moved rapidly east, not having to cope with ravines. Consequently, the flanks of the 16th Infantry, advancing in the northern half of the brigade sector, were soon exposed. The 18th Infantry had moved about five hundred yards farther south of its assigned boundary and had taken Cravançon Farm, leaving the 1st Moroccan Division behind at that point. By 8:30 A.M. these two regiments had crossed Route 2, where the intense German defense had stopped the 26th and 28th Regiments. They were far enough south of the machine guns in the Vauxbuin Position to be free of their fire. The regiments reformed and advanced through the Chaudun Position to arrive at the fields north of Chaudun, a distance of three and a half miles, in about four hours. At the end of the day, the 18th Infantry, north of Chaudun and beyond the Paris–Soissons road, held the most advanced position in the 1st Division zone.

Cravançon Farm was short of the 1st Moroccan Division's first bound. The division's rate of advance to the intermediate objective was the same as that of the 1st Division—a hundred meters in two minutes—but beyond that point the Moroccans slowed to a hundred meters in four minutes. Assuming they kept pace with their barrage, that would automatically open a gap between the two divisions. Furthermore, the two divisions' intermediate objectives were not the same. The Moroccans' first bound stopped eight hundred meters west of Cravançon Farm, while the 1st Division's first objective was the line La Glaux Tillieul–La Glaux. The two lines were some twelve hundred meters apart. If that was not enough, the 1st Moroccan Division planned to fire a box barrage from H to H-plus-35 around the Dommiers position, then lift on command of the infantry commander, who would be employing signal rockets. Thereafter, French forward movement was left in the hands of the French infantry commander. From there to the next position the rate of advance was to slow to a hundred meters in three minutes. The Americans made no provisions for controlling fire support in this fashion and made no attempt to synchronize their forward movement with their neighbor to the south. Staff coordination thus failed even before the attack got underway.[33]

To that brief summary, which in no way indicates the pace and intensity of the action in Hines's sector, we note that by about 8:30 A.M., only four hours into the historic battle, the commander of the 1st Battalion, 18th Infantry, Maj. Joseph Dorst Patch, ran into hard luck. Hit in the lungs and spitting blood, he was carried to a shell hole. "Before I passed out," he wrote later, "I remember that the hole was a big one, and sitting across from me was a dead German . . . his sightless black eyes were looking right at me." Patch's account of the battle in *A Soldier's War,* was not written until 1966, and by that time it was acceptable for an old soldier to recall what might have been some of the human frailties within the 1st Division. Although he left the scene early and honorably, Patch included some hearsay in his book that will be worth considering in tracing the subsequent fighting. It will come up in due course.[34]

In one way, these opening hours were made for the Americans. Dashing into the midst of a stunned enemy's positions, the American infantry overwhelmed those who stood and fought and marched the survivors to the rear as prisoners. Command was personal and forward at battalion and lower level as long as the leaders were upright. Everyone knew that the direction was forward as long as forward movement wasn't too difficult. Some became misoriented, but they pressed on to do whatever needed doing wherever they were. But as the leaders fell, the reports to the rear became fewer and what information did flow rearward tended increasingly to come from the wounded—whose perception was hardly positive, and very narrow. Every step forward brought with it a bit more disorganization, a bit less cohesion. At about 9 A.M. the 1st Division units paused, without orders or having planned to do so, be-

cause of a need to reorganize and regain their forward momentum. The somewhat more battle-wise Moroccans had planned on the need for such a pause
early in the attack and had incorporated it in their operations order. But the
Americans did not look at that order and rebuffed French attempts at coordination, thus insuring separation of the divisions.

1ST MOROCCAN DIVISION

The 1st Moroccan Division, one of Mangin's favorites, first had to clear the
Dommiers Ravine and pass through the Bois de Quesnoy. After the division
cleared Glaux Farm, just beyond Dommiers, the next major obstacle would
be the town of Chaudun, which, unknown to the Americans or the French,
was the heart of the so-called Chaudun Position, sometimes referred to in
German reports as the "Paris Position" as well. It was not a thoroughly developed position.[35]

The Moroccan Division was one of only three French divisions still having
twelve battalions. It had been fighting on the same ground since May and was
well below strength. General Mangin, of all Frenchmen certainly the most
qualified to assess it, called it one of the best: "*la division marocaine Daugan,
une des meilleures troops d'attaque.*" ("General Daugan's Moroccan Division is
one of the best assault units."—author's paraphrase.) Having a relatively narrow front, the division attacked in column of brigades. In the lead and on the
left side of the division's zone, adjacent to the 1st Division, was the French
Foreign Legion Provisional Regiment with a Senegalese battalion attached.
On the right, two Senegalese battalions attacked alongside the 2d Division. In
the following brigade, six battalions were organized as the 7th Tirailleurs and
the 8th Zouaves.[36]

The Foreign Legion Provisional Regiment or *régiment du marche Légion
étranger* (RMLE) is worthy of notice. The French Foreign Legion was swamped
by adventure-seeking volunteers in the opening months of the war. So many
men volunteered (forty-four thousand from fifty-one nations other than France)
to serve in the Legion that three and later a fourth RMLE were formed "for
the duration" as opposed to the normal lifelong commitment. The bulk of the
NCOs were long-service Frenchmen, and the officers were almost exclusively
French. The 1st RMLE was brigaded with the 1st Moroccan Division, which
consisted of Moroccan and Senegalese soldiers. At the time of its commitment
to the Soissons offensive, the RMLE was well understrength, not having been
brought back up after its earlier battles.[37]

The 1st Moroccan Division's operations order, reflecting greater experience
and extensive familiarity with the attack sector, devoted three entire pages to

the regulation of the artillery—including when and how it was to move forward and upon whose command.[38]

Supported by forty-eight Schneider tanks, the division fought what appear to be two separate battles on the morning of the eighteenth, and two more in the afternoon. From the attack's beginning, the 1st RMLE and its attached Senegalese battalion advanced north of the small Bois de l'Equippe. The two Senegalese battalions, in liaison with the 5th Marines in the northern portion of the 2d Division sector, passed south along the Route Quesnoy through the Bois de Quesnoy.

The Legionnaires, coming up a bit late, made contact with the 18th Infantry and eventually fought their way across the heavily defended Soissons–Paris road, which slanted across their zone. Just east of that road was Cravançon Farm and, a few hundred yards farther east, the town of Chaudun, both villages situated just within the 1st Moroccan Division's northern boundary. But it was Americans who moved through Cravançon Farm, and it was Americans, for the most part, who wrested Chaudun from the Germans.

The taking of Chaudun is a disputed passage of arms involving errant marines from the south, 18th Infantry soldiers from the north, and the Senegalese. The 18th Infantry's historian wrote casually of "the village of Chaudun, which was captured by the regiment and later turned over to the French." Actually, the 18th's soldiers had stopped in the fields north of the village. The American Battle Monuments Commission version states, "At 8 a.m., the Germans had been driven out of Chaudun by an attack from the south in which troops of both the 1st Moroccan Division and the American 2d Division participated." Marine Corps historians stoutly proclaim "That the town was taken by Company A, 5th Marines, with some hangers-on, none of whom were from the 1st Division." This is not simply marine bravado; it is the truth as best the American Battle Monuments Commission could determine it from the testimony of participants.[39]

As matters developed that morning, by about 8:30 A.M. the 1st Moroccan Division had been, for the moment, virtually "pinched out" by the American 1st Division encroaching from the north and the 2d Division moving into its territory from the south. This mixing of troops from all three divisions will be addressed in the subsequent narrative of the 2d Division's action.

The German 28th Division, with three infantry regiments—including the 110th Grenadier Infantry—had been ordered into the XIII Corps sector on July 16 to back up the badly weakened 14th Reserve Division. A 10 A.M. Moroccan attack in the direction of the Rapiere, at the southern edge of Villemontoire Ravine, aided by tanks, caused the ad hoc defenses to collapse. Elements of the 16th Reserve, 53d and 159th Infantry, and 14th Reserve Divisions broke and ran to the rear past Villemontoire. By noon, the 2d Battalion, 110th Grenadier Infantry, which had occupied the western lip of Chazelle Ravine, was isolated with both flanks "in the air" and was forced to withdraw to rally positions east of the Soissons–Paris highway.

The 3d Battalion, 110th Grenadier Infantry, was ordered forward from its reserve position at 10 A.M. to defend the northern portion of the sector facing the Moroccans (Lechelle to Hill 140). The battalion was attacked thirty minutes later by what was reported to be a mixed force of Americans and black French assisted by about fifteen armored vehicles. Further enveloping attacks lapped around the south of the German position in the direction of Charantigny. Then German artillery mistakenly fell heavily on its own troops in Barbast and Lechelle, causing serious losses among the defenders. At 3 P.M. the battalion was withdrawn to a position north of Buzancy. The German defenses in this section of the battlefield had dissolved, but they would not remain in that state for long.[40]

By midday the Moroccan Division had advanced according to its own schedule but had been aided significantly by the rampaging Americans. The Moroccans must have been scratching their heads over the behavior of the strange fellows who evidently felt no particular need to follow the normal rules of combat—like adhering to established boundaries—and who fought without sophistication but with such incredible élan! The French admired élan. With the overwhelming success that had been achieved in the first eight hours, who wanted to pause to critique the methods? The Germans were on the run to safety in the east or moving in prisoner columns to the Allied rear. That was all that mattered.

Thursday Afternoon, July 18
1ST DIVISION

The 1st Division maintained adequate control for further commitment, albeit at the cost of strenuous personal exertion by most commanders. There is a tantalizing but otherwise unmentioned notation in the 2d Brigade files recording a 6:20 P.M. telephone call from General Summerall to General Buck, in which Summerall directed 2d Brigade to "advance this evening to the crest overlooking the Ploisy Ravine." How Buck responded to that call is unknown but at 9:35 P.M. another phone call directed 2d Brigade to "make no further advance . . . until further orders from division." The chain of command was more or less intact but the requisite information was not flowing properly. The 28th Infantry was utterly unable to cross the Paris–Soissons road, a full kilometer

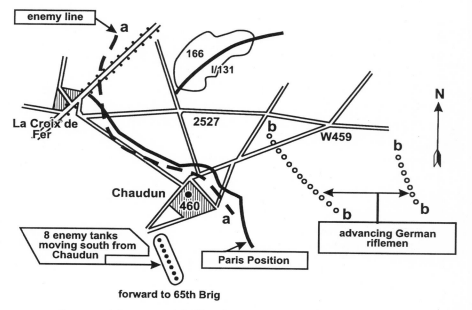

map 7. *German defenses around Chaudun, 11:15 A.M., July 18, 1918*

east of Ploisy Ravine because of the flanking machine-gun fire. It could not secure artillery support to suppress or neutralize that strong point. The 26th was likewise stymied. The inability of the 2d Brigade units to move forward served to anchor the 1st Brigade, which had to hold back its northern flank to maintain contact.[41]

1ST MOROCCAN DIVISION

July 18 had been a hard day for the Moroccans. One of the most experienced divisions in the French Army found itself stalled during an immensely successful attack when its American allies, encroaching from both sides, cut willy-nilly across the entire division sector. At such times it is best to let the commanders and soldiers on the spot work it out. That they did so without comment in official reports proves the point. However, it begs the question what effect this had on the German defenders. Surviving reports from the units opposing the Moroccans—and from those thrown into the gaps in the German line where there were no defenders—simply note that the attack paused along the eastern edge of what had been the Paris Position, south of Chaudun. That was the position all reinforcements in the center sector had been sent to secure. By the end of the day, the German 42d Division opposing the Moroccans reported

114 officers and 2,150 soldiers killed, wounded, or missing. Although Allied reports make no mention of it, it is evident that the attackers paused in part to sort themselves out. Thereafter, the German units reported attacks repeatedly forming up and being launched directly east from the Missy–Chaudun–Vierzy line. Despite foiling attack after attack, the defenders gave way to the north and south of the Chazelle–Lechelle sector belonging to the Moroccans, and the entire German line drifted back roughly to that line by nightfall. In order to consolidate its lines, the 1st Moroccan Division withdrew slightly in the north to connect with the 18th Infantry just north of Chaudun. It then had to stretch southeastward to connect with the 5th Marines, who were on the southern edge of the Lachelle Ravine. That flank connection was tenuous. In fact it was tenuous for both sides.[42]

The 1st Moroccan Division ended the day facing a stiffened German defense, although it could best be described as porous in places and none too firm on either flank where the Americans lay.

Second Lt. Herbert Sulzbach's 9th Division was snatched out of the Reims sector and thrown westward to the vicinity of Soissons, where it had fought so bitterly, if successfully, in May. On July 18, Sulzbach recorded in his journal: "In the evening orders arrive for the 9th I.D.—that's for us—to proceed to the rear! . . . our morale is quite terrible . . . all we can guess is that this great offensive hasn't come off! . . . we really feel desperate." Two days later he wrote: "It looks as though we are being thrown onto the largest enemy offensive of all time—and it was supposed to be *our* offensive! We couldn't have dreamed that this would happen—never."[43]

CHAPTER 3

Break-in

July 18—2d Division

South of the 1st Moroccan Division lay the zone of the American 2d Division, bringing with it a record of less in-country training but more sustained, bloody combat than the 1st Division. Elements of the 2d Division arrived in France piecemeal between June and December, 1917, and were put to work building roads, piers, rails, and buildings. Training began after the division was assembled in September. It first entered the lines in March, 1918.

On July 15, Maj. Gen. James Guthrie Harbord took command of the division. He was an officer who had been on the AEF's fast track from the beginning. Fifteen months before he was a major attending the Army War College when Pershing selected him for the key position of AEF chief of staff. A boyish, friendly extrovert, polished, and with an air of aplomb, he first caught Pershing's eye when they were both serving in the Philippines. By way of image, he affected the wear of the French "tin helmet." Anxious for a field command, Harbord, during an April, 1918, visit to a 1st Division training exercise, asked the commander Major General Bullard, for command of one of the brigades. Instead, Pershing surprised Harbord—and stunned marines on both sides of the Atlantic—by giving him command of the Marine Brigade that had been implanted into the U.S. Army's 2d Division. Harbord commanded that brigade throughout its storied attack at Belleau Wood. The division as a whole gained considerable experience in those three weeks in June, but it had taken terrible casualties: 170 officers and 8,739 men, of whom 112 officers and 4,598 men were marines. In the three-week respite since that time, the stream of replacements made up most of the numbers but it could not begin to make up the experience.[1]

On July 11, Harbord was notified of his promotion to major general. The next day he had lunch with General Pershing, who intimated the 2d Division commander's impending relief. On the thirteenth, Harbord and his aides went to Paris for a five-day rest knowing that the fourteenth was Bastille Day, the celebration of French independence. Their revelry was interrupted, however, by a call from General Pershing's chief of staff conveying orders to take command of the 2d Division immediately. Harbord left the next morning, July 15, and arrived before Maj. Gen. Omar Bundy, the 2d Division's commander, had awakened. Harbord assumed command at 9 A.M. and shortly thereafter received notice of the division's expected move to begin about 4 P.M. the next day. He immediately headed for Tenth Army headquarters at Carrefour de Nemours for a briefing.[2]

There, Harbord learned that the division was being assigned to Major General Berdoulat's XX Corps. Harbord and his chief of staff, Col. Preston Brown, eventually found XX Corps headquarters at Rétheuil, where they were finally given a copy of the attack order. They then traveled to the headquarters of the newly formed American I Corps at Taillefontaine, where they spent the night of July 16–17 writing the 2d Division operations order for an attack to be mounted the morning of the eighteenth.

While at the XX Corps headquarters, the group was approached by French staff officers and the G-1 of the 1st Moroccan Division, who offered to write or help write the division's attack order. The Moroccans, who had fought over the same area in May and June and remained in the line there, knew the terrain and had a fair appreciation of the enemy—all unknowns to the 2d Division. The offer was refused and with that refusal was sown the seeds for some of the confusion that would attend the next day's operations. The 1st Moroccan Division's orders were very detailed, as previously noted. They also established a completely different operational tempo, which, in ignorance of each other's plans, guaranteed the two divisions would be unable to maintain more than sporadic liaison on their flanks although both were specifically enjoined to ensure it was solid. The Moroccans planned a solid, measured advance with pauses between phases whose length was to be determined by the officer commanding the attacking brigade. The Americans were hurled headlong into the attack with a uniform rate of advance irrespective of terrain or enemy, and without consideration for pauses to consolidate and reorganize, much less pass fresh units through so as to maintain the momentum. The attack was to include French tank support, which was a fine idea except that the division had never worked or trained with tanks.

Harbord, unaccustomed to being palmed off and kept in the dark, approached this, the most critical time of his career, with great exasperation.[3] Looking back on the experience, he later wrote: "A division of twenty-eight thousand men, the size of a British or French Corps, had been completely removed from the knowledge and control of its responsible commander, and deflected by truck and marching through France to a destination uncommunicated to any authority responsible for its supply, safety, or its efficiency in an attack but thirty hours away."[4]

Brigadier Gen. Hanson Edward Ely commanded the 2d Division's 3d Brigade (also known as the Infantry Brigade), made up of the 9th and 23d Infantry Regiments. He was another new arrival, having been promoted and moved over from the 1st Division, where he commanded the 28th Infantry at Cantigny in late May. At West Point, Ely had shone in athletics but not at the blackboard. He was hard to like, gruff, pugnacious, heavy, a complainer, humorless, overbearing, and described by Laurence Stallings (who was not above some florid writing himself) as "tougher than alligator steak . . . six-feet-two, with 220 pounds of bone and gristle."[5]

The Marine Brigade, following Harbord's short but historic tenure, was assigned one of its own as commander: Brig. Gen. Wendell C. Neville, long reputed to be one of the Marine Corps' most competent officers. He commanded the 5th Marine Regiment during Harbord's tenure as brigade commander. Returning from the hospital so that he could be present for the Soissons offensive, he would have little opportunity to influence what happened, quite separately, to his two regiments of marines.[6]

If it was difficult for Harbord to take command, essentially in absentia, life in the division during that week had to be an exercise of intense faith. First, the division artillery was ordered off, even before the new division commander arrived. That was not an unusual occurrence as the guns were always in demand. If not actively in support of their parent division, they would frequently be called away to support someone else. Then came the alert order. The infantry units were to be ready to move at 4 P.M. on July 16, destination to be announced. The supply trains were to assemble at 9 P.M. and march overland separately. Since the trains included the kitchens, the eventual recombination of elements was of considerable importance. The evening meal on July 16 was truly the last supper for many 2d Division soldiers. However, the 9th Infantry, having experienced the consequences of failure to recombine before, made special provisions to take at least one complete kitchen along with the regiment.[7]

According to various accounts some French trucks arrived at the appointed hour. But there were delays, and units were required to march to previously unannounced embarking points several kilometers away. The first echelon thus did not actually move out until around 7 P.M., and others not move until 9 P.M. As the officers and men related their experience in later years, they told a tale akin to being taken hostage. Imprisoned in French trucks driven by Annamite (Vietnamese) drivers who spoke not one word of English and whose knowledge of the ultimate destination extended only to the next control point, the soldiers and marines bumped through the night and the better part of the next day without pause.

The perennial problem with secrecy is that if something happens to the people with the secret everything can come unglued. This movement was so secret that only a few French transportation officers knew more than a few of the details. Finally disembarking near the towns of Brassaire, Pierrefonds, and Rétheuil, the 2d Division soldiers and marines cast about for water and food. Finding neither, they were authorized to consume one day's emergency rations from their packs.

When those rations were but partly digested, the order came to move out immediately to assembly areas. Had anyone known the distance they had to move it would not have mattered, the congestion en route would have crippled their calculations. All day they marched with but a few halts and again no rations. Finally they arrived, footsore and terribly hungry and thirsty, at Taille-fontaine. There they finally encountered their new division commander. He gathered his brigade and regimental commanders together and passed out the attack order as best he could. There were not enough maps to provide more than a few per regiment—the 6th Marines received just one copy. Commanders looking for an opportunity to reconnoiter were bundled into a staff car and sent off, but the traffic was already so jammed that none ever saw even their jump-off line, much less the attack zone. The troops had enough time to refill their canteens but that was all, as the commanders realized that the distance to the jump-off line required them to start moving immediately.

As the soldiers and marines marched—perhaps stumbled and slid is a more accurate characterization—their way forward, the rain began to fall and the darkness of the forest through which they were proceeding became that much more impenetrable. The Forêt de Retz was an ancient royal forest preserve of huge, stately trees. It was cool and dark under the best of conditions; on a rainy night it was about as near absolute dark as it could be. If marching blind, hungry, and without sleep for the last forty-eight hours was not enough, the roads became clogged with all manner of motorized and horse-drawn traffic as well, including tanks. The Retz forest was jammed with men and war material struggling to get forward to the attack positions, but none as blindly as the 2d Division. There was not enough ammunition to go around at the announced resupply point, and many units went into action with less than their required basic load. Almost no one had grenades, flares, or ammunition for the crew-served weapons. That didn't matter much since most of the machine guns were lost somewhere well to the rear trying to find their way forward and many did not rejoin the division until the nineteenth. It is a minor miracle that the 5th Marines and 23d Infantry made it into the line at all. At every halt, commanders at every level had to exert great effort to restart forward movement.

Only those who have experienced such a situation can fully understand how easy it is to fall asleep on one's feet, or what a shock it is to the system to be awakened from that sleep while still upright. In one instance, an officer returning to find the missing half of his column found that a horse had stepped sideways in front of a tired marine. The marine had gone to sleep with his head pressed against the horse's flank and had thus broken the line. The French guides who were supposed to lead the units into position were not all present, and units became intermingled as they approached the jump-off point.[8]

Atop all this, time was running dangerously low, so low in fact that the last units had to double-time through the last hundreds of yards to meet the jump-off time—the 23d Infantry's attack battalions had to double-time over a mile. General Mangin could claim that the 2d Division did indeed achieve surprise, but he achieved surprise with the 1st Division as well, and that division was afforded a full day to reconnoiter its jump-off positions.[9]

Morning, July 18
5TH MARINES

The 5th Marines, advancing on the division's northern flank, were assigned the attack frontage of an entire brigade because the 6th Marines had been designated XX Corps reserve.[10] Harbord could use that regiment only if and when released by General Berdoulat, which was tantamount to release by General Mangin himself.

Of the twelve regimental commanders in XX Corps, none faced a more daunting situation than did Lt. Col. Logan Feland in bringing his 5th Marine Regiment onto the battlefield and directly into action. His regiment had dismounted from the French *camions* (trucks) some twelve miles short of its destination. It was 4 P.M. before a division staff officer appeared and verbally gave Feland his proper location in the attack formation—the division's left flank. The map accompanying the 2d Division's field order showed an attack frontage wide enough for both of the 4th Brigade's regiments. Feland was thus required to attack with two assault battalions abreast rather the usual formation of assault, support, and reserve battalions in column. Further complicating matters, the marines' line of departure was well back in the forest and angled southeast to join the 3d Brigade's jump-off line, which was out in the open fields. Colonel Neville did not issue a written order since only one of his two regiments was attacking. His marines double-timed the final stretch to bring the

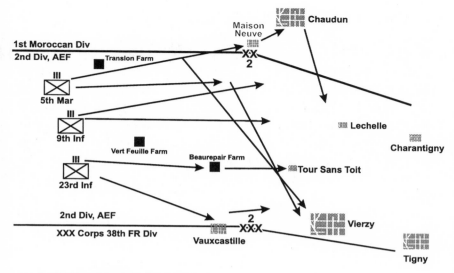

3. 2d Division Attack, July 18, 1918

lead battalion to the jump-off line soon after the barrage started. The following battalion then deployed to the right and began advancing without pause.[11]

The map also showed that soon after emerging from the forest the direction of attack was to veer sharply from northeast to east and then lean farther to the southeast. That change would have to be managed on relatively featureless terrain by officers who had not been afforded an opportunity to make a personal reconnaissance.

Feland's headquarters detachment, including his telephone communicators, was lost somewhere in the chaos to the rear, so he established a command post consisting of himself, Captain Schuler the adjutant, and two runners at a forest crossroads. By 8 A.M. on July 18 he had a telephone line to the rear. Feland had directed that Maj. Julius S. Turrill's 1st Battalion would attack on the left and Maj. Ralph S. Keyser's 2d Battalion on the right, with Maj. Maurice E. Shearer's 3d Battalion, still notably understrength after Belleau Wood with only twenty-three officers and 438 men, in support. That would virtually end Feland's command impact on the 5th Marines for that day. His regiment was about to detonate, with control fragmenting to battalions, companies, and errant detachments.[12]

Emerging from the forest, clearing German snipers and machine-gun nests as they went, the marine battalions should have made their distinct turn to the southeast at a point marked on the map by Translon Farm, south of the Bois de Quesnoy. Major Turrill deployed 17th Company on the left and 66th Company on the right, held 67th Company in support, and dispatched 49th Company, his trail element, to furnish the all-important "combat liaison" contact with the 1st Moroccan Division to the north. Second in command of 49th Company was a lanky Texan, 2d Lt. John W. Thomason, Jr., who, in later years would write and illustrate books of Marine Corps history, legend, lore, and fact. He also served for a period as an editor writing the official record of Soissons. In the retrospect of 1929, he observed that in the advance of infantry units beyond the point of the prescribed turn to the southeast, order had been largely lost. Another marine historian wrote a delicate explanation: "In the enormity and swiftness of attack, many of the fine points had been necessarily sacrificed."[13]

Thomason put it bluntly:

> The battle does not become coherent again until late afternoon. The reasons for this are evident; there was the haste and confusion incident to the last-minute concentration for the attack—all made inevitable by the French Army and Corps instructions wherein order and deliberation were compromised to the end that a surprise might be achieved. Thus, no reconnaissance by the American officers was possible . . . changes of direction in the course of action, especially on a terrain without prominent natural land marks, are difficult under the most favorable circumstances and to the best trained troops. Finally, the division orders enjoined rapidity of movement, and an advance without long halts on the successive objectives. The attack waves got off on time, they advanced, and continued to advance. They lost formation but retained so much individual energy that the German formations on their front were destroyed or rendered incapable. It is, therefore, impossible to assess exactly the results achieved although the mechanics which achieved those results was not always apparent; the front of the German 9th Army was, in the forenoon of 18 July, cleanly breached.[14]

A break-in is one thing, a breakthrough is another altogether, a thing implying penetration beyond the forward battle area and into the enemy's rear.

Forty-ninth Company lost contact with the 1st Moroccan Division's Senegalese liaison elements soon after emerging on the open plateau. There, most—but not all—of the Senegalese turned north to flank the Bois du Quesnoy, and the marines at the same time received heavy fire from the northeast, from Chaudun and the nearer Maison Neuve. Chaudun was on the northern edge of the 1st Moroccan Division's zone and Maison Neuve was near the southern boundary. Seventeenth Company—accompanied by part of the 2d Battalion's

55th Company, which was detailed to maintain liaison between the battalions and consequently was stretched over a kilometer, and a small band of about twenty Senegalese—also moved in the direction of Chaudun. On the way, about a kilometer due east of Translon Farm, they came upon a detachment led by an officer from the 1st Division's 18th Infantry that had halted and was digging in. It wasn't only the marines who were disoriented that day. The soldiers had crossed the entire 1st Moroccan Division front and were almost on the 2d Division boundary. What today might be called the "55th Company Team" took Chaudun about 9 A.M. after sharp fighting as large elements of the 18th Infantry appeared in the fields to the north of the town. Other marine elements cleared Maison Neuve and vicinity.[15]

About half of the two frontline marine battalions failed to make the proper change of direction to the southeast and instead went north, out of their sector. At the other extreme, three of the 2d Battalion's companies turned too sharply to the right, veering southward across the 9th Infantry sector, and joined elements of the 23d Infantry clearing out Vauxcastille, two miles south of Chaudun and slightly south of the division's southern boundary. When the gap between the two frontline battalions developed, several companies from the reserve 3d Battalion were sent forward, with no better result than more fragmentation.

It is clear that despite orders to move without regard to alignment, extreme efforts were made to maintain close alignment in order to preserve a coherent front and to provide sometimes vital flank protection. The result was a constant drawing upon the slender resources of the reserve formations, which compromised any hope of later exploitation. This is called "piecemeal commitment" and is not how matters are supposed to transpire. The reserve is supposed to be retained intact so as to provide the commander the wherewithal to decisively influence the battle. The most extreme troop dislocation occurred about noon, when the Germans on the Soissons–Paris road between Missy and Soissons captured a group of Americans from the 5th Marines and 23d Infantry. These soldiers and marines, having crossed the fronts of the entire French XX Corps and two German corps, caused great confusion among German order of battle experts.[16]

Between 8 and 9 A.M., fragments of the 5th Marines came up to the north branch of the Vierzy Ravine, which was the second objective. With Chaudun reduced, the major resistance on the 2d Division left was broken and the battalions took the opportunity to reassemble and work their way back into sector.[17]

American soldiers in France were fascinated by foreign things, intrigued even by their long-haul *camion* drivers' yellow race and slanted eyes, never imagining that their grandfathers would fight each other for almost ten years on the other side of the world. On this first morning of the drive toward Soissons, the Americans's direct encounter with the fierce fighters from Senegal implanted indelible memories. There was an element of admiration, an element of fear, and a great curiosity as to what might happen next. From his personal experience, and with some embellishment, Thomason set down his impressions in *Fix Bayonets!*:

> Later . . . he [the semifictional JWT himself] was caught up in a fighting swirl of Senegalese and went with them into an evil place of barbed wire and machine-guns. These wild black Mohammedans from West Africa were enjoying themselves. . . . Killing which is at best an acquired taste with the civilized races, was only too palpably their mission in life. Their eyes rolled, and their splendid white teeth flashed in their heads. . . . They were deadly. Each platoon swept its front like a hunting pack, moving swiftly and surely together. . . . They slew with lion-like leaps and lunges and shrill barbaric yapping . . .with the bayonet were terrible . . . they carried also a broad-bladed knife, razor sharp, which disembowelled a man at a stroke. . . . The lieutenant [Thomason] saw . . . unwounded fighting Germans who flung down their rifles when the Senegalese rushed, and covered their faces, and stood screaming against the death they could not look upon. And—in a lull, a long, grinning sergeant, with a cruel aquiline face, approached him and offered a brace of human ears, nicely fresh, strung upon a thong.[18]

The Senegalese reputation for fighting for the sake of fighting seems borne out by the experience of Sgt. Matej Kocak, with 66th Company, 5th Marines. Kocak, after joining what came to be known as "The Solo Club"—which required taking out a German machine-gun position by himself—found a couple of dozen unattached Senegalese. He organized them and led them on to eliminate another machine-gun emplacement.[19] A fight was a fight and the enemy had to be killed. Who cared under whose direction?

Gradually, the separated segments of the 5th Marines came together at the deep ravine that ran north to south roughly from Vauxcastille to Maison Neuve, completely across the division zone. At the bottom, near Vauxcastille, the ravine turned straight east and ran to the town of Vierzy, beyond which lay the line representing the XX Corps objective. The entire low ground complex became known simply as the Vierzy Ravine. There, among the wreckage of horse batteries and motor transport, Thomason recalled, the dead, clad in German *feldgrau,* American khaki, and the mustard-colored uniforms of the 1st Moroccan Division, were thickly scattered. Under a protective cliff, a 9th Infantry surgeon had taken over a German dressing station staff and all, and tended all comers. The ravine became "a sort of backwash of the war, into which it drew a melancholy drift of wounded men, prisoners, and exhausted men who had gone to the far edge of human endurance." For the 5th Marines, the battle had ended for the morning—but not for the day.[20]

3D BRIGADE

In contrast to the 5th Marines, the 3d Brigade had an attack frontage of about a thousand meters—roughly five hundred meters per regiment. On the night before the attack, the 9th Infantry had the good fortune to come through the Forêt de Retz before the greatest crush of congestion, and Col. LaRoy Upton had most of his battalions in their assigned positions before midnight. Two companies, L and M, did not close into position until 4:15 A.M. and 3 A.M. respectively.[21]

The brand-new brigade commander, Brig. Gen. Hanson Ely, had greeted Upton with a most forthright statement: "Higher authority has warned me that you are in an depressed condition and that it is affecting your regiment. We are going into battle in two days and if you cannot brace up and get a little more spirit into your regiment, I will have to relieve you."

Upton was upset because he had learned just a few days before that he had been passed over for promotion to brigadier general, and that the promotion list, received on July 12, included officers junior to him. He had overdone his complaint that "someone in a swivel chair in Washington" could stick a knife in his back. Harbord, who had been briefed by Ely's predecessor, Brig. Gen. Edward M. Lewis, personally made Upton aware of that fact. After the war, in response to Upton's search for vindication, Lewis wrote a favorable letter from Camp Pike, Arkansas, on September 20, 1920, that included this passage: "As you are doubtless aware, if you have seen Efficiency Report of you by me, I have spoken of your expression of perhaps excessive chagrin and disappointment at seeing your juniors promoted over you."

LaRoy Upton would have to demonstrate a high order of personal leadership—as evidenced by the performance of an infantry regiment in full-scale attack—or he would be on the road back to Blois, "the human salvage depot," where officers were reclassified for rear-area duties or sent home. He appears to have gotten hold of himself because Ely later wrote, "The man came to himself and the regiment did splendid work."[22]

Ely's other regimental commander, Col. Paul B. Malone of the 23d Infantry, was in exactly the same boat. Although Malone's name was also absent from the July 12 list, he did not scream loud enough to attract unfavorable attention. Pershing was furious that many of his recommendations for this list had been ignored by Peyton March in Washington. Harbord, too, considered the list "an outrage."

As the jump-off hour neared, Upton, who had seen nothing of the eighteen tanks assigned to support his regiment, began to think there would be no attack. Then, at 4:35 A.M., "hell broke loose" and the tanks lumbered up a bit later. As the lead battalions moved out, Upton was behind a hill. "However," he wrote, "I could not stand the strain so when everything was going all right I went forward about a kilometer and witnessed a wonderful sight. Off to the right was the 23d Infantry while in front was my regiment and to our left a column of tanks going along the edge of the woods swatting every Boche machine gun that they could find. . . . I saw one shell apparently wipe out a small column but the next moment I saw the whole column get up and go forward. It was full daylight and an inspiring scene."[23]

Evidence that he was bracing up is contained in a 5:40 A.M. message Upton sent back with a runner: "Everything went on the dot so far as we were concerned. Tanks late, did not wait for them. . . . 12 prisoners in first batch. 23d has much more."[24]

The vulnerability of battalion commanders in the 9th Infantry (not a unique case, as evidenced earlier by the 28th Infantry) is all too well illustrated. The 1st Battalion, commanded by Capt. Charles E. Speer, led with two companies on a five-hundred-yard front. Major Arthur E. Bouton's 2d Battalion followed as support, and Capt. Henry H. Worthington led the 3d Battalion in reserve. Bouton was killed by German artillery just as his battalion started the assault. His replacement, Capt. John L. Taylor, was killed later in the day, and Lt. Melvin H. Leonard led fragments of the battalion through the last phases of the attack. In the lead battalion, Captain Speer was wounded and evacuated less than half an hour after the attack commenced. The 3d Battalion's Captain Worthington would, at the end of the day, have a premonition of his own death.[25]

The 9th Infantry's leading 1st Battalion was soon taking casualties from machine guns on the left because the marines had been a few minutes late and the tanks weren't up yet. The 9th Infantry's infantrymen did the natural thing and faced left against the enemy's hot fire, just as Huebner's 2d Battalion, 28th Infantry, had done. They then fought north toward Verte Feuille Farm, arriving there at about the time the marines came through to capture it. By then the 1st Battalion was set on a direction of its own and it continued to the northeast across the 5th Marines's zone and on into the 1st Moroccan Division's sector to fight at Maison Neuve Farm.[26]

The 2d Battalion, coming up in support, also missed the turn southeast and veered sharply north to join the combat at Maison Neuve Farm. Here again, as in the case of the marine battalions, the Americans, north and south, were well within the Moroccans's zone. Later in the morning, elements of the 1st Moroccan Division arrived at Maison Neuve and the men of the 9th Infantry found their bearings and set off almost due south to rejoin the many other elements that had gathered in the north-south depression of Vierzy Ravine.[27]

The malignant benefits of launching an attack without reconnaissance or adequate maps were beginning to tell there as well. In 1925, Lieutenant General Bullard published extracts of his memoirs in the *New York Tribune*. In them he included a statement that the 2d Division at Soissons had been, among other things, "scattered." This incensed Major General Harbord, who by then was an executive with the Radio Corporation of America. Harbord obtained a splendid letter of rebuttal from Major General Berdoulat, the erstwhile XX Corps commander, in which Berdoulat stated that Harbord's troops, at the time they were relieved on the afternoon of the nineteenth, "were absolutely in no greater or lesser disorder than the rest of the troops." Although a very accurate statement, they were nonetheless scattered.[28]

Logan Feland, commanding the 5th Marines, addressed the point in his after-action report prepared July 30, 1918. According to Feland, "there was as little confusion as could be expected, considering the coming into our sector of attack of elements of other brigades and divisions. Those units of the regiment which went out of the sector did so in order to better attack the enemy and were forced to do so by the presence of the other elements mentioned and by the great narrowing of our sector at the first intermediate objective."[29]

First Lt. Ludislav T. Janda, a six-foot-two and of Czechoslovakian parentage, was the only officer present with Company M, 3d Battalion, initially held in the rear as the regimental reserve. He remembered Upton's briefing to the assembled regimental officers (". . . a deadly serious talk, brutally to the point, that left everybody with the feeling of 'we may get it but who cares.'") in which Upton specifically warned about the abrupt change of direction. It was 4:30 A.M. before Janda had his men into final position and in touch with the 23d Infantry to his right. The rain had stopped and the first gray streaks of light were just beginning to show when 1st Sgt. Andy Lauer suddenly popped to life saying, "Lieutenant, it might be a good idea to take a look at that map." Janda later credited the sergeant's foresight with helping to keep the 3d Battalion on proper course. "I believe very few company commanders, in the press of getting their men placed, had a chance to look at their maps [in daylight] and this may account for the scattering of units."

Soon after the jump-off, while his company was moving through heavy artillery and machine-gun fire, Janda noticed that the units ahead of him were veering left and troops were approaching from the right. He sent a runner to the right. "I realized then that M Company was advancing in the first wave when the runner came back with the information that the men on our right were the first wave of the Twenty-third Infantry." Continuing steady on course, Company M seized Beaurepaire Farm (almost exactly on the regiment's right boundary) at about 5:15 A.M., capturing the few surviving Germans just as the friendly barrage passed the farm. They then encountered a stray platoon from Company I. It was less than an hour after they had jumped off, and chaos had set in everywhere. Janda now had a chance to take stock: "My Company had shrunk to fifty or sixty percent of its original strength due to having passed thru the German barrage three times as it was dropped back and also to the fact that the enemy was organized in depth to such an extent that every crest seemed to be covered by machine gun fire up to the time we reached the [Beaurepaire] farm."[30]

Another Soissons veteran wrote, "He had walked into and through a German counter-barrage and come out the other side! When you came out the other side, you were an old timer."[31]

Next came one of those battlefield incidents that defy logic. Captain Worthington was commanding the 3d Battalion because Lt. Col. Alfred C. Arnold, the assigned commander, had earlier been evacuated for physical exhaustion and voice loss after being gassed. Suddenly Arnold appeared, "roaming the field as a free lance," pointed out to Janda in a whisper that the direction should be changed to the southeast, and then disappeared. Janda took his troops in the prescribed direction but did not see Arnold again that day. In fact, he did not see the remainder of the 9th Infantry until 5:30 P.M.[32]

Within a few hundred yards after leaving Beaurepaire, Janda's men, with no one else in sight on their right or left, began taking heavy casualties from artillery and machine-gun fire from across Vierzy Ravine. Janda had just halted his men on the near edge when they were hit with a salvo of tear gas. "Almost without orders, what remained of the men literally plunged down the slope with eyes streaming and cursing a blue streak. We scrambled up the opposite slope where the guns were located, but the gun crews were running off through the wheat ahead."

The company stopped there to recover and the men quenched their thirst from a keg of sauerkraut, then moved out to a point well beyond the ravine near a tower marked *"Tour sans toit"* five hundred yards north-northeast of Vierzy. Arriving there at about 9:20 A.M. and looking back with his binoculars, Janda was hoping to see at least one of the fourteen divisions mentioned in Colonel Upton's briefing as participating in the overall attack. He saw no troops at all; the fields were barren except for scattered stretcher bearers! Janda filled out a message form, giving his company's position, strength, and opposition, and requesting support. He gave the message to two runners with instructions to find regimental headquarters. He never learned what happened to either of them.[33]

As the fight developed, American ground troops all over the Soissons battle-field groused that German airplanes were having at them without effective opposition, and at this early hour Company M got a taste of their sting. Twenty brightly painted aircraft flew low overhead, strafing the company, then circled around and flew over singly to drop grenades. Despite the ground-hugging period of terror, no one was wounded. The Tenth Army aviation commander's instructions were to emphasize supporting the French tank force and recon-naissance. Other aircraft were to secure the skies, but a mix-up in orders sent them to Reims, denuding the main attack of its air cover. Brigadier Gen. William "Billy" Mitchell commented in his memoirs that he discovered this con-dition and then assured the senior headquarters that he and his men would handle the matter. As far as the American infantry were concerned, Mitchell never showed up.[34]

At about this time Janda saw his battalion commander, Captain Worthington, approaching, accompanied by only the battalion gas officer, Lt. German W. Rice. Worthington had no idea where the remainder of the battalion was. After an hour, the two visiting officers left in search of other units. Thus ended the morn-ing for Company M, 9th Infantry. When Janda counted again, he discovered he had only thirty-five of the 229 men who had jumped off, including some strays from other companies. Janda's use of this figure in his postwar account high-lights a situation that is probably widespread in battlefield narration. At first glance, the reader might think that Company M had experienced 194 battle casualties, which was not at all the case. A 1919 accounting of the company's per-sonnel going back to September, 1917, showed that at Soissons there were four killed, 68 wounded, and one missing, for a total of seventy-four casualties.[35]

Janda could hardly have known that he and the few stalwarts still with him were, at that moment, making history. They were the leading edge of the French XX Corps at the turn of the tide in World War I.

Meanwhile, Col. LaRoy Upton had remained at his command post in the rear throughout the morning, interesting himself in the arrival of German prison-ers and his own walking wounded. According to Allied command practice he could justify his presence there at what should have been the center of infor-mation. Sometime before noon, Upton left most of his staff in place and set out to get himself more actively involved in command. En route he encountered the problem of stragglers—men who used any excuse to depart the front lines for the safety of the rear. He later reported picking up "about 30 stragglers on the way. I came near . . . shooting a corporal and a private, as they were in a trench feigning to be wounded. My language[,] as I yanked them out was more vitriolic than polite."[36]

Straggling at Soissons is dealt with in several after-action reports, most realistically in those of the 2d Brigade, 1st Division, signed by Brig. Gen. Beaumont Buck, who recorded: "Our most serious short-coming appears to me to have been our failure to grapple with the problem of straggling. This evil increased daily as the battle progressed." Major General Bullard also noted the problem in his postwar writings: "The French villages were full of them. . . . we had in our army dead-beats and stragglers, evaders of battle and danger. . . . The hardest works that I did or saw done by others in France was the holding of men to duty in service and battle."[37]

Upton was taken aback by the scene when he arrived at Beaurepaire Farm, a place of "utter desolation," filled with wounded and dead, with no water to be had. By this time most of the 9th Infantry had, after various diversions out of its own boundaries, reached the Vierzy Ravine, but none were as yet up to the town of Vierzy. Janda's company was, of course, on its own, pinned to the ground about a kilometer east of the ravine.

Upton's principal staff officer, Regimental Adjutant Capt. Hanford MacNider, had his own view of the action. Two days earlier he had been sent to a Paris hospital with violent intestinal problems. However, when an acquaintance told him of the division's hasty commitment to action, he caught a ride to the Villers-Cotterêts forest. Dressed in his best uniform ("my striker's last tribute to a sick man"), and toting a musette bag and trench coat, he set out on foot to find Upton's headquarters. Following ammunition going one way and wounded the other through the woods, he made it to open ground. "Our infantry," wrote MacNider, "had left a trail of ruin and disaster behind them. One could see dark heaps everywhere lying among the poppies and wheat."[38]

He passed a battalion of the division's supporting artillery just opening fire to support a new attack (therefore sometime about 6:30 P.M.?) and, in an incongruity on a battlefield where oddity was becoming normal, found a Ford supply vehicle with a driver willing to take him up forward. MacNider soon spotted Upton with the headquarters commandant, Captain Gill, and exclaimed, "Whoa! We seem to be home!" The Ford immediately attracted machine-gun fire and Gill's greeting, "This is the front line, you fool. Get that damned Lizzie out of here before we all get blown to hell. How the devil did YOU get here?"

Hanford MacNider had resumed his place of duty. He later observed, "The

Colonel seemed moderately pleased at my return, though neither he nor Gill could understand my leaving Paris. I couldn't now myself. I felt very sick all over. The machine gun bullets whined incessantly overhead. A bashed-in baby tank just across the road became the target for an annoying enemy battery who salvoed it first with gas and then with black and ugly shrapnel."[39]

23D INFANTRY

The 2d Division's 23d Infantry Regiment was the southernmost unit in XX Corps. A man of Hanson Ely's bulk might have questioned the physical capability of the diminutive Col. Paul B. Malone to command a regiment in combat. However, Malone had been doing so in fine style since February 15, when he came down to the division from AEF headquarters, where he had been the AEF's first G-5 training officer. Malone, too, had a gripe about missing out on his star, but he apparently hadn't been obnoxiously vocal in expressing his disappointment.

The 23d Infantry was to move along XX Corps' southern boundary with the French 38th Division on its right. Major d'Arly Fechet's 2d Battalion led the column of battalions during the morning attack. His men reached the jump-off line exhausted after double-timing to ensure they were on time. They began the attack without machine guns, 37-mm one-pounders, Stokes mortars, hand grenades, or rifle grenades. Malone, realizing the significance of this, sent a message to brigade: "I cannot probably reduce Vierzy which is strongly organized. As you know I have no M.G.s no grenades."[40]

A French officer had come forward to announce that the allocated tanks were stuck in a ravine somewhere to the rear. Fechet's battalion made about a thousand yards in the first fifteen minutes, but the German counterbarrage eventually cost him five officers, including a company commander and two staff officers, and about half his command group. Fechet himself was slightly wounded but remained in command. Although there was no contact with the French on the right, no trouble came from that flank either. Unlike several elements of its sister regiments, most of the 23d Infantry's units made the turn to the southeast, although some elements joined up with the 9th Infantry and even the 5th Marines to the north. Eventually, many members of the nomadic 5th Marines latched on with the 23d Infantry.[41]

Consequently, the bulk of the 23d Infantry moved in fair order to be caught up in stiff defenses covering the town of Vauxcastille, on the division's right boundary. There the north-south ravine cutting through the division sector joined the larger east-west ravine that went on toward the larger town of Vierzy. Message traffic indicates that elements of the 1st and 2d Battalions were actually well across the division boundary south of Vauxcastille, and elements of the reserve 3d Battalion had been sent forward piecemeal to join the action. Some small groups reported they had been into Vierzy itself by midmorning, but they were driven back.[42]

Malone's detailed report of the morning's action invites comment on the capabilities and limitations of command, control, and liaison at the regimental level. It fits well with previous examples of control at brigade and division, although the commanders on this battlefield showed a lack common thinking on where they should be in a given situation. To some extent, as noted earlier, they were influenced by orders for regimental and higher commanders to stay near the communications network installed in their command posts.

In October—reacting to the AEF's experiences at Soissons, Saint-Mihiel, and in the opening phase of the Meuse-Argonne campaign—Pershing sent a message calling for "Division and Brigade Commanders [to] place themselves as far up toward the front of the advance of their respective units as may be necessary to direct movements with energy and rapidity in any attack." In the same message he told his senior commanders that they should not hesitate "to relieve on the spot any officer of whatever rank who fails to show the leadership required."[43]

At Malone's initial regimental command post in the ravine at Chavigny, about six hundred yards behind the jump-off line, there was a liaison officer from the French 38th Division, the division operating on neighboring XXX Corps' northern flank. A 2d Division staff officer was also there, charged with returning to his headquarters as soon as the location of attack battalions had been determined. Malone was "in constant contact" by runner with Upton's 9th Infantry on the left—at least with the regimental PC. However, he soon saw the need to set up an advance CP close to the main road leading back to brigade and division, from which runners could be dispatched, "no other form of liaison existing." At 6:45 A.M. Malone advised adjacent units that he was displacing forward to Beaurepaire Farm. By 8 A.M. Malone was located there, and Upton collocated with him later in the morning. Not long after, Upton reported that he had no contact with the marines to his left, and Malone had lost touch with the French on his right.[44]

Brigade Commander Ely had also made successive moves forward until he added his command group to those at Beaurepaire Farm. Mobility for communications was limited to Ely's own automobile, as there were "no motorcycles, horses, or other vehicles." Ely's telephone and wireless units were still in some rear-area traffic jam.

Even in its earlier experience of relatively static operations, the AEF had experienced communications problems. Field radios were heavy and unreliable, and buzzer codes sent over telephones had limitations. It all came down to telephones and runners and, in the fast movement of Soissons, rear-area phone lines were torn out by the unprecedented number of tanks. Forward-area linemen couldn't keep up with the demand for their services, leaving runner's as the primary means of communication.[45]

As for Harbord's understanding of his role as division commander, we must take into account this statement regarding the morning of July 18: "The attack began at the appointed hour of 4:35 A.M. It was out of my hands when they went 'over the top,' and there was nothing to do but pray for victory, and wait for news."[46] For a while that was the proper course of action.

The 3d German Division had been in the process of relieving part of the already collapsing 115th Division when the attack struck. The 115th's sector was split by the XX Corps' boundary, so it was hit by both the 2d Division's 23d Infantry and the French 38th Division. The 34th Fusilier Regiment of that division lost its entire 3d Battalion save fourteen men, and the 2d Battalion lost two-thirds its strength attempting to defend Villers-Helon in the French 38th Division sector.[47] When not encumbered by old fortifications, the French Army could strike hard and fast.

Noon, July 18

The 2d Brigade, 1st Division, operating in the northern half of the XX Corps' zone, was held up by strong German defense at Missy Ravine and from positions in the French sector farther north, where the 153d Division had failed to progress. The 1st Brigade had fought its way across the Soissons–Paris road and was about a kilometer ahead, which required that it bend its line back with connecting units in order to maintain contact. The 1st Moroccan Division's zone had been encroached upon from the north at Chaudun and from the south at Maison Neuve, but by noon it had moved forward, linking the two American divisions. The 2d Division was pulling itself together in the Vierzy Ravine, not yet having tackled Vierzy, which lay just west of the line of the third objective. There was no doubt the German Ninth Army's front had been broken. But had it been broken all the way through?

At this early juncture, the violent rupture of the German lines demonstrated the success of General Mangin's elaborate plan for striking with surprise. He had done this by launching one and hurling another American division into the attack. They had both gone in hard and in doing so became disordered.

With their flanks exposed by the inability of French units to match their dash and determination, and with command fragmented by their very success, the two were divisions in name only. The casualties were in keeping with the loss of control and would get worse.

In a musty corner of the American accounts of the battle is a statement, albeit second-hand, that is of prime importance to understanding what happened at Soissons. Following the war, an officer who had been with 1st Division Artillery recounted: "I was talking a short time ago with General Bjornstad, who was acting as chief of staff of our Third Corps, and he told me . . . he went to Mangin [on the night of the seventeenth] and told him it was a physical impossibility for some of the [U.S.] units to reach their places for the attack, but that General Mangin had said that a surprise attack by exhausted troops would be more successful than an anticipated attack delivered by fresh ones, and he was so convinced of the ignorance of the Germans of the impending attack that he would rather attack with a portion of the [XX] corps than to hold up the attack for the arrival of all of the organization."[48]

Afternoon, July 18

The history of the Soissons operation for the afternoon and evening of July 18 centers on the 2d Division's attempt to pull together its command structure, consolidate and reorganize its troops, and push ahead against frantic opposition. The division was working against the clock as the Germans scrambled desperately for more reinforcements. The division's first lunge was so stunning a surprise that local German reinforcements were consumed in their reserve positions or were hurriedly thrown into the yawning gaps that kept springing up in the line. In the frantic fighting of that first day the Germans lost entire units. Representative of the scale of losses reported by the Germans is this extract from the 11th Bavarian Division's report: "Only 2 officers and 25 men of the 3d Inf. Regt. came back. There is no information concerning the regimental staff." This report is from the division, which had been alerted early. Not until the nineteenth was there any significant reinforcement of the German line, and that too was quickly eaten away despite some initially successful counterattacks.[49]

The 2d Division received the XX Corps order for exploiting the morning's success, issued at 11 A.M., shortly before 1:30 P.M. Harbord's command post was still well behind the jump-off line at Carrefour de Nemours. Shortly thereafter his staff had the division order ready to pass down. In the absence of telephone or radio communications, the written order had to be hand delivered. At about the same time Harbord decided to cut loose from the command post and seek

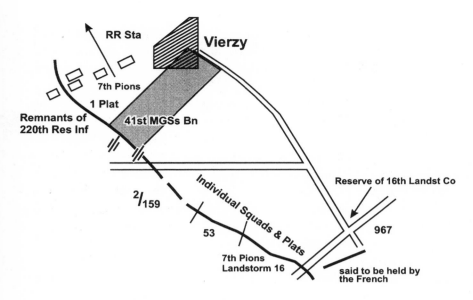

map 8. German positions southwest of Vierzy, 4:30 P.M., July 18, 1918

first-hand information. In doing this he violated what had become common practice for senior officers in the Allied armies. On the other hand, he was acting in the better American tradition of going forward to get the true sense of the battle and to convey to his principal subordinates the overall picture they could not otherwise obtain. If, in the process, he found it necessary to brace up some of the laggards, that sort of thing was always best done face to face. In a 1991 post–Gulf War interview, Lt. Gen. Calvin Waller, deputy commander in chief of the U.S. Central Command, made the point that there can be no substitute for looking into a man's eyes when giving him an order to lead his unit into battle. If he flinches, it is time to look for his replacement.[50] That sort of thing cannot be done telephonically.

Brigadier General Ely found out early that, with traffic cutting off normal access forward, he had made a mistake in placing his command post so far back. He worked his way forward and arrived at Beaurepaire Farm thirty minutes after noon. There he found both Upton of the 9th Infantry and Malone of the 23d Infantry already established. They briefed him on what they knew of the situation.[51]

Having caught up with the regimental situations, Ely knew he had to get a situation report to the division commander. With neither telephone nor mounted messenger available, Ely himself set off to make the report in the only vehicle available—the one in which he had come up. En route, he met a division staff officer coming forward with a message from Harbord requesting a status report. Evidently this was the first request for information, yet the battle was already six hours old. Ely noted that this was the first message of the day to reach him from division headquarters. About half an hour later, within two kilometers of the division command post, Ely motoring west, met Harbord motoring east. Harbord advised Ely of the attack order for the following day, July 19, which had a jump-off time of 4:30 A.M. The problem was that the assumed start positions had not yet been captured, which meant that the day's efforts were not yet finished.[52]

This is the first of several instances in which the next day's plans and orders were written early—possibly with the end in view that the attacking units would receive them early enough to take appropriate preparatory action. However, these attacks were routinely nailed to the artillery fire plans, which were created on the assumption that the day's objectives had been taken. The flow of information from front to rear was terribly slow, of dubious accuracy, and fragmentary, but it was equally slow from the rear forward. Infantry airplanes were supposed to verify the frontline trace of friendly troops, but they could not report their observations to every headquarters up the line and therefore only added to the uncertainty in the intervening headquarters. Since the 6th Marines could not be released from reserve, the 3d Brigade and whatever of the 5th Marines could be found, would have to try again—and once again without any ammunition resupply, organic auxiliary weapons, food, or water. The elements of the 5th Marines were placed under Third Brigade control—but an attack hour of 4:30 P.M. obviously could not possibly be met.[53]

The Harbord-Ely encounter was noted in the following blunt and sharply judgmental entry (not at all usual in this context) in Book 3 of *Monograph Soissons:* "It is not too much to say that [on July 18] liaison within the [2d] division broke down completely, and that the usual means of communication failed to function from the first. Generals and colonels delivered their orders in person. . . . Over the action as a whole, the division command had no control whatever, nor any accurate knowledge of its progress except that obtained by the casual encounter of the division commander and brigade commander on the battlefield."[54]

Actually, the division staff had sent the order to Ely by an officer on a horse borrowed from the artillery and, as a backup, by a courier on a motorcycle borrowed from a French liaison post. But the motorcycle broke down, and the horseman did not arrive until 3:45 P.M.—fifteen minutes before Ely managed to fight his way back through the traffic.[55] That fact notwithstanding, there is little reason to excuse either the division commander or the brigade commander for failing to communicate with each other much sooner.

Whatever shortcomings Pershing may have had as a senior commander, he knew from experience something of the confusion that besets any attack. He knew that consolidation after the successful capture of an objective, or restarting a stalled attack, always requires extraordinary energy. Because the immediate commander is usually involved in the issues of the moment, it is necessary that the impetus to recover forward momentum come from the rear—from the next higher commander. This could not be accomplished if senior commanders remained in the rear, tied to their telephones, and Pershing eventually made it clear to all what his expectations were. However, those expectations were not published until August 29, 1918, when they were published as secret instructions.[56]

At this point, while Ely was returning with the order for the day's second attack, Lt. Lud Janda and the remnants of Company M were located on the open plateau east of the Vierzy Ravine and northwest of the center of Vierzy. He and his men were the leading edge of XX Corps. In the middle of the afternoon, Janda became involved in a misadventure that removed him from the battlefield.

The 1st Moroccan Division had kicked off its second attack at about 3 P.M. and had advanced toward Lechelle, only to be driven back.[57] In another case of severe misdirection, elements of the Moroccan division had slanted down into the 2d Division zone. Janda's account follows:

> At 3:30 P.M. three small French tanks, supported by about sixty black Moroccans [Senegalese] in squad columns fifty yards behind the tanks, moved thru us from the left rear and headed straight for Vierzy. There was some confusion as M Company had some difficulty in keeping from being run down by the machines, lying, as we were, hidden in the wheat. . . . The black men just followed along stoically—and too close. . . . The machine guns in Vierzy opened up a terrific burst of fire and we were right in the path of it. The Moroccans were simply mowed down but kept on until I did not see a single one left standing. This was literally the case. The tanks turned around and vanished to our left rear. M Company had several casualties due to this foolish maneuver. How they happened to come there in the first place, I don't know. I got a bullet in the knee.[58]

At 4:30 P.M. a runner arrived with a message instructing Janda to bring his men back to a regimental assembly area immediately to the rear in the Vierzy Ravine. It was Janda's first contact with "the outfit" since he had left the roving Lieutenant Colonel Arnold in the morning. By 5:50 P.M., his leg useless, "as it was bent to a right angle," Janda, aided by another wounded soldier, had returned to find his battalion commander, Captain Worthington. Janda then prepared to hobble on to an aid station at Beaurepaire Farm. "He [Captain

Worthington] bade me goodbye and said he would never see me again. I asked him why and he replied that the Regiment was going to make another attack at 6:00 P.M. and that he knew that he would be killed."[59]

Preparing for the afternoon attack, Ely, out of contact with the headquarters of the Marine Brigade but in possession of essentially all of the 5th Marines, placed them as previously indicated. The regimental commanders reported they could get off at 6 P.M. The French tank commander said he couldn't be ready before seven. Ely therefore ordered that the infantry attacks be made whenever ready but not later than six, with the tanks to follow as soon as possible. The attack actually got underway at 7 P.M. in what was wryly reported as "a rather ragged manner."[60]

9TH INFANTRY

LaRoy Upton's reinforced 9th Infantry had the northern sector, and was to move east from the upper horn of Vierzy Ravine. It might be fair to conjecture that Upton, as he had listened to Ely's attack order, still had a part of his mind focused on Ely's recent suggestion that he "brace up" or be sent packing. Upton indeed felt the call of duty: "I knew that to make the attack start I would have to start it myself so I jumped in my recently brought forward car and rode to the advance line and told the officers and men the situation." The regiment was deployed on a front of over a thousand yards, two battalions up, two in support, all very weak in strength.[61]

Moving out at seven, they met resistance from the outset, first from the right front. After about a mile, heavy enfilading machine gun fire came from Lechelle Woods and Ravine, on their left flank. The 2d Battalion, 5th Marines, on the left of the line, turned northeast toward the fire, a factor influencing movement on practically every battlefield since the advent of gunpowder weapons. They had begun to move slowly toward the machine guns when the tanks that had been preceding the marines withdrew through their lines, followed in their wake by a barrage of intense artillery fire, which had caused the tanks to reverse direction in the first place. After many casualties from this artillery fire, which also destroyed three tanks, the marines cleared out the enemy pocket and continued east. Unknown to them, they had turned the German defensive positions that had been holding up the Moroccans's attack. As the pressure from the 1st Division's attack in the north had eased, the Germans elected to hold fast and refuse their partly exposed southern flank. Now it was wide open.[62]

Upton and a small command group that included six runners followed the assault line on foot. He was surprised at the enfilading fire from the left front because he had been told the French were advancing in that portion of the sector. The murderous flanking fire was evidence that was not the case. He watched as the battalion of marines launched their attack on the machine guns, then set out across the field. It was the last he saw of them until that night. As he crossed the field, an artillery shell killed a nearby runner and took off the foot of another.

Daylight was fading when Upton heard incessant machine-gun firing from the right front. He continued forward, policing up stray troops as he went. At the road running northeast from Vierzy to Charantigny, Upton dispatched a message to brigade that his regiment was in "a serious position" with lines broken. He then went on to the front, where he found a total of about three hundred men from the 2d and 3d Battalions. He also learned that all three battalion commanders had been killed or wounded.[63]

Upton was in the correct place, for there was no one left with the big picture. He could not have known at the time that this was also his redemptive move. Ely wrote later: "In the attack, when one of your battalions was faced to the north flank, friendly troops not being up, and the remainder of the regiment was about 1½ kilometers to the front of it, the establishment of you and your P.C. practically in the interval, reassured your men and materially assisted in enabling them to hold their lines against strong counterattacks, for which you were awarded the D.S.C."[64]

Among those officers down was Captain Worthington, he of the premonition, who with cane and pistol had been in front of his 3d Battalion only a short dash before being killed. On August 23, the Company M first sergeant, Albert W. Anderson, wrote to the still-hospitalized Janda to bring him up to date on developments in the company: "I do not know whether you heard that Capt Worthington was killed or not. It sure is fine to hear the men tell how brave he was. . . . he was killed by a shell while leading his men forward."[65]

Any reader who has been at or even near ground combat has to pause and wonder how a person who has a genuine conviction that he is going to be killed in an attack brings himself to move forward at the appointed time and place. Pleading shell shock or outright refusal and direct transportation to the disgrace of Blois would have been alternatives. John W. Thomason, Jr., wrote that he only knew of two soldiers who stated a premonition of death and then actually encountered it.[66]

Readers who have never been under fire should go to Gettysburg and stand among the guns in the field west of the Robert E. Lee memorial. From there, look across that mile or so of open, rolling ground to where the Union Army withstood the attack by Richard Anderson's division on Cemetery Ridge on July 2. Imagine that the ground is strewn with dead and now, July 3, 1863, you are going to march across that same ground with George Pickett's division. Ask yourself, as you stand there, how they did it—then ask yourself if you could.

At Soissons, Colonel Upton decided it was time for this part of the 9th Infantry to dig in, and some engineers came up to help. It was the first command decision he had the opportunity to make in this second attack. As a matter of fact, he hadn't made many in the morning attack.

5TH MARINES

Unbeknownst to Upton, Major Keyser's 2d Battalion, 5th Marines, well to the north, was also in a serious position. The marines were about a kilometer behind Upton, between his remnants and the Moroccans. At 10 P.M. Keyser sent a runner to his own regimental commander (probably because the PC location was known). The message starkly depicts what it is like to be out on a very dangerous, lonely limb: "Will you please communicate C.G. 3d Brigade, under whom I am operating that I am occupying old trench line with about 120 men. . . . I have just received word from my left company that it is unable to proceed. . . . My right company I have no news of. . . . We have had no tank support or grenades, and I consider it highly impracticable to clean out M.G. from wheat or woods without at least one of these weapons. I shall remain here holding line until further orders. My whole battalion is utterly exhausted."[67]

In a portion of the above message not quoted, Keyser says the battalion was delayed by heavy shelling controlled from an airplane. That would bear out Shipley Thomas's statement that by late afternoon Richtofen's Flying Circus had driven Allied [French] planes from the skies.[68]

23D INFANTRY

In the southern half of the division sector, Colonel Malone's 23d Infantry and attached marines fought a separate and even more violent war that took them through and beyond the key town of Vierzy. Some American elements had approached Vierzy and most of the Germans fled early that morning, but the long defense at Vauxcastille kept the 23d Infantry from getting forward in force. The fight for Vauxcastile lasted until nearly 6 P.M. when, surrounded by the 1st and 2d Battalions, 23d Infantry, and with French tanks in their rear, remnants of the German 220th, 219th, 218th, and 169th Regiments and fragments of the 115th Division finally surrendered—some two hundred soldiers. Meanwhile, the Germans reoccupied Vierzy and resisted strongly all afternoon. Some German troops were trapped in a cave, some in a railroad tunnel.[69]

That was not the picture higher-level French and American commanders had of the situation. Both American and French reports said the town was in American hands. To add to the confusion, the French 38th Division of the XXX Corps, operating south of XX Corps' right boundary, was successfully attacking to the north and east from a line Montremboef Ferme–Bois de Mauloy toward Parcy-Tigny, well ahead of the Americans. These French troops unwittingly helped force the Germans out of Vierzy by threatening to envelop it from the south. The 2d Division order, issued at 1:30 P.M., directed both brigades to move their command posts to Vierzy.[70]

Recently promoted Brig. Gen. Wendell Neville, commanding the Marine Brigade, approached the town at about 3 P.M., but his car was fired on from houses in town. Prudently heading back toward Beaurepaire, he encountered Ely going forward and warned him to delay. When Major Turrill, commanding the 1st Battalion, 5th Marines (by now little more than a hodge-podge of marine companies), received the order to join Ely's command to support the 23d Infantry, he was far to the northwest, on the Mauberge road. He was not able to start his men on the long march to get there until 5:30 P.M.[71]

Malone had come up to Vauxcastille Ravine at 6:30 P.M. to find his exhausted battalions. In what developed into a converging attack that could not possibly have been planned in detail, the 23d Infantry moved out with the 2d Battalion on the left and the 1st Battalion on the right (each already having parts of the 3d Battalion and some men from the 9th Infantry intermingled). Most of the battle line was north of Vierzy, but the right of it extended to the division boundary well to the south. By 7 P.M., with the 9th Infantry on the left "advancing in excellent order," the leading elements of the 23d Infantry had reached the crest of the hill overlooking Vierzy. Malone reported the action thus: "In the ravine west of Vierzy I found a battalion of Moroccan troops and 15 tanks which were to support me in the attack. At about 7:15 the attack, supported by the tanks, which had rendered such exceedingly valuable service in the morning, moved forward in conjunction with a heavy fire of machine guns and artillery. The attack continued with great vigor until after 8:00 P.M."[72]

Most likely those Moroccan troops, the remnants of the ones who brought such ill fortune to Lieutenant Janda, "were to support" simply by the fact of their badly misdirected presence. The 1st Moroccan Division had shown its willingness to fight earlier with the marines and the 1st Division, now it was their turn to join the 2d Division. Can anyone complain of such Allies?

Sometime during this period Major Turrill's long march ended when, southeast of Vierzy, he encountered Ely. Ely and his staff had tried to advance into the town and, like Neville, had been forced back by German fire. Ely's idea of a commander's battlefield location was simple: "It is better to err on the side of being well up among the troops to take personal command in emergencies than to be . . . in the rear perhaps under the idea of keeping constant touch with higher authority." This had been the command philosophy of the American Regular Army almost since its inception. Freed from the constraints of trench warfare, the Regulars naturally reverted to this somewhat more effective habit. In any event, Ely ordered Turrill and his 150 men to eliminate the resistance in Vierzy and keep going toward to Hartennes-et-Taux, about five kilometers distant.[73]

Evidently it did not occur to Ely that this order would shift the division's northernmost marine element to its southernmost flank. However, Ely was a pragmatist and took whatever assets came to hand and put them where they would have the greatest effect. Besides, the 5th Marines seemed to be everywhere: from just south of Soissons to south of Vierzy. Turrill, detached from his own command since early morning, turned to with a will—as all marines are expected to do.

Given the already established rivalry between the 2d Division's two brigades, disagreement arose over who should get credit for taking Vierzy on the night of July 18. A fair statement would be that it was taken by both the 1st Battalion, 23d Infantry, coming down from the north, and the 1st Battalion, 5th Marines, moving in from the west.[74]

After Vierzy fell, the 1st Battalion, 23d Infantry, then pushed on well to the east, finishing their advance well short of the Soissons–Château-Thierry road three kilometers beyond the town. They arrived on their final position under command of Major Fechet. By one account, the strong point he set up was manned by a composite "battalion" of eighty men from three different regiments.[75]

Colonel Malone, after observing the attack, moved to high ground north of the town in an effort to get a fix on frontline positions. In the dark he looked at German flares and concluded that the troops of the 9th and 23d Infantry had fought themselves into a salient, pushing far beyond the French units to the north and south. He was more or less correct. Ely later complained that misinformation had caused many casualties because he had sent his units forward based on erroneous reports that attacking elements on the division's right and left were out in front and that the French cavalry had been pushed forward ahead of the infantry lines.[76]

Major General Harbord, arrived at the Beaurepaire Farm at 10 P.M. to find the wrecked main building and its yard serving as an advanced dressing station with "some hundreds of wounded and dead men, infantry, marines, artillery, Moroccans, Germans and Americans all lying on the ground in the common democracy of suffering and death."[77]

Lieutenant Lud Janda was among those in the aid station when the general arrived. He recalled the frantic doctors sorting out the worst cases, with even the sides of the building being bloody: "The men were being sent back in ammunition trucks for lack of ambulances. I found a place on the front seat with the driver of one of these jolting agony boxes. It took us all that night of the 18th to get back thru Villers Cotterets Forest. So ended my part in this one."[78]

The XX Corps order required the divisions to go a kilometer or two *beyond* the Soissons–Château-Thierry highway and capture a line from Buzancy Château through the Bois de Concrois south to the village of Hartennes-et-Taux. The forward bulging frontline trace on the map shows unit dispositions for the end of July 18th.

The first day of fighting at Soissons was at an end. In all of James G. Harbord's extensive writings, his close-of-the-day description of his experience stands out as an understatement of lasting note: "It was a hectic day for a new Division Commander."[79]

Open warfare à la 1918 France was a fact. It was not open warfare as Americans had known it on the western plains, nor in the steaming jungles of the Philippine Islands, nor in the northern Mexican wilderness. It was warfare of movement across open ground unencumbered by strong trench positions buttressed by thickets of barbed wire and carefully sited, mutually supporting, machine-gun equipped strong points and massed artillery. There was room to maneuver—and the tanks helped, even though they drew uncomfortable quantities of fire. Some things the Americans had yet to learn, such as taking the time to work around the flanks of machine-gun positions rather than simply charging them wherever found. Charging straight ahead increased the speed of the attack to be sure, but the cost was beginning to mount. Fragmentary but stubborn German defenses, the loss of leaders, and exhaustion had combined to drain strength from the attack until it reached its culminating point—that wonderful term Clausewitz employed to denote the point at which the strengths of the opposing forces come into balance. It is the point beyond which progress becomes fragmentation and invites a devastating counterstroke. But there would be no counterstroke from the Germans this day.

The Germans were naturally reluctant to admit publicly that they were unaware of their vulnerability to a trap that was, after all, of Ludendorff's own making. German press official Georg Wegener issued the following statement as an explanation for what happened at Soissons on July 31, 1918: "Despite that [Mangin's deception efforts], we were not deceived regarding his intentions. We knew he was preparing to attack and that every wood and gully was full of troops and materials. Only regarding the exact time of the attack had we no knowledge. We can accept the belief, however, that as *our offensive* [of 15 July] *was to take place further to the east, its effect would be to make the enemy renounce the execution of his plans for an offensive* [emphasis added]."[80]

That statement comes down square on the proposition that the major impact came directly from the surprise made possible when Foch overruled Pétain's order to postpone Mangin's attack because of the July 15 German push. Quartermaster General Ludendorff addressed the question twice. On August 4, 1918, Ludendorff issued this "official" statement: "We figured with an attack on July 18th and were prepared for it. The enemy experienced very heavy losses and the Americans and African auxiliary troops, which we did not underestimate, suffered severely. By the afternoon of the 19th we already were fully masters of the situation. . . . We left the abandoned ground to the enemy according to our regular plan."[81]

The following 1919 Ludendorff statement offered a different assessment: "[On July 18] He employed masses of infantry and a greater force of tanks than had ever before been concentrated in one drive. . . . South of Soissons our infantry did not resist this attack as firmly as I had hoped . . . the success of the enemy came to me as a shock, and I sent immediate reinforcements, which, however, owing to the difficulties of transport, were slow in arriving. On July 19th our situation was much more satisfactory. Even the troops who had been surprised on the preceding day now rallied and fought well. The reason they gave for their former failure was the wholly unexpected nature of the attack."[82]

Since the victors write the first histories, the losers take every possible opportunity to turn the unwary to their version. Ludendorff misspoke himself on the issue of surprise. On tanks he was correct. In fact, as reported by the 28th Division, the Germans were so surprised by the timing of the attack that two divisions were in the process of being relieved when they were hit: "The greatly depleted organizations of the 14th Res Div were relieved by the 47th Res Div, those of the 115th Div by the 3d Res Div. Into these movements the enemy on July 18 thrust his attack. . . . French and American divisions went forward . . . supported by numerous tanks. They encountered either worn-out or still unoriented German troops, who lacked every semblance of protection such as offered by established positions."[83]

The records of the German 110th Infantry Regiment of the 2d Brigade, 28th Division, establish beyond any doubt that what front existed for the next twenty-four to forty-eight hours was wherever the Allied soldiers chose to stop—there was very little opposing them and in some cases nothing at all. The 1st Battalion's after-action report records: "Later . . . on the evening of July 18, it became more and more apparent that the right flank of the battalion was in the air. . . . At 10.30 PM the left flank company (8th Co) sent word that at the Rapiere Ferme and points south thereof our own troops are in the act of retiring to the woods south and west of Taux. Scattered members of the 16th Inf, . . . in all about 50 men, are put into the gap between the 2d and 3d Bns."[84]

The soldiers and marines of the 2d "Indianhead" Division had created a proud memory indeed. Literally flung into the attack as if they were a handful of gravel, they had shattered the German defense and driven its fragments almost five miles backward. But the strong cords of command had snapped at the outset and by evening only strands remained. They were enough to keep the senior commanders in touch, but to really understand what was going on, commanders had to walk forward about three miles and attempt to sort through the chaos of the battlefield. While brigade and regimental commanders struggled to find the remnants of their commands, the soldiers and marines they sought simply longed for water, rations, ammunition, and sleep.

CHAPTER 4

Edging Forward

July 19 — 1st Division and 1st Moroccan Division

Second Lieutenant Sulzbach's diary recounts: "19 July So here near Soissons, the bastards are at it on a large scale! Taking the 7th and 9th Armies by surprise, the enemy . . . is said to have advanced six to eight kilometers in the first phase alone. And so the very places have been recaptured which we, the 9th I.D. [Infantry Division], took with so much effort and paid for so dearly with our blood. Chaudun has been lost. The fact that they are driving us back here at such a pace must mean that the situation has got really ticklish."[1]

The Situation

General Mangin sent out his written order for the second day's attack at 8 P.M. on Thursday, July 18, even as the 2d Division was getting its dusk attack under way. At 11 A.M., Major General Berdoulat (apparently acting on verbal information from Tenth Army) issued the XX Corps order stating, the attack on the day's objectives having succeeded, the advantage "should be exploited energetically and as quickly as possible" eastward to move to and beyond the north-south Soissons–Château-Thierry road. The corps was to support "as closely as possible . . . the cavalry corps which is going into action to pursue the enemy." Despite French optimism, the Americans came to realize at Soissons and later that the elegant French cavalry, forever poised like a dagger to attack the German rear, served mainly as a target for German aircraft and machine guns and as an obstacle to traffic in rear areas. As Lieutenant Butler, Summerall's aide-de-camp, put it: "The French cavalry manoeuvered around the battlefield behind our Inf today & the enemy avions knocked many of them out of their saddles with machine guns. Tonight this cavalry all marched out, having accomplished nothing but to block the roads."[2]

The Cavalry

General Pétain first mentioned II Cavalry Corps as a participant in the attack on July 8, at which time he placed it at the disposal of Tenth Army "for exploitation." By 10 P.M. July 18, General Fayolle, commander of the French Group of Armies of the Reserve, knew full well that the cavalry was not going to succeed, so he issued an order directing its withdrawal. Somewhere in between, however, the cavalry made some kind of an attempt. At 7:15 A.M. General Mangin gave Major General Robillot, the II Cavalry Corps commander, the order to take up a position from which he could advance for full exploitation of the developing situation. It is worth remembering that at this time XX Corps was bowling over any German forces left standing by the rolling barrage and would continue its rampage through the German defenses for another two hours. Likewise, the 130 Renault light tanks held in reserve were ordered up, with the 1st and 2d Battalions allocated to XX Corps and the 3d Battalion to XXX Corps.

Although terrain is seldom an obstacle to cavalry units in the movies, the reality is that they are road-bound to some extent and become just like infantry when they have to pass through dense forest. Congestion in the Tenth Army's rear area was such that the cavalry was unable to reach the rear edge of the battle area before 2 P.M. By that time the 1st Division was gathering itself together for another try if so ordered. The French 153d Division was just completing its relief of the 2d battalion, 28th Infantry, just outside Breuil in order to allow the latter to return to its own sector. The attack in the 2d Division sector had likewise come to a halt as it too prepared for a second lunge. It might still have been possible to push the cavalry through, but the situation looked touchy.[3]

Harbord recounts that at about 6 P.M. the commanding general of the French 6th Cavalry Division appeared in the 2d Division headquarters and said he was going to attack to the southeast from Vierzy. The French cavalryman then asked if he could obtain artillery support. Harbord promised fire from six batteries. For reasons unknown to Harbord the attack did not take place, even though a second encounter resulted in a promise of 50 percent more artillery for a morning attack.[4]

Despite the apparent loss of the moment, some of the cavalry moved forward and the Germans immediately sent back reports as increasing numbers entered the Missy Ravine. There is nothing in existing German records to indicate the cavalry did anything more than move into forward assembly areas. To one American observer, looking "back across the Paris road, the field seemed suddenly alive with horsemen." However, he does not report seeing them attack.

Fayolle's order removing all cavalry from the area explicitly included those horsemen who had dismounted to fill the line. Once again the truth of the cavalry's irrelevance to modern warfare had to be played out—should anyone have had the clarity of vision to notice. At his remote III Corps headquarters, Robert L. Bullard noticed: "Sometime in the forenoon . . . I received a message from our army commander, that he was thinking of sending in his cavalry! I groaned, It was too late; they should have started two hours before. . . . Two hours later, perhaps, the cavalry began to go past me. . . . I was perfectly sure they would do no good, and they did none."[5]

It is improbable that the French army or corps commanders knew the actual location, reduced strength, and organizational disarray of the leading troops. But that was normal for them. Even the American division commanders had only an approximate idea of where their troops actually were. The XX Corps order, by being issued too early was more out of touch with the prevailing situation to which it sought to give direction than the Tenth Army order finally issued some nine hours later. Just the same, there was no possibility that an American division commander would protest the order in the midst of this under-the-magnifying-glass test of national will and ability. This was the very first American multidivision attack. They would continue the attack no matter what the reality was on the ground.

None of these orders reached the divisions until very much later, and the 1st Division order was not issued until 1:35 A.M. July 19. The two operative sentences in Tenth Army Order 301 were simple: "I. Tomorrow, July 19, continuation of the attack for the purpose of gaining the objectives announced for July 18. II. The attack will be launched at 4 am. with the assistance of tanks under the same conditions as for July 18."[6]

Tenth Army correctly deduced that the day's objectives had not, in fact, been attained. The first objective, the "Crest to the west of PERNANT–SACONIN-et-BREUIL–CHAUDUN–VIERZY–VILLERS-HELON" had been essentially attained in XX Corps' sector before noon. However, the second objective, "The plateaus between CHARCRISE and OULCHY-le-CHATEAU," or the western edge of the valley through which the Soissons–Château-Thierry road ran, was still some distance ahead.[7]

Describing the situation in 1925, Major General Berdoulat, the XX Corps commander, expressed some interesting memories with regard to what had already taken place: "The most striking point is the enormous advance of the first day, with its relatively slight losses, and the slight results afterward at the cost of such great losses. The reason is that on the first day we profited by . . .

surprise. Moreover, the attacking troops were well under control of their chiefs, advancing in order."[8]

Yes, there was surprise. But to describe the first day's losses as slight and taken by troops advancing in good order is valid only for about the first half hour, and only in certain sectors. For one comparative casualty count, the 1st Division lost about fifteen hundred men on the first day and three thousand on the second. The degree of actual command likewise varied sharply from some to none. The 2d Division's 5th Marines were operating in two sectors other than their own, and both 1st Division brigades had troops well into their neighbor's sectors. In fact, control had broken down in interesting ways. From division to brigade, command, communications, and control were generally adequate, at least until the brigade headquarters moved forward. Thereafter, communications were erratic for the most part. From brigade to regiment, command could be described as adequate even if communications were primarily by muscle power. But forward of regiment, command existed only on the initiative of individuals. Communications really existed only when the commander went forward in person, and only when the troops had halted long enough for someone from the rear to find them. The divisions moved forward until they could no longer do so, then they paused and regrouped. Ordered forward, they lunged forward again to the limit of their collective abilities.

The German crown prince presented a more accurate—and realistic—summary of the difference between the two days: "On the first day the enemy was able to gain a great success, as figured in ground gained and men and material captured, but did not know how to exploit it to the limit on the same day. As the defense which had been formed quickly in the rear became effective and as counteraction against his tanks constantly grew in effectiveness, his advance already began to waver on the second day."[9]

1st Division

The 1st Division's mission on July 19 was to reach a line slanting southeast from Berzy-le-Sec to Buzancy, both towns *exclusive,* but attempts to carry out the order produced little.[10] Every attempt, in Sir Basil Liddell Hart's apt phrase, "founder[ed] on the rock of the machine gun." In particular, the northernmost 28th Infantry Regiment still could not make progress. "Owing to the continued failure of the 153d French Division, adjoining the corps sector on the left, to come up abreast of the 1st U.S. Division, the 2d Brigade was unable to advance beyond the second objective. At every attempt it was enfiladed from the north and northeast." Bullard noted later that:

Before, at, and after Soissons, American troops fighting beside them had quite regularly declared that the French lagged, failed to keep abreast, in the attack. That, it is true, is the sure cry of the inexperienced, the excuse of those who themselves have not gone forward—"Our flanks were exposed because our neighbor would not advance with us; we couldn't advance."—but the uniformity and number of these claims carries some conviction of the truth. The ill feeling . . .which I found existing between the French and the Americans in the French Sixth Army when I entered it as U.S. III Corps commander and in the remainder of the Aisne-Marne campaign was due very largely to the Americans' belief that the French would not stand beside them in the face of the enemy.

However, Jennings Wise counters, "The difficulties encountered by the French Divisions on the flanks of the Americans must not be underestimated by those who seek to understand their relatively tardy progress."[11]

2d Brigade

Summerall's headquarters had moved at 7:30 A.M., July 18, into a large quarry cave ideally suited to the purpose. As sketched by Summerall's aide-de-camp (and journal keeper–artist) Lieutenant Butler, the orderly layout was a tribute to the professionalism of the division chief of staff, Col. Campbell King.[12] Neither the Tenth Army attack order for Friday, July 19—which, as previously noted had started down through the chain of command at eight o'clock the night before—nor the XX Corps order of 11 A.M. on the eighteenth reached the 1st Division's forward elements until sometime before 3 A.M. And zero hour was 4 A.M.! It appears the army order took three hours to reach corps, and the corps order took fourteen hours to reach 1st Division, after which the Division order took another two hours to reach brigade. It is impossible to pinpoint the cause of the delay because there is nothing in the existing records to reveal the truth. However, the 2d Brigade Duty Log includes two telling entries: "3:10 A.M. Order for attack 4:00 A.M. July 19 telephoned to 26th Inf. Could get no connection with 28th Inf. . . . 3:55 A.M. Order for attack 4:00 A.M. July 19 delivered by Lieut. Witherspoon."[13]

The 1st Artillery Brigade received the order at approximately the same time, but since it was in position and had been resupplied with ammunition, it opened on time, with the 75-mm guns providing another rolling barrage and the howitzers firing more distant concentrations. Unfortunately, they were firing in support of the *assumed* jump-off line, which had not been reached. Further-

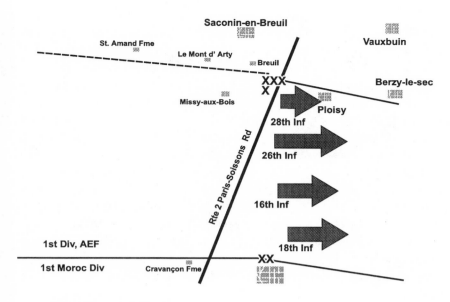

4. 1st Division Attack, July 19, 1918

more, Lt. Col. Maxwell Murray states that the barrage was limited to one gun per twenty-five meters per minute—not exactly the kind of wall of fire one might have expected. While it is possible to criticize the French army and corps commands for failing to dispatch their attack orders expeditiously, this terrible failure to have located the front line correctly within the 1st Division suggests the blame may lie partly with the Americans. This unfortunate error, repeated all too often, demonstrates a systemic rigidity in American thinking. It can be understood to a degree by considering the limitations inadequate communications imposed.[14]

Ravines! The 2d Brigade had taken a terrible beating passing through Missy Ravine. Now it had to look ahead to Ploisy Ravine. However, to get there it had to cross Route 2, the strongly defended Soissons–Paris road. "Defended" may have sounded odd to the soldiers having to cross it, for there were relatively few troops directly before them. The ingenious German defense rested upon a massive concentration of machine guns entrenched on the high ground in the 153d Division's sector, the Vauxbuin Position. The machine-gun fire from this position swept the gently sloping ground all the way south into the 1st Brigade sector. Beyond Ploisy Ravine lay the critical terrain, the key to the whole operation: the village of Berzy-le-Sec, overlooking the road and railroad in the valley of the Crise. The attack order specified that the village lay outside the division sector—the French 153d Division to the north was still charged with taking it.[15]

To the south, the 1st Brigade—already having fought across part of the Soissons–Paris road—was to attack eastward, maintaining contact with the 1st Moroccan Division to its south the 2d Brigade to the north. The division was again to attack with four regiments abreast.[16]

Fragments of the 28th Infantry's 3d Battalion began the attack shortly after 4 A.M. on the division's northern flank, with remnants of the 2d Battalion following in support. The untouched 1st Battalion, led by Maj. George Rozelle, remained in division reserve. The assault force moved forward toward the flat, treeless terrain traversed by Route 2, swept by both artillery and machine-gun fire now intensified by German reinforcements. Fire from the front was bad; fire from the north flank, still unprotected because the French 153d Division had again failed to advance, was even worse. As mentioned earlier, the Germans had available to them some old French entrenchments, but they also had apparently constructed or adapted several key points as strong points into which they had jammed a horde of heavy machine guns to make up for their dearth of artillery. From these very strong positions they were able to pour devastating flanking fire on the Americans as they attempted to cross Route 2. In a command failure of major proportions, no senior officer other than Colonel Babcock seems to have noted the location of or taken any action to neutralize the flanking fire. It was as if a mental wall existed. The guns were firing from the French sector, so the French should have to deal with them. This blindness is even more unusual considering that the 28th Infantry's very first action after crossing the jump-off line was to change course and attack out of sector to deal with just such a problem at Saint Amand Farm. The situations were somewhat different, however, as frontal fire in that first hour of the first day's attack was negligible; that was not the case on the nineteenth. Still, there is no evidence anyone other than Babcock attempted to place artillery fire on the strong point, or ask permission to attack it otherwise. Babcock sent division two messages describing the problem. The first was sent at 7:15 and the second at 9:32 A.M. He also attempted to coordinate adequate fire support with Major John F. Ruggles, commander of the 28th Infantry's supporting artillery, but to no avail.[17]

Actually, Babcock's July 28 report states that heavy "fire for destruction" was twice placed on these positions, but he completely omits any mention of support in his August 4 report. We have discounted the full accuracy of the July 28 report, as Babcock must also have done. In it he first lauds the artillery support given. Then, in the August 4 report he discounts his artillery support almost entirely. The second report may reflect the more careful examination of his subordinates' actual experience. It may also reflect his attempt to justify his unofficial relief from command, but it cites a division Special Order as its genesis. The July 28 report contains no such citation. Given the otherwise spotty artillery performance in this battle, and the testimony of Major Huebner in particular, we are strongly inclined to discount the artillery's effectiveness. It is this kind of thinking that has led the U.S. Army to develop a concept called "Battle Space." The intent of this concept is to make it more likely that commanders will think beyond lines drawn on the map since it proposes to do away with those lines altogether.

After several attempts to force the road, the 28th Infantry was reduced to digging in on the flat ground and refusing an open left flank. Of the tanks initially supporting the regiment, all were soon out of action. As a general rule, the tanks that had such impact on the first day across the entire corps front seemed to have expended their strength and hardly appear at all in Allied accounts of events on the nineteenth. Of the 324 tanks allocated to Tenth Army, 225 actually arrived on the battlefield July 18, of which 102 became casualties, 62 by artillery fire. Personnel losses were 25 percent. A total of 109 tanks entered combat on July 19, of which 50 were hit, with 22 percent personnel losses. On July 20, 32 tanks attacked and 17 were hit, with 52 percent personnel losses. A hundred tanks attacked on July 21, of which 36 were hit, with 27 percent personnel losses. Although they had suffered serious casualties on the order of 25 percent, there were still hordes of them from the German perspective.[18]

Along Route 2, and as a general case over the entire Soissons battlefield, German machine guns were causing massive American casualties. At this stage Americans soldiers took pride in their ability to charge—singly or in groups—into machine-gun fire and capture or destroy the gun positions. It had happened all too often with the Marine Brigade at Belleau Wood, and it highlighted the inadequate training of the AEF. The division's official account of the 26th Infantry's attack toward the Paris–Soissons road reads: "From what seemed like hundreds of machine guns was heard the rat-tat-tat-tat that was so deadly in its significance, and the air was torn by the shriek of bullets. The losses came so rapidly that for a moment the forward echelon seemed to be withered. The officers dashed to the front of their men, and with shouts and gestures they led their units straight into the successive lines of machine guns."[19]

What a pity that the 2d Brigade soldiers could not benefit from the example of the Senegalese from whom the 1st Brigade soldiers were able to learn better techniques. Certainly the Senegalese closed with the bayonet, but always from the side or rear.

There is nothing in the records of the battle to suggest that the 260 machine guns allotted to the 1st Division were killing many Germans. At this point in the development of AEF open-warfare tactics there was no appreciation of how machine guns might support the attack. They were given no fire support mission; they were merely told to maintain their places in the formations, plodding along under their heavy burdens, in some cases in the first waves of the assault. A postwar study described the situation as follows: "In the 1st Division at Soissons on July 18, 1918, the machine-gun companies were broken up and three guns assigned to each infantry company. These guns were practically all placed in the first wave of the company to which attached. . . . They were not interested in finding opportunity for shooting their guns. . . . The machine-gun companies suffered very heavy casualties and accomplished practically nothing. . . . One company lost 57 men without firing a shot. A[nother] company lost 61 men and fired only 96 rounds."[20]

Proper machine-gun instruction was available through the British Army school system and was roundly applauded by American soldiers who attended it—many of whom were stationed with the 27th and 30th Divisions. Those divisions remained in the British Expeditionary Force sector throughout the remainder of the war.[21] Not until later, notably during the Meuse-Argonne operation, were machine-gun units given full, sophisticated support missions. The price for unpreparedness and ethnocentric stubbornness was high. But Conrad Babcock understood at least in part and outlined a partial solution in his August 4 report: "I recommend . . . that machine gun companies do not follow their battalions into the action, but come up after the position is taken and hold it." Only Babcock and Captain Paul L. Ransom, Commander, 2d Machinegun Battalion, 1st Brigade made any such recommendations.

Informed that the French 153d Division would attack at 5:30 P.M. to reach the western edge of Ploisy Ravine, 1st Division headquarters issued an order for the 28th Infantry to attack simultaneously. In response, Summerall, who had been in command of the division for only a few days, received what he perceived to be a threat to his authority from a regimental commander. It does not matter that the regimental commander had been commanding, managing, and seeking intelligent assistance in a very exposed position for almost two days. Writing in 1953–54, Summerall recorded that "the Division was to attack by orders of the French Corps at 4:30 P.M. At 4:25 the colonel of the regiment called me and said that he could not obey the order and would not attack. I told him as calmly as possible that he must not say anything to his battalion commanders whom I knew would attack. He showed himself unsuited to be a combat regimental commander. The battalion commanders led their troops to take their objectives."[22]

Battle records make it clear that the call came from Colonel Babcock of the 28th Infantry. Summerall presumably meant that Babcock should not express his objections to the order to his battalion commanders, but that he should just pass the order along and trust that they would comply. Summerall might have been thinking of his original lineup of assault battalion commanders, who had pushed through the day before. By this time, however, Majors Huebner and Tack had been evacuated and their combined battalions were commanded by 2d Lt. Samuel I. Parker, who was awarded the Medal of Honor for his subsequent action. Summerall was correct in assuming subordinate obedience, lieutenants seldom refuse to obey major generals.[23] The other battalion, Major Rozelle's untouched 1st Battalion, was about to be released from reserve for this attack. The incident is significant in the larger view because it is probably the first time in the AEF's short history that a regimental commander appeared to balk at an attack order. For the present account it is also oddly significant that the tough-talking Summerall took no immediate action to relieve Babcock.

Babcock left behind his own version:

> About 3:15, while about five hundred yards in rear of my front line, I received a warning message . . . that we would probably attack at 4:00 P.M. [note the difference in time] . . . The [northern] limits [of the attack position] allotted to the 28th Infantry fell exactly on the ground that the French had failed to capture during the day and which was to my personal knowledge held by the enemy. I directed the attacking battalion [Rozelle] to prepare for the attack south of these limits, but not to move forward until I directed them to do so. . . . I reported the situation by phone to the division that the 28th Infantry could not form up as directed. [Fate dictated that he got a direct connection to the division commander.] I was directed to attack where I was and that troops would come up on my left. I at once notified the attacking battalion to push forward at once *when the troops came up on the left.* [Emphasis added.][24]

The string was finally taken off the 1st Battalion and it successfully led the movement forward. As recorded in the division's official history: "At 5:30 P.M. the artillery fire dropped and the 2d Brigade rose and charged forward. The 1st Battalion of the 28th Infantry, which had been in division reserve, was placed at the disposal of the regimental commander. It passed through the rest of the regiment with a dash that defied all opposition. It swept over the most stubborn resistance and clung to the barrage. Casualties were heavy, and when the objective was reached only eight officers were left to command the front line."[25]

The battalion commander, Major Rozelle, was one of the few battalion commanders to come through Soissons unscathed. Elements of his battalion were later acclaimed for having finally taken the key objective, Berzy-le-Sec, but very soon after the battle Rozelle disappears from the division's annals. Like Babcock and Buck, his is a compelling story, even though it stands incomplete.

Rozelle, a member of West Point's Class of 1903 who was then forty years old, was not one of the newcomers to command within the division. He had commanded the same battalion at Cantigny in the last days of May and was awarded the Distinguished Service Cross (DSC) for his leadership there. The citation reads: "For three days near Cantigny . . . he withstood German assaults under intense bombardment, heroically exposing himself to fire constantly in order to command his battalion effectively, and although his command lost half its officers and 30 per cent of its men, he held his position and prevented a break in the line at that point." More than the DSC, he cherished a 28th Infantry regimental citation in which Hanson Ely, who commanded the regiment at Cantigny, described him as capable of "making quick tactical decisions at critical moments and correct ones."[26]

As for his command of the battalion on the afternoon of July 19, Rozelle started out in the best "Follow Me!" tradition but lost contact with the troops he set out to lead—not an unusual case at Soissons. In an account written a week later, he stated: "During the attack of July 19th, with Lieut. Barnard, Arty Liaison Officer and four runners, we advanced ahead of the battalion in an effort to lead the hesitating troops to the final objective. We did reach the final objective but found ourselves alone on the ridge [west of and overlooking Berzy-le-Sec] and in danger of being killed by machine gun fire from the front or rear or of being captured . . . we were alone and there were no supporting troops near at hand."[27]

By separate account we know that Rozelle and his group made it back initially to join a platoon from one his companies and a French company at Mont Courmelles Farm, almost exactly on the corps boundary on the high western bank of Ploisy Ravine. Later that night he joined the battalion headquarters in the village of Ploisy.[28] A few 1st Battalion elements had made it across Ploisy Ravine and into the outskirts of Berzy-le-Sec. However, still without support on the left, they were obliged to fall back about twelve hundred yards to the west. We can only imagine the combination of relief and disbelief that greeted Rozelle and his group when he met up with the surviving company commanders. Had he been reported up the chain of command as missing in action, Rozelle would likely have received some credit for good intentions. Instead he soon became known as the commander who, after becoming lost, was completely ineffective and nowhere around when his four companies seized the objective. Still, it is worth noting that others behaved worse without sliding into oblivion.

Major Theodore Roosevelt, Jr., describes another case that parallels Rozelle's "way out front" leadership. Control is the issue here: "Another captain we had was thoroughly courageous personally, but . . . he could not keep his men under control. Once after an attack his battalion commander was checking up to see if the objectives were taken . . . in the instance of this one company, the company itself was missing. On the objective was sitting the company commander and his headquarters group. The rest of the company missed its direction advancing through the woods and got lost."[29]

As for the remainder of the 28th Infantry in this attack, the remnants of the 2d and 3d Battalions under the command of Lieutenant Parker were placed in support of Rozelle's 1st Battalion. Seeing that Rozelle's left flank remained exposed by slow-moving French troops, Parker, already wounded in the foot, closed the gap by moving up on the left to consolidate the line.[30]

The 26th Infantry, for which records are sparse, jumped off at 4:30 A.M., and got across the Paris–Soissons road, where it was halted by the fire from the front and the Vauxbuin Position. It attacked again at 5:30 P.M. and made a three-kilometer advance, assisting in the capture of Ploisy. It captured a German 77-mm battery and several hundred prisoners but had to endure another night without food.[31]

Lieutenant Col. Edmund S. Sayers was attached as an auxiliary officer to the 28th Infantry. In a 1919 letter he recounted finding his way to the 28th Regimental PC at Mont Courmelles Farm (it was actually in Ploisy), where he spent the night in a wine cellar: "Seeing hundreds of dead Moroccans, Algerians, Americans and Boche scattered through the grass in behind stone walls, some all blown to pieces, faces blown out, bowels ripped open and every terrible kind of wound that could possibly be imagined, and the stench of the dead bodies was almost unendurable."[32]

1st Brigade

To the south, the 1st Brigade's 16th and 18th Infantry Regiments ended the day with a good gain because the Germans, acting on orders issued at noon, withdrew all along their front and that of the Moroccans. The advance in this sector, albeit without infantry opposition, nevertheless faced the artillery and machine-gun fire.[33] Colonel Frank Bamford, commanding the 16th Infantry, an interior unit, tersely described the impact: "After the first day in the attack the regiment was never supported on its left. The left flank [on each succeeding day was] in the air and exposed to, and much of the time subjected to the enemy's machine gun fire from the left."[34] The 18th Infantry managed an advance of only five hundred yards against strongly reinforced machine-gun units.

Beaumont B. Buck Tours the Battlefield

After the war, Brig. Gen. Beaumont B. Buck wrote *Memories of Peace and War,* providing details that add much to the above account.[35]

Buck, perhaps because he was brand-new on the job and uninstructed in the exactitudes of brigade command, never quite decided where a commander should locate himself. Initially, he was well installed in his command post, wired into division, by the book, and he wrote:

> After the battle is launched, battalion [and lower] commanders are the men who must carry out the purposes of the higher command. . . . It is only during lulls of battle or at the conclusion of well defined phases that the master touch of the higher command [Buck himself, one presumes] is felt. . . . In these days of machine guns and long-range cannon, the place of the commander is distinctly NOT in the front ranks. [The commander must] protect himself from such hazards by remaining in the rear where he can keep in touch with his entire command by means of modern communication and direct the operation to much better advantage. . . . . [However,] There comes a time in battle when nothing will longer hold [exhausted men] to their tasks but the presence of their commander."[36]

Having professed that slightly mixed philosophy, Buck soon discovered that other considerations required him to go out and gain first-hand knowledge of battlefield conditions.

By 7 A.M. on the nineteenth Buck was up with Col. Hamilton Smith and the 26th Infantry on the Paris–Soissons road, where "gusts of machine gun bullets whistled through the branches of the trees which lined the highway, or ricocheted from the surface of the road." Smith reported that Major Roosevelt, who had gained wide respect for his handling of the 1st Battalion, had been wounded minutes before. Roosevelt, bearing a "Gunshot Wound Severe" tag on his shirt, arrived at his wife's Paris apartment in the afternoon. She was quasi-legally serving in France with the Young Men's Christian Association. According to Roosevelt, "If I could only have gotten hold of a horse, I could have gone through the day at least." Instead, with no ambulance available, he had gone out on an artillery limber, ridden several hours in a motorcycle sidecar, and finally found an "old friend" who loaned him a car for the rest of the trip into the city.[37]

In five lines of his war memoirs, Buck makes two statements that set the reader reeling. First, he says that "I never saw Colonel Smith or Captain Mood [his adjutant] again. Both were killed later in the battle." However, Smith was not killed until the morning of July 22. Buck thus is saying that he did not see this regimental commander for three days, and he had only two regiments under his command! Second, "I roamed all over the battle field that day and the next day. I wanted to see and judge the troops and the fighting." Beaumont Buck went sightseeing!

Was this worse than what Babcock or Rozelle had done? With occasional checks back to his own command post, he visited the front lines of the 1st Moroccan Division (which he wrote were on the edge of the valley of the Crise—an obvious error), "hurried on" to the 2d Division's zone of advance, observed a group of French cavalry, and "found time" to visit Colonels Parker and Bamford in their joint command post in a Chazelle Ravine dugout. Buck does not mention encountering the adjacent 1st Brigade commander, Brig. Gen. John Hines. If he had, there is little doubt Hines would have questioned his sanity. None of these side jaunts could be related to Buck's command responsibility. As a capper, Buck wrote, "I went to all these places alone and on foot."

By dusk, Buck was back at the 28th Infantry's PC. Major Clarence Huebner, the only officer from the 2d Battalion, 28th Infantry, who hadn't been killed or wounded on the first day, came in not long after Buck's return with a broken steel helmet and bloody face and shirt. Said Huebner, "Well, General, they got me at last!"

Beaumont Buck had turned in a day of patently aberrant behavior, a day in which he abandoned command of his brigade. In the coming days, he would move by foot, horseback, motorcycle sidecar, and automobile as he continued his erratic wandering tours. In the end, Major General Summerall would finally cause him to focus on vital matters within his own zone of command.[38]

1st Moroccan Division

The 1st Moroccan Division, operating on the middle axis, mounted afternoon attacks at 3:15 P.M. and again at 8 P.M. It is almost impossible to determine when attacks actually took place. The records of the German units opposing the Moroccans report widely differing times, strengths, and directions. Whenever an attack is reported as successful it is prefaced by the remark that the artillery is heavy and there are masses of tanks and men. The 42d German Division report records that a "most severe artillery preparation . . . supported by tanks" occurred at 6 A.M. and again at 11 A.M., 6:30 P.M., and 8 P.M. (German time).[39]

The Moroccans were able to overcome much of the frantic German resistance in front of them by working around the flanks of the Chazelle–Lechelle

Ravine. The vigor of the 1st Moroccan Division's attacks, coupled with those of the American 2d Division, had opened a two-kilometer gap between Parcy-Tigny and Charantigny by about 1 A.M. A.message from the German 219th Reserve Infantry to the 94th Reserve Brigade, 47th Reserve Division, on July 18, at 12:10 P.M. notes that its flanks had already been turned. Later, on the nineteenth, the 215th Reserve Infantry reported strong enemy forces were moving toward Villemontoire. The 2d Battalion, 110th Grenadier Regiment confirmed that observation. Then, at 1:30 P.M., the 94th Reserve Brigade directed that regimental staffs report to the Soissons–Hartennes-et-Taux road to police up stragglers—an indication that units were breaking up. On July 27 the brigade's parent 47th Division was disbanded and its remnants combined with the 14th Division.

By late evening on July 19, however, the Moroccans had to bear the brunt of the German 20th Division's counterattack. The German 20th Division received the counterattack warning order at 11:35 A.M., and the attack order arrived twenty-five minutes later. No attack time was noted, but subordinate and adjacent unit reports indicate the division had difficulty launching its attack before late afternoon. The Moroccans lost some of the ground they had gained earlier in the day, but the counterattack did little more than feed a weak division into the defense line, albeit at a critical time. By 6:45 P.M. the German 2d Battalion, 79th Infantry, had repossessed Villemontoire, which had earlier been abandoned by panicky German troops. By nightfall, the Germans, who had been driven off their positions along the west edge of the Villemontoire Ravine by flanking attacks from the south and by their own short-firing artillery, were able to restore the defense of Villemontoire—but little more.[40]

As a study in command, the actions on July 19 present a very uncomfortable series of images. Colonel Babcock, the cavalryman commanding an infantry regiment, was doing a remarkable job against terrible opposition to his left front and ignorant prejudice to his rear. His brigade commander, Brigadier General Buck, who should have been the connecting link between Babcock and division, was off gallivanting around the battlefield. And Major General Summerall, the artilleryman turned infantry division commander, merely frothed in ignorance, failing to make the necessary effort to understand the situation adequately. This not-so-pretty picture was partly attributable to command style, partly to communications failures, and partly to inexperience.

fig. 1. Saint-Chamond tank recaptured from the Germans by the U.S. 12th Infantry. Courtesy U.S. Army Military History Institute

fig. 2. Two Schneider tanks. The vehicles shown here are equipped with machine guns only. Courtesy U.S. Army Military History Institute

fig. 3. Renault light tank with 37-mm gun. Courtesy U.S. Army Military History Institute

fig. 4. American troops escort a captured German colonel to the rear. The officer is most likely the colonel captured by Babcock's regiment. The back of the photo bears the following inscription in French: "A German colonel prisoner of war, near Soissons, July 18, 1918." No other German colonels were captured by American forces near Soissons that day. Taken by an unknown French photographer, this photograph was donated by Avashai Halevy.

fig. 5. U.S. Infantry accompanied by Schneider tanks in the Cantigny operation. Courtesy National Archives, III-SC-16559

fig. 6. The caves at le Mont D'Arly. Courtesy National Archives

fig. 7. *The 2d Division's attack sector, looking east from a point just north of Beaurepaire Farm. Courtesy National Archives, 117-TPB-7-2-27*

fig. 8. *The 6th Marines's attack sector from north and slightly east of Vierzy. Courtesy National Archives, 117-TPB-7-2-33*

fig. 9. Brig. Gen. Beaumont B. Buck on "Coley." Courtesy U.S. Army Military History Institute

fig. 10. Brig. Gen. Frank Parker, September 18, 1918. Courtesy U.S. Army Military History Institute

fig. 11. Maj. Gen. John L. Hines decorates a Col. Hugh B. Myers with the Distinguished Service Medal, June 26, 1919. Courtesy U.S. Army Military History Institute

fig. 12. Col. Paul B. Malone, August 25, 1918. Courtesy U.S. Army Military History Institute

fig. 13. 1st Lt. Ludislav Janda (center) and friends in September, 1918. Janda's face is swollen from the premature explosion of a rifle grenade. Courtesy National Archives

fig. 14. Marines practice sending messages with a blinker set in France, February, 1918. Courtesy U.S. Army Military History Institute

fig. 15. American artillerymen firing a captured German 150mm howitzer captured near Beaurepaire Farm. Courtesy U.S. Army Military History Institute

fig. 16. The battlefield and foxholes located northwest of Vierzy. Courtesy U.S. Army Military History Institute

fig. 17. Looking down into Ploisy from the vicinity of Mont{?} Courmelles Farm. Courtesy National Archives, 117-TPB-2-1-36

fig. 18. Berzy-le-Sec as seen from the plateau south of town. Courtesy National Archives, 117-TPB-2-1-42

fig. 19. Berzy-le-Sec as seen looking west from German positions across the Crise Valley. Courtesy National Archives

fig. 20. Doughboys of the 16th Infantry Regiment, 1st Brigade, 1st Division, await the order to attack a machine-gun position in a railroad embankment near Visignaux on July 18. Courtesy National Archives, 111-SC-16497

fig. 21. An American supply column fights its way forward on a road clogged with French cavalry in the 1st Division rear area on July 18. Courtesy National Archives, 111-SC-16523

CHAPTER 5

Futile Bravery

July 19—Attack of the 6th Marines and Relief of the 2d Division

The 2d Division, having no recourse but to use its one uncommitted regiment on the division's attack frontage, was able ultimately to move some disjointed elements within rifle shot of the final objective, and in doing so lost its ability to continue the battle. There were few German forces before them and the German defense was indeed desperate. However, relatively plentiful enemy reserves were en route to bolster the defense. The French 38th Division, operating south of the 2d Division, extended its attacks northeastward to the vicinity of Tigny causing frantic reactions among the remaining German units. At times it appeared that the zone between the southern end of the Villemontoire Ravine and Parcy-Tigny was almost empty of effective German troops. But this was unknown to either the French or the Americans. The attacks in the vicinity of Tigny had so disrupted the defenders in that sector that the Germans designated the Soissons–Hartennes-et-Taux highway as the next defensive position. The German 28th Division Combat Report noted, "Toward 12.00 o'clock noon, the left contact troops retired at and beyond the Soissons–Hartennes road. . . . The flanks of the battalion were open." When the line of communications becomes the front line, the former has been severed.[1]

Early on Friday morning, July 19, 2d Lt. Daniel Bender, the 6th Marine Regiment's gas officer, went forward to check for toxic shells. Wounded in the buttocks and spine, he dispatched a message to the rear, "No gas. Shot in the ass. Bender." Search as you may, you will not likely find another humorous touch of the account of that regiment's attack on the second day south of Soissons.[2]

The French liaison officer bearing the XX Corps order to attack at 4 A.M. on July 19 did not find 2d Division headquarters at Beaurepaire Farm until 2 A.M. About an hour later, Lt. Col. Harry Lee, commander of the 6th Marines, received the division order directing him, in light of the circumstances, to attack at 7 A.M. instead of four, as the corps order directed. Accounts differ on the attack time, with marine accounts stating that it was at eight o'clock, which is more realistic.

It is interesting to follow the orders for this attack. The XX Corps order was issued at 11 A.M. on July 18, the Tenth Army order at 8 P.M., and the Army Group order at ten—exactly the reverse the sequence in which they should have been issued. Evidently this could be done in the French Army, but it also suggests otherwise unrecorded telephonic communications between headquarters staffs, which is fully in keeping with what staffs are supposed to do—talk to each other to keep the information flowing smoothly. The disparities between these orders suggest that while the staff work was not all it should have been, the senior headquarters were well aware of the need to get something into the hands of the attacking units as quickly as possible. Neophyte armies delay issuing orders until they "know" everything. The troops who have to "do" whatever is ordered are then deprived of any planning opportunities. The existing records do not provide enough information to indicate where the breakdowns in this process occurred throughout this battle. The only clearly established fact is that the orders consistently arrived late. The corps order also returned to division control those battalions held out of the first day's fight to support the anticipated cavalry attack.[3]

The obvious question is whether this was the proper time to commit the reserve. Or should it have been sent in at noon on the eighteenth to exploit success? Mangin apparently saw the situation with enough clarity that he intended to send in the cavalry but strangely did not pursue that effort with much vigor. There is also the question of how much of the truth of the situation was known accurately. The corps order suggests very little. How much greater success could have been reaped had the 6th Marines been committed around noon and how much more again if the cavalry division had followed on the regiment's heels? The 6th Marine Regiment was in decent condition, was organized, and could have moved forward with relatively little confusion. It might have broken through had it been committed at a specific point rather than being spread across the front as the second day's attack demanded. We may only speculate.

The physical condition of the three regiments in the line at the end of July 18 made it imperative that they be replaced if the attack was to be continued. But since that could not be done in the time available, Major General Harbord's staff issued the orders to meet the requirement the only way possible: by sending in the marines. There is no record of their release from XX Corps control, and Harbord noted that he had no telephone communications to XX Corps. We must assume he simply ignored the corps order, seized his own troops, and ordered them forward. They did not hesitate or quibble over out-of-date orders. Instead, like Colonels Strong Vincent and Joshua Chamberlain at Gettysburg, they acted as the situation dictated.[4]

6th Marines

Lieutenant Col. Harry Lee's 6th Marines, and the 6th Machine Gun Battalion (organic to the Marine Brigade) had been held in corps reserve for the entire first day. They were rested, well fed, and fully equipped. The 1st Battalion, 2d Engineers, and the 2d Division's 4th Machine Gun Battalion would constitute the new division reserve. Twenty-eight French tanks were assigned to the July 19 attack. The basic task—to cut the great Soissons–Château-Thierry road—had been attempted the day before by the 3d Brigade plus the 5th Marines. Now a single regiment would try to finish the job. The ground was flat and open, commanded by higher elevations from the north and east. The high point in the division's front line was Elevation 132. Due north, directly southwest of Charantigny is Elevation 149. Directly east of the Second Division center is a ridge, elevation 160. The 6th Marines alone would attempt to accomplish the mission against more and fresher German defenders brought up overnight.[5]

The 6th Marines moved out from their assembly area southeast of Beaurepaire at 6:30 A.M. The 4 A.M. attack directed by the corps order was completely out of the question. Located about two and a half kilometers to the rear of the front line, the battalion commanders elected to follow a partially concealed route to the jump-off line, which extended their march about an additional kilometer. Using this longer route through the ravine to the west of Vierzy, they arrived there without incident. But once again because of infantry-artillery coordination failures, the artillery barrage began falling at 6:30 A.M.—the very hour the battalions were just beginning their approach march. At 8:15 A.M., at the railway station in Vierzy, Lieutenant Colonel Lee issued his order deploying the regiment. Two battalions formed the assault echelon on the three-kilometer division front: Maj. John A. Hughes's 1st Battalion on the right, and Maj. Thomas Holcomb's 2d Battalion on the left. Major Berton W. Sibley's 3d Battalion was in support. There remained yet another two kilometers to go just to reach the front line. All three battalion commanders had been through the ordeal at Belleau Wood in June. Hughes had just returned from the hospital, where he was being treated for a wound he received in that operation. The 2d Battalion moved off to the north, and the 1st went through the town and up the ravine to the level plain with the tanks following. The day was clear and bright, the barrage had long since passed, and every German defender was alert to the threat of a new attack.[6]

When the marine battalions began their advance from the ravine at about 8:30 A.M., they were still two kilometers behind their own front line and about four kilometers more from the objective, the western edge of the Bois de Concrois. At the very outset of the advance, enemy artillery fire began to blast the advancing men. The scathing, galling machine-gun fire from the elevations to the east and north came a bit later. The accompanying French tanks seemed to act like artillery magnets.[7]

Colonel Upton of the 9th Infantry, in his lonely command post from which he had declined to go back to a meeting at division headquarters, was up at 5 A.M. to watch his thin line "smear" a German counterattack. He observed that "at 9:00 a.m. the 6th Marines and some tanks went through us." He did not elaborate. He was more concerned with his own personal woes: "We lay there all that day in these shallow trenches with the Boche artillery pounding the life out of us, with the sun roasting us, with gas choking us, and with the Boche airplanes swooping down and firing machine guns into us. Taking it all around it was as unpleasant a day as I have spent in my life."

Upton's behavior begs explanation. Other commanders seemed to be able to circulate about the field of battle, but he seems to have remained locked in place. Of course he had no orders to do otherwise. Late that night he moved his P.C. back about 500 yards and had begun to reorganize when he received orders to move to the rear. He received a Distinguished Service Cross for "extraordinary heroism in action."[8]

The story of Major Holcomb's 2d Battalion on the 6th Marine left is succinctly reported: "The zero hour was 8:20 and we were supported by tanks. The advance to our front lines, a kilometer distant, was across perfectly open wheat fields. Our pace, because of the necessity of following the tanks, was slow, and the advance over the entire distance was through a heavy barrage put down by the enemy. When we had passed through our front lines his machine guns proved most troublesome. We were halted after a gain of about one kilometer because we had nothing left with which to continue the attack."[9]

Sergeant Don Paradis, in Company G of that battalion, found himself in the first wave with Major Holcomb, and his account fills in some of the human element. The German artillery concentration, he wrote,

> . . . was so great that it seemed like a black curtain, and it seemed to me that [Major] Holcomb was headed for the thickest and blackest part. . . . Captain Lloyd always carried a cane. I could see him in the first wave formation swinging that cane and urging his men forward. . . . A man was hit about twelve yards back of me and he yelled, "Paradis, help me!" I started back but Holcomb yelled, "Let the medics take care of him."

. . . from that time on I am not very proud of my actions. We reached the German front lines and found a series of foxholes they had abandoned. . . . I never saw a German. What few of us that were left piled on top of each other to seek cover from that murderous fire. Our advance had not taken long. We were in the German foxholes probably 9 or 9:30 and from then until about 4 P.M., the shell fire, machine gun, and rifle fire never let up.[10]

Another writer described the advance of Hughes's 1st Battalion, on the right flank as follows: "The French tanks, dispersed at fifty-yard intervals among the infantry, drew the bulk of artillery fire coming from guns only four thousand yards away as the waves of Marines passed through the forward foxholes of the 23rd Infantry. The doughboys urged the Marines to take cover, but the lines of men pressed forward. Tank after tank burst into flames, showering the wheat with burning gasoline and bursting ammunition. The Marines skirted the pyres and marched forward. . . . The 75th Company collectively decided it could go no farther when the last tank in its area exploded from a direct hit. Almost immediately, the remnants of the company fell into the thin concealment of the wheatfield."[11]

At 8:55 A.M., Lieutenant Colonel Lee sent a runner to tell Major Sibley that as soon as the lead elements reached the division's previously established front lines, the 3d Battalion would be partially committed to reinforce the assault battalions, and the 1st Battalion, 2d Engineers, would be designated the reserve. The 83d and 84th Companies were sent to fill the gap that had developed between the two lead battalions, 83d Company to the right of the 2d Battalion, and 84th Company to the left of the 1st Battalion. The 97th and 82d Companies remained in support behind the 84th and 83d Companies, respectively.[12]

The early piecemeal commitment of reserve battalions, sometimes not directed by a higher echelon, appeared prevalent in the 2d Division, and is in contrast to the 1st Division's very tight control of designated reserves. Although circumstances were by no means identical, recall that the 2d and 3d Battalions of the 1st Division's 28th Infantry fought throughout the day on July 18, at times as a consolidated unit. They even made the morning attack on the nineteenth before that regiment's 1st Battalion was released for commitment. A more extreme example is that of the 2d Battalion, 18th Infantry, which was held intact as division reserve and then brigade reserve through July 20, even though the 1st and 3d Battalions were reduced to consolidated shreds. Part of the 2d Battalion, 18th Infantry, eventually was assigned to help the 2d Brigade take Berzy-le-Sec on the morning of July 21.[13]

Even Major Sibley's battalion command post, located well to the rear of the assault echelon, was subject to the battering those elements were taking. Low-flying German observation planes spotted the comings and goings in the ravine his headquarters occupied and called heavy artillery that caused many casualties among the runners, scouts, headquarters company personnel, and machine-gun units. "In 10 minutes we had ten men blown to pieces and twenty wounded within fifty yards of us," wrote Capt. David Bellamy, adjutant, 3d Battalion, 6th Marines.

At 10:30 A.M., the battalion scout officer, Lieutenant Marshall, reported from his forward post that the advance line was about a kilometer beyond the old front lines, but getting heavy direct enemy artillery fire and cross fire from machine guns emplaced in the woods to the front and flank. It is worth noting how this organization took the initiative to provide a detached observer to fill the inevitable gap in reporting that must accompany an advance. Note also that there is no other mention of such innovative practice—although it seems to have parallels with the Germans. This practice is sometimes referred to as a "directed telescope," a means for the commander to verify the locations of friendly units without having to bother the attacking commands. It came into fullest practice in the American Army with Lt. Gen. George S. Patton, Jr.'s Third Army in France in 1944.[14]

Ten minutes later, the two companies sent forward into the gap reported that they had suffered about 60 percent casualties. Sibley responded by sending 82d Company forward, soon to be followed by elements of Headquarters Company.

Sergeant William Scanlon left a colorful account of the terror of the attack:

> Tanks now come up from the rear and pass through us. The German artillery swings into action with a vengeance. . . . We curse the tanks. . . . We advance continuously. The machine gun fire encountered before the town of Bouresches was bad but the fire now is a thousand times worse. . . . It is like a hailstorm. . . . My body is bent forward as though forcing myself through a heavy rain. . . . There are crooked little paths through the wheat . . . at the end of each little path lies a dead soldier. Sergeant McFadden has the group next to me on the left . . . he is leading. All of a sudden he swerves around, facing our group. He has a terrified, surprised look of agony on his face. . . . His hands clutch the air one moment, then they wrap themselves about his stomach. . . . His teeth gnash. . . . Biting the air, he staggers back and falls.[15]

Lieutenant Colonel Lee reported to division at 11:45 A.M. that: "Reports indicate growing casualties, amounting to heavy, say about 30 per cent. . . .

First Battalion reports no French troops on right, and are held up 300 yards in front of Tigny. . . . Have in line from right, First, Third and Second Battalions, Reserves, Battalion Engineers, Headquarters Company and two companies Sixth Machine Gun Battalion."[16]

In the center of the action, a Lieutenant Mason had taken over as commander of 84th Company. He led his remaining men on a dash across open space to take an elevated strong point about six hundred yards due north of Tigny—Côte [Hill] 160, seven hundred yards short of the Soissons–Château-Thierry road. It appears that this band of marines had made the 2d Division's farthest advance in the battle of Soissons.[17]

Sibley continued to serve as a hub of communication. His scout officer brought back word from Major Hughes, the 1st Battalion commander, that the Germans still held Tigny, that he had about a hundred men, and, as for getting on with the attack, "Major Hughes stated he needed reinforcements badly, nothing less than a regiment sufficient." Grim humor, indeed.[18]

At 12:40 P.M. a runner appeared before Sibley bearing a very direct question and a very welcome order from Lieutenant Colonel Lee: "Has the town of TIGNY been taken by our troops? If you don't know, find out. If you are stopped dig in." Sibley was soon able to inform regiment that Tigny had not yet been taken. Not until 8 P.M. however, did Lieutenant Marshall complete another of his perilous trips across the front lines to compile the battalion's status. The 3d Battalion had started the morning with thirty-six officers and 850 men. Now Sibley could account for only twenty officers and 415 men. The fields between the battalion command post and the front were littered with dead and wounded, and there were no facilities for getting out any but the walking wounded. One officer lamented: "We entered the attack without an adequate supply of stretchers, stretcher bearers, morphine, or bandages. . . . If it had not been for the captured German supplies in Vierzy, we would have been all but destitute. . . . Men died on that account."[19]

At 6:40 P.M., Lieutenant Colonel Lee, sent position sketches to Brigadier General Neville at Marine Brigade headquarters. He added: "It is impossible to move from one position to another without drawing all sorts of fire. Losses are placed by Battalion Commanders at from 40 to 50 per cent. Their appeals for doctors, ambulances and stretcher bearers are pathetic. Cannot the ammunition trucks, and other transportation that may appear tonight, be used to evacuate the 200 or more cases now on the Regimental P.C. under Doctor Boone? Some may be saved by prompt removal."[20]

During the course of the day, the command posts of the division and division artillery remained at Beaurepaire Farm, with all subordinate headquarters established in and about Vierzy. There appears to be no record of any officers

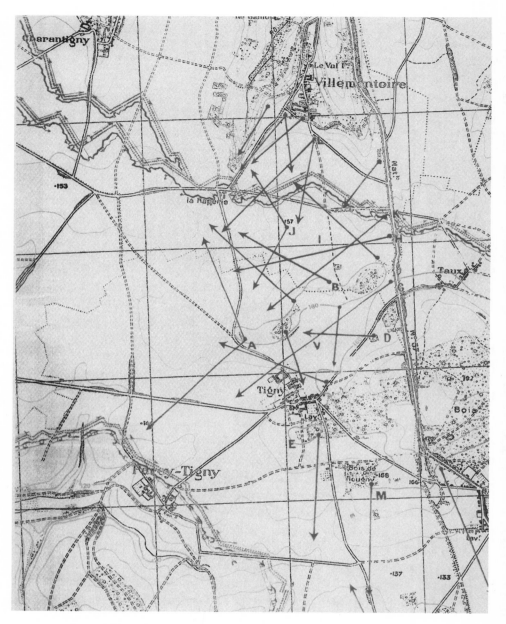

map 9. Machine-gun defenses between Villemontoire and Tigny

from higher headquarters coming forward to assess the 6th Marines's situation or to suggest further actions. The word of impending relief did not reach the forward elements until 9 P.M.[21]

How did the 6th Marines endure? Major Robert I. Denig, later a major general, recorded the following in his diary:

> At 8.35 A.M. we jumped off. . . .Wallace, hit in the legs, went down in the short wheat. . . . Overton was hit by a big piece of shell . . . his heart was torn out . . . a man near me was cut in two; others when hit would stand, it seemed an hour, then fall in a heap. . . . Captain Woodruff . . . his hand all tied up, coat torn in rags, left arm helpless, thigh cut up and in general a mass of blood, but his eyes were sparkling. . . .
>
> At 10:30 we dug in; the attack just died out. Watched some men . . . in the beet field near dig in. You don't know how fast it can be done till you have to. Cates, with his trousers blown off and slightly wounded said he had sixteen men of various companies. . . . Another officer reported he had or could see some forty men all told.
>
> A Marine in a trench by himself had fallen heir to a German machine gun with apparently unlimited supply of ammunition. He amused himself all afternoon in shooting at planes. . . .
>
> In a shallow trench . . . I found three men blown to bits, another lost his legs, a fifth his head. At one end of the trench sat a crazy man who . . . with a shrill laugh, pointed and said over and over again, "Dead men, dead men."
>
> The man who had lost his eyes wanted me to hold his hand. Another with his back ripped open wanted his head patted.[22]

Relief of the 2d Division

The 2d Division, having arrived within rifle shot of the Soissons–Château-Thierry highway but still two kilometers short of its new objective, was relieved from further action. This was at the specific request of the division commander and with the approval of an army commander not noted for compassion. The French 58th Division moved up from XX Corps reserve to take over the 2d Division sector on the night July 19–20. The occasion requires some explanation.

The AEF's planners decided early-on that a "square" division made up of four regiments of infantry divided into two brigades would be best suited to a grinding war against the Germans. They did not use the word attrition but their intent was clear. With an authorized strength of more than twenty-eight thousand men, more than twice the size of European combat divisions, it would have "staying power." Once committed, a division should stay long enough to make its full weight felt by delivering really effective, successive blows before needing to be replaced. Replacing a division in the attack could produce a loss of momentum. Theory had it that a big division should be able to hit harder, stay longer, and endure more than a small one. The extent of that staying power was not specified, but came to be thought of as something like four days. At the same time, it came to be recognized that there were many, many factors that could limit the power of that unit's offensive punch. There was also the significant consideration that there were too few trained senior staff officers to allow proliferation of smaller divisions. All of this assumed the division could be brought into line as a complete unit. That was hardly the 2d Division's experience.[23]

Although there is no record of when Major General Harbord made the decision to request his division's relief, he is on record as being professionally outraged at the manner in which his division was taken from his control and hurled into the battle. It is also possible that his mindset was influenced by his having had to keep the Marine Brigade in the fight for Belleau Wood far beyond reasonable expectations of endurance. There, both he and Maj. Gen. Omar Bundy, the 2d Division commander, had requested relief and been turned down by Gen. Jean Degoutte, commander of the French XXI Corps. In neither of his books does Harbord provide any particular insight to this decision. All we have is the following terse comment: "It seemed evident to me that the force of my division was spent and that it had done its red-blooded best. I so informed the 20th Corps."[24]

In a different book, Harbord recorded: "[The 6th Marines] in a hard day's fighting advanced our line to within a few hundred yards of, and commanding, the Soissons–Chateau-Thierry road. Here the attack reached the limit beyond which it could not be supported by artillery unless the artillery changed position. This was not considered advisable under existing conditions. The French Command therefore decided to relieve the 2d Division the night of the nineteenth. It was thrust out ahead of its neighboring divisions like the long middle finger of a giant hand."

It is perfectly clear that this bit of selective memory is badly off the mark. Artillery support was hardly a factor in the soldiers' or the marines' success after the opening barrage. In fact, the opening barrage on July 19 was wasted, having been fired at 7 A.M., well in advance of the actual attack. Evidently no one told the artillery the time had been changed from the original order, and no one took position to observe. There was yet a lot of learning to do.[25]

Harbord must have made his decision about noon, when he saw that the high, critical terrain at Tigny and vicinity had not been taken—and wouldn't be. He sent the XX Corps commander, Major General Berdoulat, a letter titled "Report on Attack." In it he told Berdoulat:

- The [July 19] attack was late because the corps order was late.
- He used the only not-exhausted troops he had, the 6th Marines and the engineers, "a force regarded by me to be inadequate to the task, but no other was available."
- The attack "is now held up on the right from the direction of PARCY-TIGNY, a place previously reported to us as being in French possession. On the left it is being held up and our left flank threatened, due to the fact that the Moroccan 1st Division has not apparently advanced as far as CHARANTIGNY."
- The division can hold what has already been gained, "but I desire to insist most strongly that they should not be called upon for further offensive effort."[26]

In regard to flanks left open by adjacent French units, only nine days later Maj. Gen. Hunter Liggett, commander of the U.S. I Corps, wrote to the French Sixth Army commander regarding the continued exposure of the American 42d Division. He said he would continue the ordered advance, "with the certainty that if the enemy is retiring contact will be maintained, and with the equal certainty that if resistance is serious and the units on the right and left do not perform their full part in keeping abreast, the move will be stopped almost on its inception."[27] In this case, however, the French were indeed in advance of the 2d Division although they no more held Tigny than the 23d Infantry held Vierzy early on July 18.

By 3:15 P.M., Harbord was still in the dark about his division and about his request for relief. His 3:15 P.M. message to Hanson Ely let the latter know that the 6th Marines had been ordered to dig in where they were. However, he then directed that Ely dispatch a marine battalion reported to be "available," to move to cover the 6th Marines's left flank, which was believed to be in the air. He then charged Ely with the defense of the division front and directed him to rearrange the division at dark and reconstitute a reserve.[28]

It is not evident that Harbord left his forward PC that day or that he was in effective communication with his senior headquarters to the rear. It is most painful to see that he did not go forward to find out the state of his division or to observe the terrain and the enemy defenses. If he had, he would have seen that the road to Vierzy was certainly available. Why wasn't Ely forwarding reports of the 6th Marines's progress or halt? Were there other observers beyond the immediate resources of the attacking 6th Marines? Was everyone else behaving like Upton—too concerned with their own situations to contribute to the overall effort? Was the trauma of the eighteenth too much to handle? It seems as though the command echelon had been overcome by some pernicious inertia.

The division's operations log carried this entry: "At 5 P.M., word arrived that the 2d Division was to be relieved by the 58th Colonial Division. The troops were notified at once and by midnight the relief of the elements had begun."[29]

In this war where success was perversely measured by numbers of friendly casualties, the converse of Vietnam's enemy "body count," it appears that the 2d Division was very successful during the period July 18–20, having lost 4,135 officers and men killed, dead of wounds, or wounded.[30]

There is one fact that has been omitted thus far from the account of operations on July 19: At 5:45 A.M., General Mangin released the 58th Division to XX Corps "with the relief of the American 2d Div. in view." It would appear Mangin anticipated Harbord's request by more than half a day.[31]

CHAPTER 6

Try Again

July 20—1st Division Continues the Attack

At 2:30 A.M. on Saturday, July 20, General Mangin's headquarters passed along the word received from the Allied commander in chief: "The battle in progress should have for its object the destruction of [all] the enemy forces south of the Aisne and Vesle. It will be conducted with the greatest activity and energy, without loss of time, in order to exploit the success realized."[1]

The element of surprise was gone. The swarms of tanks that had been instrumental in making the breach were no longer a major factor. Worst of all, masses of German reserves were moving rapidly toward Soissons in an attempt to secure that place and protect the line of communications from Soissons to the German forces in the salient—or at least to secure the route that would permit their safe withdrawal. The Allies's faint hope for a chance to cut across the base of the Marne salient had vanished completely "as the armored weapon had not yet reached the state of mechanical reliability—or mobility—for such a long, and indeed tenuous, advance."[2]

Lieutenant Alban Butler's journal entry for July 20 records: "This morning the 20th Corps ordered this division to take Berzy-le-Sec. It is in the zone of the 153d Div. but they cannot take it. . . . The 2nd U.S. Division to our south were relieved last night. The Moroccans will come out tonight."[3]

The trace of 1st Division positions at dusk on July 19 shows the dramatic northwest-to-southeast slant of the front line. The 28th Infantry was down in Ploisy Ravine, while the 26th Infantry was facing mostly north as it struggled to maintain the connection between the 28th Infantry and the 1st Brigade. The 1st Brigade connected with the 2d Brigade at the edge of the Ploisy Ravine and extended southward to join the Moroccans near Chazelle. By the end of the twentieth, the Moroccans moved up to Charantigny, putting them close to the line hard-won by the 6th Marines but then held by the 58th French Division.

Berzy-le-Sec was heavily defended by the Germans for the same reason it was so necessary to Mangin's, Berdoulat's, Summerall's, Buck's, and Babcock's

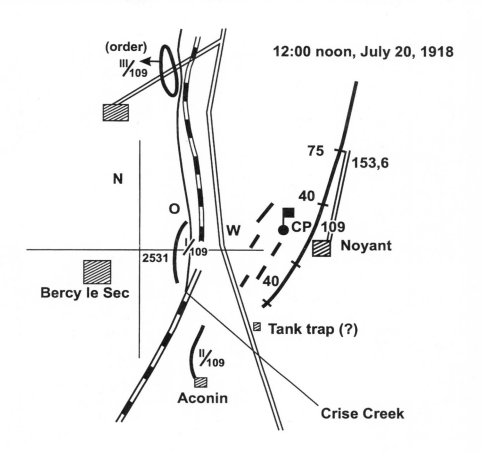

map 10. Trace of German positions east of Berzy-le-Sec, 10:00 A.M., July 20, 1918

success. To its north, Soissons lies at the northeast corner of a long, high plateau. Coming south down the Crise Valley there are four overwatching knobs. The Montaigne de Paris, with an elevation of about 155 meters, gives direct access to Soissons and controls its southern exits. The knob south of Vauxbuin and west of Courmelles at about 158 meters elevation is on a line roughly parallel to the Montaigne de Paris and approximately the same elevation. The highest point of both of these knobs is well back from the Crise and the road net, about three kilometers average. Berzy-le-Sec is the third and sits on the end of a similar knob with an elevation of 153 meters, but the town itself is only about 140 meters high. It then tumbles down to the valley floor, where it connects with both the railroad, for which it has a station, and the highway. The knob east of and higher than Berzy-le-Sec, the Noyant Plateau, elevation 164 meters, offers the potential to control that town by fire but cannot secure the road network. Berzy-le-Sec looks directly down on the Soissons–Villers-Cotterêts railroad and the adjacent Soissons–Château-Thierry road. Looking to the north from that knob, Soissons is actually in sight. Possession of Berzy neutralizes the two arteries to the north and south.

It was useful that the 2d Division got up to Tigny; taking Berzy-le-Sec was essential. Mangin was determined to take it. It was he who changed the boundary and assigned it to Major General Summerall's 1st Division. Having the order in hand, Summerall arranged a meeting at his headquarters to coordinate with the French 153d Division. He now released the long-husbanded 2d Battalion, 18th Infantry (a 1st Brigade unit), from division reserve, and assigned it to Buck's 2d Brigade for the thrust at Berzy-le-Sec.[4]

The account for this day focuses on the 2d Brigade. Indeed, the remainder of the chronicle might well be subtitled "The Taking of Berzy-le-Sec."

The 1st Moroccan Division attacked late in the morning, before the 1st Division's primary afternoon move, and during the day the Moroccans moved some units across the railroad, slanting back to the west and south of Berzy. The 1st Division's 1st Brigade moved with them, with little opposition until the Americans started down the bluff, at the foot of which was the railroad. Parts of two battalions of the 16th Infantry made it east of the railroad, about six hundred yards southwest of Aconin Farm. Elements of the 18th Infantry, operating along the division's southern boundary, organized positions along the railroad tracks several hundred yards northeast of Bois de Maubuee. The opposing German 20th Division reported a first attack at 9 A.M. (German time) that commenced after an artillery preparation fired an hour earlier. The Germans reported beating off the initial attack and retaking some previously captured guns. The German records claim five separate attacks were launched by 2 P.M., with three more later in the day. Neither French nor American records reflect these actions.[5]

Brigadier Gen. Beaumont Buck responded to the new situation by riding off into the blue. Having issued the brigade attack order, Buck set off "reconnoitering the front line positions" by motorcycle sidecar. Intending to reach the southern end of Ploisy Ravine in his own zone, he instead got into the 16th Infantry's sector at the north end of Chazelle Ravine. In fairness to Buck, the two ravines aren't all that far apart. It could have happened to anybody. Buck had short conversations with Col. Frank Bamford, commander of the 16th Infantry, and Col. Frank Parker of the 18th Infantry, their advanced PCs being only two hundred yards apart, then found the way to his own brigade's reserve position. His report of this morning activity states, "No definite and satisfactory information of the Second Brigade troops was obtained so returned to Brigade P.C. to see what information had come in." This is a rather startling admission from a commander who apparently spent about four critical hours again knowingly out of touch with his own troops. If he was lost initially, how could he possibly justify spending precious time continuing to survey his sister brigade's positions, which were of no relevance to him or his assigned undertaking? The smell of cowardice is faintly present. If not that, then of considerable mental confusion.[6]

In the early afternoon, Buck, his aide Lt. Percy R. Pearce, and two orderlies went forward on horseback to observe the 2d Brigade's 2 P.M. attack. En route they dodged a flight of five German planes, which strafed them and a well-marked aid station. Buck and Pearce left the horses with the orderlies and went over open ground behind the 26th Infantry, which had started the attack. Buck concerned himself with the control of an assortment of stragglers drifting to the rear—some claiming to have been gassed, other that they had been sent back for ammunition or water. Many times two men were found helping one wounded doughboy. He also found a hysterical lieutenant going for reinforcements because his company had been "shot to pieces" after advancing into the deep valley beyond Berzy and opposite Aconin Farm. Buck settled the lieutenant and put him charge of returning a group of thirty stragglers to the fighting line. And that, apparently, was the full extent of Beaumont Buck's supervision of the main attack of the French XX Corps on July 20. Buck made no contact with any of his regimental commanders, battalion commanders, or anyone of higher rank than the hysterical lieutenant. Nor did he make contact with higher headquarters. Instead, he "then sent Pearce to get the horses and orderlies, and we returned to my P.C., where I learned that the attack on Berzy-le-Sec was a failure and that the men were digging in for the night." These are not the actions of a leader in full control of his faculties; they are rather more suggestive of mental dysfunction from fear or exhaustion.[7]

The action this brigade commander had missed took place in two parts: a slight effort by the 28th Infantry from the northwest, and a larger, foredoomed effort by the 3d Battalion, 26th Infantry, from the southwest.

When Colonel Babcock received the attack order at his rear command post, he was told that the supporting barrage would be light, serving to "mark a line for the troops." He then notified the Buck, in person according to his account, that without a heavy barrage he would sustain heavy losses crossing the flat ground under heavy artillery and enfilading machine-gun fire. Nevertheless, he wrote later, "The attack was not altered." This was the second day in a row that Babcock had protested an attack order and been told to do it anyway without any consideration of the possibility of placing suppressive artillery fire on the enfilading strong point. His analysis was correct in both cases, but he seemed utterly unable to prevail—in both cases over telephone lines—against

Summerall or Buck. It is worth remembering that Babcock had protested the conditions of the division attack order the previous afternoon, which Summerall interpreted as a refusal. As a result, Babcock was at once eliminated, in the division commander's mind, as qualified to command the regiment. Nevertheless, he remained in command.

And where was Buck in all of this? He seems to have always been south of his own brigade sector—except that he would periodically reappear at the 28th Infantry's or his own headquarters. Even when he says he visited the 28th Infantry, it must have been without any effect upon him. Babcock later wrote: "At 1.15 P.M. I received an order to attack Berzy-le-Sec at 2.00 P.M., (at this time I was in Missy-aux-Bois, which was as far as telephone communication then reached. . . .) I went immediately by [motorcycle] sidecar to Ploisy to arrange for the attack."[8]

There seems to be no explanation why Babcock did not receive the early morning order until afternoon—ten hours in transit—although Buck's absence could have been a factor. This is particularly odd since he maintained his rearward communications at the expense of communications with his subordinate elements operating forward.

Complicating matters even further, the division's final report on the operation states, "The Divisional Artillery, which had been moved into forward positions, delivered a powerful preparation of two hours, and a rolling barrage from H hour."[9] This report is completely at variance with the previously noted plan to deliver light fires that would mark the forward line of troops. Moreover, all of the infantry reports confirm the absence of any effective fire support. There might have been a preparation that the infantry could not see because Berzy was at the edge of a plateau and every round fired that went over the edge of the plateau would disappear into he valley below. But a barrage would have been noticed if it was located anywhere near friendly troops. The infantry reports are consistent on this point: there was no supporting barrage.

To muddy the waters even more, the division order indicates a completely different set of instructions. The "Special Instructions for 2nd Brigade" indicate no rolling barrage, but rather that "a powerful artillery fire for destruction" was to fall on Berzy-le-Sec and its environs. Then, at 8:30 A.M., the brigade was to advance and the fire was to lift. Following the seizure of the town, 2d Brigade was to pass into division reserve. However, only the 1st Brigade actually attacked at 8:30 A.M. The 2d Brigade attack did not begin until 2 P.M. The original French order called for the attack to jump off at 4:45 A.M. The 8:30 attack hour came into being after the commander of the French 69th Division, one brigade of which was reinforcing the 153d Division specifically for the attack on Berzy, refused to attack at the appointed hour and demanded a three-hour preparation.[10]

After resolving an ambiguous directive received earlier by Maj. George Rozelle, who commanded the 190 remaining men of the 1st Battalion, Babcock put 1st Lt. Soren C. Sorenson in charge of three sixteen-man "infiltration groups" to attack behind the scheduled 2 P.M. barrage. Why not Rozelle? Perhaps because he was the only other field grade officer left in the regiment who was forward. The infiltration groups would try to get into Berzy by going through the trees bordering Ploisy Ravine, enter from the north, "and then to bring over more groups until he had passed the entire battalion over. This attempt," continued Babcock's report, "was made and Lieut. Sorenson reached the outskirts of Berzey-le-Sec till the machine gun fire, in this opinion, made it impracticable to enter the town until after dark."[11]

Babcock then arranged with Brigadier General Buck to make a night infiltration attack, but, "about 11.00 P.M. just before the company left, I received notice that an intense bombardment would fall on the town at 4.45 A.M. and as no method of signalling the capture of the town could be arranged with the Division at that hour, the night attack was abandoned."[12]

Here is another tragic demonstration of inadequate communications and the regrettably standard failure of connection between infantry and artillery that had dogged the attacker for three years. But the British and Germans were both showing signs of learning how to make the coordination work. Once again, one must ask why this could not have been corrected since the telephone lines rearward seem to have been intact—or is Buck the problem again, or Babcock, or Summerall's staff? A brilliant opportunity wasted.

An observer back near Chaudun watched as a unit—he did not know it was the 3d Battalion, 26th Infantry, coming up from a reserve position—moved toward Berzy from the northeast edge of Chazelle Ravine. So far almost unmolested, the leading waves approached the crest of the ridge before Berzy, following their barrage (evidently the barrage landed properly for the 26th Infantry's attack), each individual soldier distinctly visible against the grassy hillside. A single battery of enemy 150-mm. howitzers then opened with

time shells, obviously with observed fire on the target. This was followed almost at once by many other batteries of 150-mm. and 105-mm. howitzers, all firing time shell . . . our infantry was shrouded in smoke and dust. Great gaps were left in the ranks as shells crashed among them. Nevertheless, the advance continued in the most orderly way. . . . Many of our infantry passed out of sight over the ridge. Men struck by the enemy's fire either disappeared or ran aimlessly about and toppled over.

Then began to be heard also the rattle of machine guns. . . . The thin lines lay down in shell holes, while long files of wounded hobbled painfully back. Then appeared a sight which at first seemed inexplicable. Individual men and groups of twos and threes began to wander about all over the field. They were the unit leaders, reorganizing their groups against counterattacks. Thus the afternoon passed and night fell.[13]

The 1st Division did not take Berzy-le-Sec on July 20. Actually, the Germans reported losing the town around 12 A.M., but evidently they recaptured it shortly thereafter. It is impossible to determine who captured the town from the Germans because neither French nor American troops reported getting anywhere near it in the morning, and the 28th Infantry did not attack until 2 P.M. Nevertheless, records of the German 65th Infantry Brigade show that the town was not in German hands at 12 A.M. German time (11 A.M. Allied time). The diagram accompanying the brigade's report shows defending units to be intermingled at this time, but they are clearly portrayed as occupying positions east of the town and west of the railroad and highway located east of Berzy. Furthermore, the German lines at that time are depicted as highly porous but developing in depth.[14]

Meanwhile, Lt. Col. Maxwell Murray recalled that "on the morning of the 20th, the request of the French division commander on our left, that we take the town of Berzy-le-Sec in his sector, was followed by definite orders from [XX] Corps to extend our division sector and take that strong point."[15]

Late in the afternoon General Mangin, Major General Bullard the U.S. III Corps commander, and General Pershing arrived and insisted on the necessity for the capture of Berzy. Arrangements were made for the relief of the division for a twenty-four-hour rest after the attack, and orders were issued to renew the assault the following morning, July 21.[16]

In the actual sequence of events, Mangin first visited Summerall's headquarters, without doubt to discuss the necessity of taking Berzy and Summerall's ability to carry it out. Summerall then departed on a tour of his front lines. General Pershing was making a day-long circuit of his own troops, touching base with five divisions and I Corps headquarters. Pershing recalled: "In the middle of the forest, at the main crossroads, I met General Mangin, the Army Commander, trudging along on foot, followed by his automobile, which was working its way through the jam. . . . Although we talked but a moment, it was long enough for him to speak in high praise of the brilliant dash of the American divisions under his command. Moving on toward the front, we soon found ourselves at the command post of the 1st Division."[17]

Colonel Campbell King, the division chief of staff, briefed Pershing, who left congratulations for Summerall, "who was still somewhere out on the battle-field." Upon being informed of the impending visits, Summerall left for the front—perhaps to avoid both of his senior officers—telling his chief of staff he had to go forward to see the troops.[18]

There is a postscript to Pershing's visit to the still-very-much-engaged 1st Division: "At the headquarters of the 2nd, I saw General Harbord, who always wore his tin hat [from the first he had affected the French helmet]. I recall saying to Harbord that even though the 1st and 2nd Divisions should never fire another shot they had made themselves and their commanders immortal."[19]

This may have been the inspiration for an interesting memorandum Harbord issued later that day to his two brigade commanders. It read: "The Division Commander is especially desirous of re-forming the infantry brigades at once in order to enable them to take up the pursuit, and continue to establish the record they have already gained."[20]

Major Gen. Charles P. Summerall had come to a decisive point in his military career. He had every right to expect some help from the French on his left flank. Instead he had been told to take over their hardest task. To the south, Harbord had requested and received relief for the 2d Division. That division had gone farther east than Summerall's men but still hadn't taken its final objective. Furthermore, with regard to casualties and overall effectiveness, the Second was probably no worse off than the First. What was Summerall's responsibility up the chain of command, in contrast to his responsibility to the men in the ranks? Should he protest or continue the mission? Summerall set down his attitude on the issue of asking for relief a few months later, while he was a corps commander. It is unclear whether he held that attitude on July 20 or developed it as a result of the Soissons experience. In any event, the opinion he articulated was: "Don't ask for relief. Those in higher command are constantly considering the matter of relief. It is expected that the full measure of the organization's strength will be demanded of it before it is pulled out. It must be so if we win. When you have reached the stage that the gains you are making do not justify the losses you are sustaining, you will be taken out."[21]

Hanson Ely had some thoughts of his own on the relief of a unit. He fought his troops to the last fragments and pushed them hard, especially at Blanc Mont in early October. Nevertheless, he believed that a time came when the troops had had enough. He told a War College audience in 1938 about his experience at Cantigny where, after three days, he had asked Bullard for relief. The division commander responded by sending a staff officer to investigate. Ely recalled having the following conversation with the man:

"How many men do you have?"

"About sixteen hundred, losses eight hundred or so."

"You are pretty well off."

"What do you mean? Let me tell you one thing and put it down in your notebook. These men have been fighting three days and three nights and have been successful. . . . There are three other regiments that have had their sleep right along. It is an injustice not to relieve these men."[22]

They were relieved that night.

When he left division headquarters, Summerall set out to visit each regiment to explain the mission and his expectations. According to his aide, Lt. Alban Butler, "he was shot at with everything—shells, M.G.s rifles . . . they promised him they would take Berzy-le-Sec. He promised them they would be relieved tomorrow night." Summerall didn't get back to his command post until 1 A.M. His trip, however, was marked by two more confrontations that, until he wrote of them in 1954, were only mentioned in old-soldier war stories. Summerall's account of his long inspection trip on July 20 includes these passages:

> One brigade [Buck's 2d Brigade] had not reached its objective. On leaving the division command post, I met the lieutenant colonel of a regiment of this brigade. [Lieutenant Colonel Clark R. Elliott, commander of the 26th Infantry]. He told me he was taking supplies to his regiment. I told him to come with me. . . . On reaching the brigade command post I found the brigade commander much confused and worn. I told him to get some rest, that the attack would be resumed the next morning and that he would lead the attack. On reaching a regimental command post, I found the colonel [Hamilton Smith, commander of the 26th Infantry] exhausted. He was sullen and defiant. I asked him why his regiment had not attacked. He replied, "The order was impossible and I did not try to obey it." I could have relieved him but it was evident that he was overwrought and scarcely responsible. The strain had been too great for him. I told him I had brought the lieutenant colonel who would be on duty while he rested. The colonel was killed the second day after this. The next morning the attack was successful but the lieutenant colonel whom I took to the lines was one of the first men killed.[23]

It is no surprise that Summerall considered Buck confused; it is more surprising that he did not relieve him on the spot. Instead, already having little or no faith in Babcock's ability to lead the July 21 attack on Berzy, he told Buck to get some rest because Buck, himself, would lead it. That conforms to a 1st Division legend that achieved circulation in Henry Berry's *Make the Kaiser Dance,* written in 1978. In that collection of interviews, an articulate veteran of the 18th Infantry, Jeremiah M. Evarts, passed along another version of the event: "Now this was the third day of the battle and I understand that Summerall, then commanding the division, told Buck to go over there and take Berzy le Sec or he'd send him back to Blois in disgrace. Oh, that wa[s] a dreadful thing to do. You should not have had a brigadier general down there acting like a junior officer. But that's what happened."[24]

The 26th Infantry attacked as directed and as described above. However, retired Maj. Gen. Joseph D. Patch, writing in 1966, presented a different version of this visit. His conclusion was that Summerall had treated Colonel Smith unjustly. According to Patch: "On a front line tour he [Summerall] formed the opinion that Smith was too far to the rear and told [him] so, ordering him to go up and take personal command of his forward units. Smith got the idea that Summerall thought him lacking in courage. The result was that he went up and got himself killed. The men of the 26th never forgave Summerall for this. . . . I was with Hamilton Smith all through the trying days in the Ansauville Sector and knew that he possessed all sorts of courage, and so did everybody else in the 26th."[25]

The official history of the 26th Infantry describes the attack on the afternoon of the twentieth in forthright terms: "[The attack on the railroad line south of Berzy] involved desperate work, and that day we failed." The account continues and is quoted here, out of time sequence, to supplement Patch's sensing that Summerall had reached a snap conclusion and acted unjustly:

> The Division Commander himself came to the front line battalions that night. . . . "Early in the forenoon of July 21 Lieut. Colonel Elliott, beloved by all because of a fatherly interest in each, was killed by a shell on the plateau above Berzy-le-Sec while directing the attack . . . July 22 on the very eve of the relief after he had personally conducted the Scotch reconnoitering party over his area, Colonel Hamilton Smith was killed by a machine gun bullet while directing an attack on machine gun emplacements near the sugar mill in front of NOYANT. Colonel Smith spent a greater part of those last two days [July 21 and 22] in the front lines with his men, and by his courage and happy spirits worked wonders among them. His death brought gloom and a grim determination to avenge all."[26]

Summerall's memoir chapter on Soissons records one more visit to a regimental commander. The resulting confrontation turned into more of an effective counseling session than an episode of defiance and threats:

. . . when I reached a regimental command post, the colonel [Frank Parker, commander of the 18th Infantry] at once said in a most resentful manner, "General my regiment has lost 60 percent of its officers, nearly all of its old non-commissioned officers and most of its men and I don't think that's any way to treat a regiment." I could have relieved him for insubordination, but I replied calmly, telling him that the tide of battle had been changed by his troops and those of the division of which his were only a part and that the attack would be resumed with what he had. In repeating the incident later [presumably in a letter to Summerall] he stated that I replied, "Colonel, I did not come here to have you criticize my orders or to tell me your losses. I know them as well as you do. I came to tell you the Germans recrossed the Marne last night and are in full retreat and you will attack tomorrow morning at 4:30." He added, "From that day, I have never questioned your orders, and I never will."[27]

After the war, Parker related to Theodore Roosevelt, Jr.:

The worst strain of battle came during the last two days when casualties had been so heavy as to take off many of the field officers and most of the company commanders, when the remnants of the regiments pressed forward and captured Berzy-le-Sec and the railroad. It is always more difficult for the juniors in a battle like this, for they generally do not know what is at stake. General Frank Parker told me how . . . when battalions of eight hundred had shrunk to a hundred and it looked as if the division would be wiped out, and even he was wondering whether we were not losing the efficiency of the division without getting a compensatory gain, General C. P. Summerall, the division commander, came to his headquarters and said, "The German high command has ordered the first general retreat since the first battle of the Marne."[28]

After Soissons, Parker moved up to brigade command, and when Summerall left in October to command V Corps, Parker was given a division command based on Summerall's personal recommendation. Considering that Summerall had effectively relieved one regimental commander on the basis of a forthright report, recognized what he thought was exhaustion in the brigade commander, and impugned the courage of another regimental commander, one is left to wonder how Parker escaped. Very likely the following passages hold the answer.

Summerall summarized all of this by saying that he had not anticipated such conditions. Of the confused, reluctant, and defiant senior leaders he wrote: "Thus, the two colonels in a brigade stated that they could not obey an attack order and the brigade commander was too worn and mentally confused to force the attack. Such was the terrible ordeal of battle on officers."[29]

Parker evidently survived because he was last in a line of exhausted men and by the time the division commander reached him the burden described in the passage above had taken hold. There is nothing in the documentation to suggest that Summerall threatened Buck with a "Take Berzy-or-it's-off-to-Blois" order, but Buck certainly acted as if that had been the case. From that point on he was a changed man who didn't rest long before he went forth. He later wrote: "So exhausted were the men that it was often necessary to take hold of them and shake them to get their attention. This was their condition on the night of July 20–21 when I went along the front line of shell holes and fox holes . . . and by flashlight beneath a shelter-half read and explained to each the order for the attack . . . and told them I expected to be with them at the jump-off."[30]

Thus, at the end of Saturday, July 20, the 2d Brigade, 1st Division, still confronted Berzy-le-Sec—now its very own problem. At the very end of the day, a highly motivated and finally focused Beaumont Buck was touring the front lines to explain the forthcoming attack.

To the south, Hines's 1st Brigade, still west of the Soissons–Château-Thierry road, straddled the ravine carrying the railroad southwest and had reached the vicinity of the Bois Gerard, Visigneux, and Aconin Farm, then bent back its flank on an east-west line to stay in touch with the 2d Brigade. Colonel Bamford, commanding the 16th Infantry, still complained that he never had a day without an exposed northern flank. In fact, his regiment was facing predominately north in order to keep connected.

The Moroccans on the middle axis had also crossed the railroad and entered the Bois Gerard. They were relieved during the night by the French 87th Division. On XX Corps's southern axis of attack, the French 58th Division completed its relief of the 2d Division and was planning its attack for July 21.[31]

Command and control in the 1st Division seems to have gone through a fascinating transition. An obstinate division commander fired a regimental commander, and the 2d Brigade commander moved about but not forward and was as ineffective as the properly motivated Major Rozelle. On the other hand, Summerall, after finally moving forward to find out what was going on, was time and again confronted by exhausted commanders. By the time his tour of the front was finished, Summerall was handling them with somewhat improving understanding.

It is evident that no reliable communications existed forward of either brigade headquarters. In contrast, the Germans were well informed of most of what was happening through their integrated reporting system. The Americans, despite orders to the contrary, were unable to sit quietly at their headquarters and await reports; they knew they had to move forward to find the truth in the midst of the chaos.

CHAPTER 7

Mission Accomplished

July 21—Taking Berzy-le-Sec, Consolidation, and Relief of the 1st Division

German Quartermaster General Erich Ludendorff, unwittingly having set his own trap, now faced a major disaster. His huge investment of men and material in the Marne salient had clearly failed in its attempt to break the Reims shoulder or threaten Paris. Furthermore, his planned follow-on attack against the British had to be canceled. Worse yet, he had also failed to regain the initiative—it was now his turn to dance, and General Foch was the piper: ". . . it was essential that we should not lose the initiative. . . . That meant we must remain on the offensive. We should find ourselves under the hammer the minute we let it slip from our hands. . . . From the purely military point of view it was of the greatest and most fateful importance that we lost the initiative to the enemy. . . . [The consumption of a large part of the reserves] meant the end of our hopes of dealing our long-planned decisive blow at the English Army."[1]

Ludendorff could yet avoid outright disaster by managing a deliberate, fighting withdrawal if, and only if, he could keep the Allies from cutting straight across the base of the salient. By the night of the second day of the Allied counterattack, July 19, he had ordered German forces south of the Marne to withdraw.[2]

During the next two weeks, the French Sixth Army used two American corps headquarters and six American divisions to push the Germans out of the salient from the bottom—in the direction they had already decided to go. Given the difficulty the 2d Division experienced moving too rapidly into an unreconnoitered attack position, and knowing the congested state of the lines of communications, it was probably not feasible to pull other American divisions out of the line and use them along the critical west–east XX Corps axis. Nevertheless, it might have been attempted with better success had a plan for it been developed earlier, had the degree of XX Corps's success been foreseen, and a host of other "ifs."

The relief of divisions on line, even while in the attack, was a well-developed French staff skill, but the Americans had not yet attempted it. Each relieving division pushed forward in XX Corps was identified days earlier and gradually moved forward so as to be able to relieve the attacking divisions in place without any loss of momentum. It seems to have been the French practice to relieve their divisions every three to four days, on average, in order to keep them fresh. With only two divisions in the second line, Major General Berdoulat relieved the American 2d and the 1st Moroccan Divisions on successive days, but was unable to move the 15th Scottish Division up fast enough from army reserve to relieve the American 1st Division until after the fifth full day. Generally, the artillery of the relieved division remained to support the relieving division for several days. But the opportunity to actually achieve a complete breakthrough of the German defenses was lost at Soissons, as is often the case with unexpected successes.

For Sunday, July 21, Berdoulat's XX Corps attack order differed from the previous day's in only one particular: it established 4:45 A.M. as the attack hour. On the 1st Division's southern axis, Hines's 1st Brigade went forward behind a rolling barrage at the appointed time, maintaining contact with its new neighbor to the south, the French 87th Division, which had relieved the 1st Moroccan Division the preceding night. Once again there was a requirement to bend back to maintain contact with the 2d Brigade, which was still taking heavy enfilading fire all the way to the heights north of Buzancy.

The battered remnants of the 2d Brigade had yet another extenuating circumstance and could not move at the appointed hour. Tenth Army had sent forward a regiment from the French 69th Division to reinforce the 153d Division, more specifically to push the attack to protect the Americans's flank as they moved to seize Berzy-le-Sec. The commander of the 69th Division declared his utter inability to attack at so early an hour and demanded a three-hour artillery preparation. He got it.[3]

Not only did he get a heavy preparation, other French divisions were likewise receiving extended preparations before their attacks. One must ask, in view of the 69th Division's success, how it could obtain the obviously required fire support when the 1st Division, commanded by a field artilleryman, could not?

Ironically, Summerall, as a member of the Baker Board sent to France ahead of Pershing's headquarters, in July, 1917, drafted the initial requirements for field artillery support for the AEF. Pershing's staff complained that his calculations were 50 percent too high. Later, his estimates were proven correct. It is worth noting that the success of almost every American attack in the war was proportional to the level of fire support provided to it. Cantigny and Saint-Mihiel were comparative walkovers because of the overwhelming fire support provided by the French. The worst of the casualties at Cantigny were sustained while holding the ground gained—*after* French artillery support was withdrawn. The opening days of the Argonne attack foundered in part from a lack of artillery support. The French had learned from long years of experience that throwing men against machine guns without proper planning and support was stupid. The Americans in their early operations were considered "imprudent" at the least.[4]

The German XIII Corps headquarters telephoned a message to all commands late in the evening of July 20 saying, "Not a single Frenchman will be permitted to advance eastward beyond Ploisy-Chazelle. . . . The high ground at Bercy and south thereof must be held without fail."[5]

To the south, the French 87th Division's attack jumped off with a heavy artillery preparation beginning at 4:30 A.M., followed by the ground attack at six. The attack was immediately successful and by 6:45 A.M. the enemy had been driven across the highway south of Villemontoire. Short-firing artillery again hampered the German defenses and counterattacks. Buzancy changed hands several times during the day. The German Fifth Division's arrival was announced in orders at 4 P.M. (German time). Its mission to retake the high ground east of Charantigny was foiled by the Franco-American forces, who stopped the attack cold before it could clear Buzancy—although it did succeed in securing that place for the remainder of the day. Among the Allied POWs taken in the counterattack were several 6th Regiment marines, operating well out of sector, who apparently did not get the word they were being relieved.[6]

The 1st Division attack order arrived at 2d Brigade headquarters twenty minutes before midnight on Saturday, July 20. By 2 A.M., Brigadier General Buck, as previously noted, was personally carrying the brigade order forward. It directed the 28th Infantry to take Berzy-le-Sec to the center of the ravine east of town, and assigned the 26th Infantry the task of taking "the Sucrerie [sugar factory] and the line in advance of it from confluence of little streams 500 meters S-E of Sucrerie to, point on railroad 600 meters N-W of Sucrerie." In simple terms, these regiments were to move over the plateau crest and down into the steep valley, across the railroad, and then across the main north-south road. For the 28th Infantry, the "center of the ravine" would be at about Berzy railroad station; for the 26th Infantry, the sugar factory was well beyond the railroad and east of the road. No matter how specified, the purpose of the attack was to have the hillside town of Berzy, looking straight north to Soissons, firmly in American control.[7]

It appears at this point that Beaumont Buck eliminated his regimental commanders, Conrad Babcock and Hamilton Smith, from the chain of command.

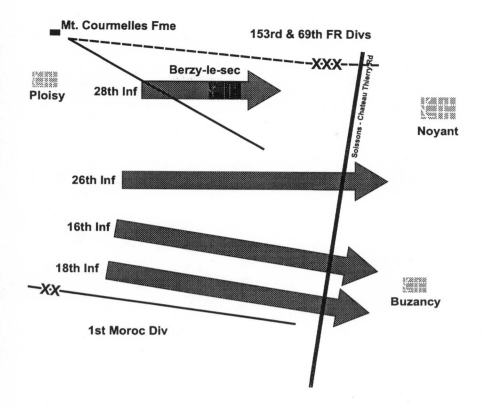

5. 1st Division Attack, July 20 and 21, 1918

He mentioned neither of them, by name or position, when he described his after-midnight briefing of *battalion* commanders: "The officers of each battalion were assembled and by a screened light under a shelter half in little trenches the maneuver was explained. . . . Watches were synchronized."

Buck then records: "The 1st Bn. 26th Infantry was not personally visited because daylight overtook the Brigade Commander before it could be located. . . . The Brigade Commander with two staff officers went to the assembly point of the 28th Infantry on the edge of the plateau south of Ploisy, arriving there about 8:00 A.M."[8]

It wasn't that simple.

Buck revealed the remainder of his travels in the book he wrote after the war. Finished with delivering orders to the battalion commanders, he returned to his own command post long enough for breakfast. He then loaded his Cadillac with the brigade adjutant, Maj. John H. Wills; Lieutenant Pearce, his aide; the French liaison officer, Capt. Pierre H. Hendrickx, and three orderlies. They went "as far to the front as we cared to risk, then we continued on foot." They were out of touch with division headquarters as a consequence, but could claim that with several orderlies and an automobile stashed at an intermediate point, essential reports could be rendered, albeit late. As the party approached the jump-off line near Ploisy Ravine, they were caught by a German counterbarrage—"a hell of bursting shells"—and they hugged the slope and waited.

With time running out, the party made a single-file dash, led by Buck and ending with the orderlies. Reaching the plateau and continuing forward through what Buck thought to be the thinnest part of the barrage, the whole party was flattened by an explosion. When the dust settled, Buck recalled, "I got up and realized I was not hurt. All the others got up except Major Wills, who rolled over and sank down again. . . . I saw that he was mortally hit. I sent Lieutenant Pearce and an orderly back to notify some litter bearers at the head of Ploisy ravine . . . a hundred yards further on we saw the remnants of the 28th Infantry forming."[9]

Buck had made it to exactly the correct assembly spot and had kept his promise to be with the assault troops at the 8:30 A.M. jump-off time. By then there were an estimated 190 men from Major Rozelle's 1st Battalion in the frontline area and about ninety more from the other two battalions under Lt. Col. Edmund Sayer back at Ploisy. At 8:27 A.M. Buck found the senior officer present, Lieutenant Sorenson—the same Sorenson who, although lost on the first day, had, under the eye of Babcock and Rozelle the afternoon before, conducted the short-lived attempt to get infiltration groups into the town. Sorenson confirmed that he had his map and understood the instructions. The first wave would consist of the men of Company D under 2d Lt. William Warren on the right, and those of Company B under 2d Lt. John H. Donaldson on the left. With the first wave ready to move out, Sorenson was hit by a fragment from a shell that detonated fifteen feet away. When Buck called for the next in command, 2d Lt. John R. D. Cleland, stepped forward. He had just joined the regiment. Buck watched as Cleland led the first wave to the crest of the plateau overlooking the village, then stop. Buck started forward to investigate but turned back when the line started forward again.

The pause was because Cleland had been wounded. His DSC citation reads: "Although wounded before and in the attack upon Berzy-le-Sec, Lt. Cleland declined an opportunity to be evacuated and led his platoon to its final objective, which he consolidated and held." A postwar letter from Lt. Col. Clarence Huebner endorsing Cleland's application for a Regular Army commission notes that Cleland joined the regiment *while it was in action,* was awarded the DSC, and then was given command of Company F. Heubner added: "He is an officer of most excellent judgment, a high sense of honor and a thorough gentleman. . . . Should he be commissioned an officer in the Regular Army I should be more than pleased to have him with or under me."[10]

When the first wave began moving again, Buck looked back and saw the second line waiting for a command to move forward, so he gave it to them. The first wave was now moving down the hill into the village, and when the second wave followed, Buck went back to get the third wave (a platoon's-worth of collected men and four machine guns) and got them moving up the slope. Buck continues: "This was scarcely finished when the fighting in the village stopped. One of my men came running to me and said if I would go to the brow of the hill I could see small parties of the enemy running down the slope to the Crise. I did not go because intermittent bursts of machine gun fire were sweeping the brow. Evidently the fighting was over. . . . After a hurried questioning of [a party of twenty] prisoners, I hastened to the nearest telephone to report to the Division Commander that Berzy-le-Sec had been captured and was in our hands."[11]

Beaumont Buck's action at Berzy-le-Sec is a fine example of combat leadership in the sense that there comes a time when senior commanders must move to the point of decisive action. We will never know the extent to which he was inspired by Summerall's threat of being sent to Blois. Whether threat or long-inculcated habit was the cause—it is more likely the two worked together—this was the time when the commander's place was forward even if out of touch with the rear. The importance of the occasion transformed the deed into myth, and myth into legend.

Laurence Stallings, the very best of captivating storytellers wrote: "Beaumont Buck having lost all his field officers, was heading his brigade like a platoon leader in front-line sweeps. (All twelve battalion commanders were gone.) . . . Buck, waving his tin hat took the village on the 2nd Brigade's second try."[12]

Then a company commander in the 18th Infantry, Jeremiah Everts' version reads: "I was told that General Buck ended up taking it with *eighteen* men. He had a rifle in his hands at the time."[13]

From General Order No. 44, Headquarters, 1st Division, August 5, 1918: "General Buck . . .went along the front line of the attacking battalion, gave the correct direction to the men of the line and led the first wave."

The division's official history goes a bit further, putting "the brigade commander and his staff in the first wave."[14]

But Beaumont Buck never moved out with the first wave, did not go up to the crest of the hill overlooking Berzy-le-Sec, did not wave his tin hat, and did not lead eighteen men with a rifle in his hand. He never said he did. In fact,

Buck's is the only account, official or otherwise, that does not have him "in the first wave" of the final attack on Berzy.

What of Col. Conrad Babcock and Maj. George Rozelle? Where were they while Buck was directing the remnants of the regiment? We know that two days before Summerall wrote Babcock off as unfit for command but nevertheless left him in command. We know that Summerall told Buck to personally lead the attack on Berzy-le-Sec. When they met that morning, what did they have to say to each other? Had they even talked in the previous twenty-four hours? The day before, Major Rozelle (himself under a cloud for having become lost himself during the afternoon attack on the nineteenth) had delegated control of the 1st Battalion's attack to Lieutenant Sorenson. From Buck's account of events on the morning of the twenty-first, that battalion level of command was also eliminated—leaving the brigade commander to work directly with the senior surviving company commander, a brand-new lieutenant.

Conrad Babcock wrote two after-action reports, the first an immediate report dated July 26. The second was written August 4. The two reports differ as one might well expect, the latter benefiting from the passage of time. In the latter report, Babcock discussed the unsuccessful attack on the afternoon of the twentieth, the canceled plan for a night attack, then reported his actions on the morning of the twenty-first:

> I went to the front at about 7:00 A.M., consulted with Major Rozelle and talked to the men. At 8:30 A.M. the barrage was to fall but at that hour nothing could be heard of any barrages—however the front wave started and at about 8:40 a few shells went over (sounded as if one battery was firing). About that time I was notified that the Brigade Commander was present and I reported to him in the edge to the woods just east of the town of Ploisy. The town [Berzy] was captured about 9:15 A.M. with about 20 per cent casualties, and the final objective (on the railroad) about 10:15 A.M. From Berzy-le-Sec, I could see Soissons and the country beyond; the town had a fine view on all the country north and east.[15]

Buck, in a penciled note on records sent to the American Battle Monuments Commission by Major Rozelle during the Commission's attempts to resolve contradictory reports of events, indicated that "Col Babcock went into Berzy. After leaving me he went to the telephone at P.C. Ploisy & telephoned Berzy was taken." Nowhere in Buck's *official* report or in his memoir does he take note of having seen Babcock that morning. Furthermore, Buck reported that he himself had sought out a telephone to make the report. The two commanders might have seen separate groups start the attack, but possibly Babcock and Rozelle watched the Sorenson-Cleland group move out, not knowing that Buck was directing the action. Babcock followed the surviving 28th Infantry soldiers into Berzy-le-Sec, Buck did not.

The matter of Berzy-le-Sec having finally been settled, Buck then mounted himself, Lieutenant Pearce, and two orderlies on horseback to go south to check the progress of Smith's 26th Infantry. He stated, "I learned that on account of the severe fire of the enemy which checked the 26th Infantry's advance, the C.O. 26th Infantry had demanded the assistance of my Brigade reserve and that the entire reserve had gone to the assistance of the 26th Infantry and had enabled it to reach the Sucrerie."[16]

One is left to wonder who might have given such permission? The adjutant, who ordinarily might have been running the command post, had gone forward with Buck and was killed before the attack commenced. Had Buck left no instructions for employment of the last reserve? He certainly was in no position to direct its employment. The tone of his report is one of some irritation, but again signals his rather loose management style. That style would cost him dearly later in the war.

Then to muddle things a bit more, the German 11th Company, 8th Body Grenadier Regiment, reported it still held the sugar factory as of 8:15 A.M. (German time) July 23.[17]

For the remainder of Sunday, July 21, the division consolidated its lines and pushed forward patrols. At nightfall the line went from the heights north of Berzy-le-Sec, along the Château-Thierry road south of the Sucrerie, and well to the south and east. The 1st Brigade was far across the road, and stopped in the wood west of Buzancy Château.

While in that position, the division got the word that it would *not* be relieved that night. Lieutenant Alban Butler's journal reflects what had to be the terrible disappointment of that postponement: "The 15th Scotch Division, which was to have relieved us, cannot reach here on account of the congested condition of the roads. . . . General Summerall tried hard to get us relieved because he had promised the men yesterday that they would be relieved. He would not say that we were tired. If we go out tonight we go out with our tails up & no one knows what may happen tomorrow. The general visited the lines again tonight to explain to the men why they were not to be relieved & to cheer them & praise them."[18]

By the end of the day, Mangin's bold scheme for decisively trapping the Germans, once canceled by a cautious Pétain, then reinstated in no uncertain terms by Mangin's mentor Foch, had ground to a halt—not for lack of continued effort but because the Germans had brought to bear the necessary determined defense.

During that day, elements of the 1st Division had indeed captured key terrain on the Germans's main supply route. On the middle axis, the French 87th Division, which had relieved the Moroccans, moved east of the road and captured Buzancy, then lost it at 7:15 A.M. to a boiling counterattack coming out of the Bois de Concrois—at the cost of a thousand casualties. In the former area of Harbord's 2d Division, the French 58th Division, with reconstituted tank support, moved past Tigny and more than a kilometer beyond the road to the western edge of Bois de Concrois. The same counterattack drove it back west of Tigny, from whence it came, at a cost of nineteen hundred casualties within those few hours. Whether another American division could have done any better was certainly an open question at that point. A fully constituted, partly rested division going in against an ad hoc defense might well have torn the German defenses apart a second time, but the principal object had already been attained: The line of communications southward had been cut and the Germans were retreating as rapidly as they could, forfeiting huge stockpiles of war supplies in the process.[19]

Lieutenant Sulzbach's diary records: "21 July: I don't know the word indicating the difference in degree required to describe the wholly crazy artillery fire which the French turn on for the attack in the morning. The word 'hell' expresses something tender and peaceful compared with what is starting here and now. . . . It's as though all the barrages one had ever known had been combined to rattle down on us now. . . . I don't see how the French have managed *this*—first bringing our offensive of 15 July to an unsuccessful halt, and then, completely unobserved by us, preparing and carrying out an attack on a huge scale with such quantities of troops and equipment."[20]

CHAPTER 8

The Reward

July 22—The Last Day

There was no significant activity on July 22. The 1st Division continued to reorganize and adjust its positions. Throughout the day priority was given to removing the wounded and burying the dead, despite a stream of German aircraft flying low and strafing any available targets. German artillery was active in harassing the front lines and firing occasionally effective counterbattery missions. The advance parties of the 15th Scottish Division arrived to plan that night's relief. However, the 26th Infantry found it necessary to advance its lines to eliminate sniper fire from the sugar factory, confirming German reports that it was they, not the 1st Division, who held it.[1]

Shipley Thomas, the 26th Infantry's intelligence officer, said in a 1976 interview that on the afternoon of July 22 he was trying to reach the division adjutant when Major General Summerall grabbed the telephone:

"Hello," the general bellowed, "this is General Summerall. Who is this?"

"Lieutenant Thomas, sir, 26th Infantry."

"Well, how are things?"

"I have to report that we have broken through as far as we can. Our colonel is dead, our lieutenant colonel is dead, and all the majors are dead or wounded. And God knows how many captains and lieutenants are down. And the situation with the men is just as bad."

"Great God, Mr. Thomas! Who is commanding the regiment?"

"Captain Barney Legge."

"How is he doing?"

"Fine, sir, with what he has left."

"Well, who is his executive officer?"

"I guess I am. . . ."

Summerall then told Thomas that the 15th Scottish Division was on the way in to relieve the division and that the 26th Infantry would be saluted with a feast and a band (which Thomas says he asked for) on the way out.[2]

Starting at the top of the AEF, Pershing demanded leaders with drive. He wanted leaders who were willing to push men forward, knowing that war was a matter of will above all, and that victory, in all its appalling carnage, goes to the side with the last push—the side that, even if bloodied more than its opponent, will push one more time. These words are carefully chosen, for in the 1500s, the time of the *tercio,* the final push had bloody implications. The *tercio* was a formation created by the Spanish, consisting of a square mass of approximately fifteen hundred men armed with metal-tipped, twenty-four-foot-long pikes. In the assault, as many pikes as could reach forward were lowered to present an almost impenetrable front. This was mass in its ultimate form. When this mass hit any other formation, momentum imparted by velocity was crucial, but velocity had to be controlled in order to impart the full weight of the formation. Whichever side was able to impart that final "push of pike," that last supreme, murderous effort, would crush and slaughter the enemy's square.[3]

Commanders in Pershing's mold—or as Pershing wished them to be and as Charles Mangin fully expected them to be—had to have a cold-bloodedness that would let them expend men like cartridges and consider their own judgment nearly infallible. Pershing said, "Make men fear you." A British general regretted that his army's generals "lacked the ruthlessness, the complete disregard of individuals, the iron hand, the steeled soul and drive . . . qualities [that] are necessary characteristics of a great Captain."[4]

Hanson Ely later wrote of situations similar to the final days of Soissons, and his message rings true for the situation that Summerall had faced:

> Men must be trained that when they have been in battle for days and nights, when perhaps they have been badly handled by the enemy and have had heavy casualties, yet when the signal comes to go they will go again to *the limit of their endurance.* That is another thing that should be put in large letters—that it is *the last five percent* of the possible exertion that often wins the battle . . . not the first attack nor the second or the third, but it was that last straggling fourth attack. It has long been established that battles are won by remnants, remnants of units, remnants of material, remnants of morale, remnants of intellectual effort. . . . In the A.E.F. it was generally known that certain divisions, regiments or battalions could be depended upon to reach their objective, but others not. In France, whenever certain divisions were ordered to attack it was said,

"They will go until they get 15 percent losses and then they will want to be relieved and that will be the end of them"—and it was.[5]

Hanson Ely offers here what is perhaps the exactly proper subtitle for a description of the American participation in the battle of Soissons: "Battles Are Won by Remnants." Yet we must remember that it was Ely who successfully forestalled a staff officer with the report that the time had come for his men to be relieved. Who is to know and how is he to know when that last bit of strength has passed, that the time for relief has indeed come?

Was Babcock correct in reporting what he did? How different was his situation from that of others? He remains something of an enigma. From his reports and from his continued presence he appears to have had his regiment rather well in hand. After the initial hours, he was frequently well forward, always well in touch with his regimental headquarters, and periodically communicated with his brigade commander.[6] Although it is unclear if Babcock was aware he had been more or less relieved, it is to his credit that he did not withdraw from the field of battle. Quite the opposite, he personally made it to the final objective. And what is one to make of the confusion between Babcock and the commanding general? Where was his immediate superior, the brigade commander? The available evidence strongly suggests Babcock turned in an excellent performance for which he deserved reward; yet the 1st Division did not decorate him. As an interesting footnote, Brig. Gen. C. E. Kilbourne wrote a letter to the AEF adjutant general on November 15, 1918, in which he stated: "While serving as Chief of Staff, 89th Division . . . I was forcibly impressed by the qualifications of . . . Col. C. S. Babcock. [He is a] natural leader of men, forceful, physically and mentally apparently tireless, indifferent to danger, thoroughly versed in [his] profession."[7]

Can Buck be forgiven his abdication of command at those early critical points when, to all intents and purposes, he was absent without leave in the face of the enemy? His right was advancing and his left was stalled and taking heavy casualties. Where did he go? Not to the point of decision but off on a lark. It is difficult to give Buck any accolade for his final acts. His absence counts for more than his tardy, final presence. Lieutenant Sorenson or Lieutenant Cleland or his successor evidently would have accomplished the mission. Both Major Rozelle and Colonel Babcock were present and capable of directing the attack. After all, the French had cleared most of the brigade's northern flank, which had done so much damage and to which Buck had paid no attention whatsoever.

It would appear fair to conclude that Charles P. Summerall, even considering his huge ego and bluster, was the proper man at Soissons, with the proper determination and driving ability to win his segment of the battle, successfully driving the remnants forward.

What were Summerall's strengths? At a time when "driving" appears to have been the approved method, he was a driver. How much effect his histrionics actually had on subordinates is not clear; how much effect his challenge to their personal honor had is abundantly clear. It is equally certain that he possessed a certain touch for this level of command evidenced by the speed with which he moved his command element forward and, most of all, by his sense of timing when he, personally, should go forward. Summerall can be forgiven much for twice trooping the line to talk to the soldiers, to get a real sense of their condition and then retrace his steps when the promise he had made could not be fulfilled.

Joseph D. Patch concluded: "It is the opinion of the men of the Division that Summerall was the best Combat Commander of the war, probably one of the best of all time. . . . Summerall whether you like him or not, was a great soldier and a great American."[8]

In November, 1918, Summerall was nearly relieved over the "folly" of the "Race to Sedan" incident, which occurred while he was commanding V Corps. Summerall was among other commanders who were criticized for wasting lives immediately before and at the time of the signing of the Armistice. But Summerall's address to officers of the 89th Division shows the development of his command attitudes after intensive command experience.[9]

Another Summerall protege, Col. Frank Bamford, commander of the 16th Infantry at Soissons, was selected as a "driving" commander to replace Maj. Gen. Clarence Edwards and push the 26th Division in the final weeks of the war.[10]

And what of the Germans? The 46th Reserve Division reported the following to its corps headquarters on July 22: "at present . . . fit only for duty as a front line division in a quiet sector." Personnel present for duty: 40 officers, 339 riflemen, 48 machine guns, 8 light *minenwerfers,* 3 artillery pieces, approximately one weak battalion.[11]

Closure

In telling this story, we set out to present a new historical view of American participation in the battle of Soissons within the scope of the actions of the two American divisions serving under the command of the French XX Corps in the French Tenth Army. The final relief of Summerall's 1st Division on the night of July 22–23, did not conclude the battle, nor did it conclude the AEF campaign officially designated Aisne-Marne. At dawn on July 23, the 15th Scottish Division, supported by the American 1st Division's artillery, which had remained in place for support, attacked and received a grim initiation, making little progress and suffering heavy casualties. As recorded by the 1st Division's historians: "Unfortunately, due to unavoidable difficulty and confusion in locating the infantry front line, the rolling barrage was too far advanced and afforded insufficient protection to the troops in the assault. Later in the day, the artillery was able to place its defensive fires accurately in assisting the Scottish infantry to repel a counter-attack."[12]

One might well add that the 1st and 2d Divisions had also lost their barrages and never seemed to recover them, but went ahead anyway—at terrible cost.

Speculation as to what would have happened if Mangin had had more American divisions or a reinforcement of more French divisions; speculation about what would have happened if he had made more daring use of the ever-lurking cavalry, or if the tanks had demonstrated greater sustainability are all idle topics. Mangin was, for the moment, halted. However, his Tenth Army, still poised at the northwest shoulder of the salient, within actual sight of Soissons, would act as a hinge for the French Sixth Army to the south. Given bulk and drive by the divisions of Hunter Liggett's I Corps and Robert Bullard's III Corps, Sixth Army drove northeast to the Vesle River.[13]

An estimated 150,000 Americans acquired their combat training during that period, and most did it without having the in-country training and field experience that had been acquired by the 1st and 2d Divisions.

Soissons itself fell on August 2. When the campaign officially ended on August 6, the two opposing forces were facing each other along the Vesle River, in a straight line from Reims to Soissons. The Marne salient, it's birth begun with such violence by the Germans on May 27, offering such promise for them again on July 15, and then presenting the Allies with such an opportunity to trap the German forces in it beginning July 18, was finally eliminated.

Conclusion

Soldiers, being essentially practical people, always want to know what each past battle or war should teach them. The sooner they know, the better they may be able to adapt to the inevitable changes in warfare. If there is one thing that is absolutely certain in war it is that the conditions of battle are constantly changing. War is not a mechanical process and consequently is often badly replicated in computer-based war games. Those war games are based upon mathematical models incapable of duplicating the paralyzing effects of fear, the corrosive effect of poor leadership, and the solvent effect of panic. Numbers, upon which all present games are based, have no feelings, no personalities, no prejudices, and no character flaws. Numbers never need sleep, food, water, dry clothing, or human companionship. They can be made to replicate the effect of rain or snow by an arbitrary reduction of movement capability, but they can never duplicate genius or superhuman effort. For example, even Saddam Hussein's army presented America and its allies with unpredicted situations in the Persian Gulf War. Who would ever have thought to bury tanks under sandbags to reduce their heat signature and then kindle small charcoal fires under sheets of corrugated metal to create a diversionary signature for the $165,000 tank-killer missiles to home in on? Soldiers fight other soldiers, and both desperately want to wake up to see the next sunrise.

Consequently, when armies begin to study their battles, they often shy away from quantitative measures, seeing in them a false certainty that does not account for the central fact of a living, human enemy. One of the horrors of pre–World War I doctrine was a calculus peculiar to the French Army that demonstrated conclusively that attacking infantry would generate a higher volume of fire that would beat down the enemy's counteraction and inevitably prevail. Thus the school of the attack became a matter of religious faith to that army—a religion based on a false faith in numbers. There were echoes of that religion in U.S. Army infantry doctrine going under the name of "fire superiority"—about which more follows.

In any event, soldiers over the years have sought to reduce their actual experiences to "lessons." For some years now, the American Army has routinely produced "Lessons Learned," even though most of those have been collections of mere "observations." Nothing is truly "learned" by an organization until budget dollars and personnel assignments attach to it and it becomes enshrined in doctrine.

The Effect

The American contribution to the battle that universally carries the label "turn of the tide" had ended. The two American divisions had, in General Pershing's words, "made themselves and their commanders immortal." French staff officers would exclaim, "*Superb! Magnifique! Epatant!*" Indeed, Soissons *had* been stunning, marvelous, and first-rate! The collapse of the last German drive and the immediately successful American-fueled counterattack caused Field Marshal Paul von Hindenburg to write, "How many hopes, cherished during the last few months, had probably collapsed at one blow! How many calculations had been scattered to the winds." This moment had been long in coming, but in less than four months the Armistice would be signed.[1]

General Mangin's letter of commendation to the American divisions read: "*Camarades americains, je vous suis reconnaissant du sang genereusement verse sur le sol de ma patrie.*" ("American comrades! I am grateful to you for the blood so generously spilled on the soil of my country.") And well he should have been. In a war where success and fame seemed to be measured perversely by one's own casualties rather than those of the enemy, the 1st Division had lost roughly seventy-two hundred killed and wounded and the 2d Division more than five thousand.[2]

For students of the Great War, particularly Americans, Soissons provides special aspects that give it an absorbing, long-term interest. It was not a neat and orderly maneuver, nor was it an exemplary exercise in generalship. It was, in fact, a confused mess, what the Germans term a *schutzenbrei* (hunter's stew), a complete mix-up of men and organizations. But Soissons stands at a distinct point of transition—a transition in operations and tactics, a transition in the mechanics of warfare, and, particularly for the two divisions representing the long-awaited presence of the American Expeditionary Forces, a transition in leadership, with its terrible tests of command and control. The battle demonstrated how much the Americans had yet to learn, but it also provided hints of just how quickly some of them could learn and how long it would take others to do so. Nevertheless, after all the sources have been examined, the photographs poured over, and the maps examined, the story of Soissons comes down to just a few things: First, General Foch's tenacity and intuition; second, General Mangin's wiliness; and, finally, the American soldier's exemplary dedication and endurance.

Lessons

What then, shall we say of all this? Is this simply an exercise in dredging up the past and setting portions of the record straight for the grandsons of the participants? Hopefully it is more than that. Hopefully we have been able to illuminate some of both the good and bad practices of our forefathers from which some of us may gain some small measure of wisdom. In all of it we must remember, first and foremost, Clausewitz's dictum not to mistake the kind of war upon which one is embarking for something it is not, nor to try "to turn it into something that is alien to its nature." The art of command in battle, while based upon principles, must also respond to present realities.[3]

The American Army entered World War I steeped in its own principles but almost blind to the realities of war in western Europe. Why, when that war had been raging for almost three years, is hard to imagine. It entered the war as a junior coalition partner for the first time since Yorktown, and it was as touchy about its status in 1918 as it had been in 1781. But its leadership principles and basic leadership instincts were sound, although largely unknown to its hugely expanded leadership body. General Pershing set the stage for both of these positions when he announced to the War Department in July, 1917, that the current *Infantry Drill Regulations* (which happened to be dated 1911 with numerous minor changes) were perfectly adequate for warfare in Europe, and that the rifle-armed infantryman was the key to victory. This was myopia of the worst kind, for in many ways the rifleman was all but extinct as long as trench warfare continued. But that is going too far, just as Pershing did, for the rifleman *was* still the key if anyone could break the stalemate in which wire, machine guns, and artillery reigned supreme.

Pershing argued that American troops should be trained for what he called "open warfare." But no one, including Pershing, was able to describe just what that was in relation to the war in France. We must remember that Pershing came to France from two years on the Mexican border, where real "open warfare" had been the order of the day, albeit against lightly armed bandit gangs. Ironically, as much as Pershing believed that the Americans would be the ones to break the stalemate, it was the Germans who did so with their five spring offensives.

General John J. Pershing has gone into the myth-laden mists of ethnocentric history as the only Allied commander in chief who had it right in his insistence on open warfare. Yet he was as wrong as the rest of them, although in different ways.

In March, 1918, Pershing overrode all objections and forced the shift in training to this undefined form of warfare—an action that served principally to disrupt training that was already in progress in the United States. By the time proper training had begun to become effective, it was too late. The German spring offensives fueled an insatiable demand for men, men, and more men! Training suffered further curtailments as a result of the accelerated shipping schedule, and many of the soldiers who crossed the jump-off line on July 18 were criminally untrained. Maneuvers in open terrain were beyond their ken, and many of their officers were, in equal measure, uninstructed.[4]

Soissons thus reflected an army in transition. The "laws of trench warfare" demanded that senior commanders remain in their headquarters, tethered to the end of a telephone wire. The "laws of trench warfare" demanded that the infantry do its best to keep up with the opening artillery barrage. Company and platoon commanders were to do their best to keep the soldiers moving forward on line for purposes of control more than anything else, while sergeants were responsible for proper dress along the line. The entire American system was mechanical because no one had been able to figure out how to properly fight the poorly trained force, given the limited capability of battlefield communications, the rudimentary ability to coordinate supporting artillery fires, and the rigidity of thinking that equated a line on a map to an impenetrable wall. At least in this last regard the 1st and 2d Divisions both demonstrated an ability occasionally to transcend artificial limits and act as the situation, not the lines on the map, demanded.

Some American units and staffs had been trained by the Allies and then by their own instructors for two different types of warfare. Their tools of the trade were transitional, as was their organization. Of the two divisions employed in this battle, the First was the only one to go through the entire planned training cycle. In some ways that turned out to be detrimental. However, as Americans have always been individualistic, it seems that whatever a unit's level of training, each commander fulfilled the functions of command as he thought best.

The French had evolved a very sophisticated system of control from the highest level. It met the requirements for security and centralized effort. How many American officers shared Harbord's dismay when the division he had been sent to command was literally taken from his hands within forty-eight hours and dispatched into the blue? How often did such things happen in the French system? Evidently it was routine. Recall the reactions of the French XX Corps staff when confronted by the irate Harbord—they were used to it! Such things did not happen in the British Army as the experiences of the American 27th and 30th Divisions attest. On the other hand, it was the British who were initially so insistent that the commanders of larger formations remain within telephone contact with higher headquarters at all times.

It is perhaps instructive that when the AEF command group arrived in France and began examining the structures and training regimes of the Allied armies it reported that the proper size of an infantry company should be 250 men—of whom about 10 percent were there simply to reconstitute the unit in the event it was decimated. The British, from whom the Americans copied the TO&E, had come to expect the loss of many officers and noncommissioned officers and understood the necessity of reconstituting units around a core of surviving veterans. When the Americans adopted the 250-man company, they did so to give the unit more punch and staying power. But, like so many personnel schemes, this one worked little better than did any other.

Continuity was thrown to the winds at the senior command level. That is a price that must always be paid when a force is expanding rapidly. It may seem criminal to replace two division commanders and a number of key subordinate commanders within days of a major offensive operation, but most of those men had been tried in battle at least once before—although the tests varied sharply in their severity. In fact, the 1st Division's leaders may actually have been less well prepared for the ordeal of Soissons by virtue of their Cantigny experience. That operation was a set-piece affair of regimental size, with exquisite planning, time, and overwhelming support. It was nothing like the baptism of fire the 2d Division underwent. The Second's performance at Belleau Wood and Vaux was remarkable and arguably more instructive since it was essentially a hasty attack—unfortunately very similar to the attack at Soissons. All other factors aside, it is evident that personality may well have been the greatest single factor in determining success. Summerall and Harbord were both professional soldiers of relatively limited combat experience, but both had served their commander well and had exhibited the kind of drive he demanded. Neither had ever been confronted with a situation quite like the one they encountered on July 18, 1918.

The 1st Division had one major advantage: it was a day closer to its jump-off line and thus at least some opportunity to reconnoiter the ground over which it would attack. Leaders had time to digest their orders and at least attempt to accomplish some of the troop-leading procedures.

In contrast, the 2d Division had virtually no time whatsoever for troop leading, and no time at all for reconnaissance. Its officers and men had never trained with tanks, yet they were supported by almost fifty of those ungainly but useful creations on the first day. But the tanks followed the French method of command and responded only to higher headquarters until they were committed to action. If there was any coordination between the tank formation's commander and the division it was minimal. The cooperation that occurred on the bloody battlefield evidently was without plan or design since no commander at brigade level or below mentioned any. The air support described in the operations order evaporated within hours and ceased to be a factor. Here is another irony: Even though every subordinate commander noted the free play of German airplanes, there is not a single request for anyone to do anything about it.

The worst observation must be that there was no evident effort to control the artillery in any but the most perfunctory fashion. It is worth noting that the French Army's artillery, usually an effective contributor, is not mentioned in any of the accounts. The absence of support by heavy batteries had to be especially painful for the 28th Infantry, which suffered so terribly from the flanking fire of massed machine guns in the Vauxbuin Position. There was plenty of heavy artillery available, yet there is no evidence of any attempt, save the one message from Colonel Babcock, to deal with that position by any means other than human flesh and rifles. That Summerall, an artilleryman should miss so obvious a situation is most puzzling. It is painful to read the accounts of his subordinates as they describe the absence of supporting artillery fires after the opening barrage of the second day.

General Pershing, like most real people, was himself in transition. He knew what he knew from his own experiences and, once in France, attempted to adopt as much as he valued of the Allied experience. For all his insistence upon open warfare as the doctrine for the American Expeditionary Forces, he was never able to really define it. Nor was he able to resolve the fact that, until the Germans broke out of their entrenchments and initiated open warfare themselves, the problem of the trenches had always to be conquered first. If the Americans paid a terrible price in blood to learn their trade, their vigor and careless aggressiveness was too much for the Germans in the long run, and Pershing was counting on that.

What *was* learned and what *should* have been learned? These are very different questions because most of the lessons that need to be learned too often are not. What should have been learned was that the American instinct for forward command had been validated. The lesson that "artillery conquers while infantry occupies" was found to be a half-truth. There is, as there has always been, no substitute for working together. That tanks are effective in masses was validated, but the mechanical inefficiencies of those early weapons precluded learning greater lessons. Evidently the loss of air superiority was of little more than nuisance effect, thus stifling any learning on that issue. Infantry-artillery coordination was identified as a major problem, although not a new one by any means. Nevertheless, it was one for which no reliable technical solution was available.

Then there was the issue of command and control. Command in war is always the most important and the most difficult function. At the squad level it consists of keeping everybody moving together toward the next objective. At the company level it is more complicated because the commander loses the ability to directly influence all of his subordinates and because reports have to be rendered rearward based on fairly accurate knowledge of immediate events. At battalion, except under unusual circumstances, the commander is hard put to "see" all his companies and their supporting elements unless they are able to feed him timely and reasonably accurate reports. If the battalion commander does not receive regular reports he has two options: go forward and see for himself, or, climb high enough to see—thereby becoming a significant target. The Allied—particularly the British—system of demanding that commanding officers remain at the telephone was not adequate since the telephone lines seldom operated satisfactorily far enough forward to allow the stay-behind commander even to provide personal observation of an attack. How many runners were killed directly or indirectly as a result of this practice probably cannot be determined. For the regimental commander to remain "on the line" had some possible merit since occasionally the next higher headquarters, brigade or division, might have assets with which to influence the battle, and rapid response was key. Where no such assets were at hand, it would seem that accurate reporting should have been secondary to providing a forward, motivating command presence. This, of course, concerns issues of centralized or decentralized command. Ironically, General Pershing kept saying words that emphasized decentralized execution as the heart of open warfare, yet in practice he clearly wanted centralized control.

Perhaps it was the American Army's lack of experience with warfare on this scale more than anything else that made the difference. At Gettysburg in 1863, mounted staff officers could transmit commands rapidly from one end of the battlefield to the other, and those in turn could be augmented by signal stations, although once combat was joined the latter seldom seemed to have contributed much. But machine guns and artillery had made mounted couriers only marginally successful at those same duties, and even runners seem to have been not more than about 50 percent successful. The battlefield had become too murderous a place to physically transmit messages, yet they had to be transmitted—and there simply was no other way. And while the use of the ether for that purpose would come in time for the next great war, it was of little help in the first one. Thus command, like so many other functions during the First World War, was performed at only a fraction of the level required. Intelligence moved rearward too slowly, operations reports moved rearward too slowly, and orders moved forward quickly to a point, but seldom far enough forward to have any significant effect. Martin Middlebrook has described this tragic effect in his classic work about the first Somme offensive.[5]

Opportunity after opportunity was lost because of the lack of flexibility of the command and communications functions. It is instructive to see how General Pershing summed up the World War I experience: "There is no situation which can justify a commander for remaining in ignorance of the situation on his front. The necessity for communication with the rear must not so tie him to a fixed post as to prevent him from keeping in touch with the situation by personal reconnaissance or from exercising his direct personal influence on the troops in action."[6]

Infantry in Battle, published at Col. George C. Marshall's urging by the Infantry School, was the first real step toward learning these lessons—but that did not occur until 1934.[7]

Really Learning?

Late in World War I, the AEF's G-5 Training Section began issuing *Notes on Recent Operations.* The title was much more appropriate than the current practice of issuing "Lessons Learned." The AEF G-5 issued four such *Notes* prior to the end of the war, and then attempted to incorporate them in a 1919 AEF version of the *Infantry Drill Regulations.* That "provisional" regulation eventually became U.S. Army doctrine.[8]

As one might expect, most of the *Notes* dealt with tactical matters. After the war, larger units submitted Reports of Operations that addressed higher level matters. The culmination of that attempt to profit from the immediate past came to rest in the AEF's *Superior Board on Organization and Tactics.* Published in 1920, the result was a controversial document to which even General Pershing voiced objections. As is so often the case, wrong lessons emerged from the observations incorporated in the report, and outside interests seized upon portions of it for their own purposes.

When Doug Johnson was detailed to work on what became known as the "Tait Report" following the Gulf War, those same pernicious influences were once again present, distorting the conclusions for narrower purposes. The report was named for Maj. Gen. Thomas T. Tait, who was placed in charge of an analysis group at Fort Leavenworth, Kansas, with full access to all Gulf War records. Because the report was critical of problem areas—the expected function of an after-action report, it was suppressed. In its place, Brig. Gen. Robert H. Scales Jr. was assigned a different group with the charge to produce a new report with a more positive spin. The army's official history of the Gulf War, *Certain Victory,* was the result. While the latter is accurate, so too was the former.

The AEF Superior Board made no mention about the function of leadership; its charge was to address organization and tactics. But, as previously noted, Pershing had strong feelings about leadership: he wanted leaders forward. As Kenneth Hamburger has noted, one of the salient lessons of the war should have been that forward leadership requires deep reserves of leaders, especially junior leaders. We have seen in this battle narrative that almost every officer below the regimental level became a casualty. Therefore, masses of well-trained junior leaders were essential, yet how is one to produce such men in adequate numbers? The honest answer is that it cannot be done. The best remedy may well have been that hit upon by the Readiness advocates before the war: civilian training camps for anyone interested enough to pay his way to the nearest one. The Reserve Officer Training Corps (ROTC) performs that function to a certain extent, but what is really needed is junior officers with real experience leading units in exercises as near real as can be created. Today, those exercises are conducted at the Joint Readiness and National Training Centers. But even those excellent facilities do not condition more than a fraction of the junior officers required.

So what was learned from the battle of Soissons? The third *Notes on Recent Operations* clearly had Soissons in mind, for it was published in late August, 1918. As such it should have focused on offensive operations and did. It complained that attacking formations were too tightly bunched; that soldiers needed to spread out; that infantry units needed to employ their auxiliary weapons better, 37-mm infantry cannon being particularly effective against enemy machine guns; and that better coordination between infantry and artillery was necessary. It bespoke an inadequate training program without saying so. It bespoke immature command and control practices. Later evaluations would attempt to place some blame on French management of the battle, but of course that would never have appeared in official reports during the war.[9]

The G-5 training officer's final report was, as one might expect, congratulatory for what had been accomplished with so little time. Although the AEF was capable of powerful blows, the report noted, they were "delivered with an awkwardness and lack of resource that made them unduly costly and rendered it impracticable to reap the full fruits of victory." This was certainly the case at Soissons.[10]

Relatively few after-action reports remain from this battle. In the 1st Division there was an order directing their submission. In the case of Brigadier General Hines's 1st Brigade, the commanders followed their brigade commander's lead and reported there was little to be learned. In fact, so sparse are 1st Brigade reports that one has to turn to the 1st Engineer Regiment's after-action report to discover that Company B, 1st Engineers, was ordered to advance with the 16th Infantry, with which it attacked in the second wave, later taking up front-line positions and eventually suffering ten killed and 72 wounded.[11]

Conrad Babcock, on the other hand, provided a detailed and specific report on August 4. It was a good report that correctly identified significant short-comings particularly relevant to the employment of machine guns and artillery.

What follows is a sampling of the participants' views.

Colonel Babcock wrote:

> I recommend that the front waves be replaced by well trained combat groups of about twenty men. That machine gun companies do not fol-low their battalions into action, but come up after the position is taken. . . . That more ambulances be used. . . . That Divisional Staff officers remain with Regimental Commanders and by personal observation gain impressions of the fighting, and report these impressions...to the Divi-sion at intervals. . . . That a much lighter wire be furnished the Regimen-tal Signal Detachment. That Battalion and Regimental Headquarters be furnished a light Ford truck. . . . A fast car . . . would have been of inestimable use. That Brigade and Regimental Commanders be called upon to give their ideas about tactical situations in their own front . . . that each tactical situation be dealt with by the Regimental Commander and that he be given sufficient time to arrange his attack before H hour.[12]

Colonel L. R. Holbrook, 7th Field Artillery, but commanding the 1st Field Artillery Brigade, saw the "Absolute necessity of putting the best available offic-ers in charge of liaison work between artillery batteries and the front line sup-ported and keeping in communications at all hazards even at the expense of the communications to the rear."[13]

Lieutenant Col. Maxwell Murray of the 5th Field Artillery wrote: "Batter-ies were subjected to considerable harassing fire from the north after the first day of the attack. The positions were well in sight of enemy balloons near Soissons. . . . strongly recommend that regiments of 155mm Howitzers be equipped with one sending set (wireless) for Regimental Headquarters."[14]

Lieutenant Col. Courtland Parker of the 6th Field Artillery concluded: "These operations emphasized the necessity for closest liaison. . . . There was always a great deal of doubt about the exact positions of our front lines. . . . It is believed that our inventors can, if the necessity is properly shown, devise and instrument whereby communications can be effected from the front to the rear under almost any circumstances."[15]

Several reports complained of an absence of friendly air cover. In fact, although it was the main attack, it had no air support whatsoever. Contrast that with the support later provided at Saint-Mihiel, where Brig. Gen. "Billy" Mitchell assembled some fourteen hundred aircraft and swept the skies clear of any German interference.

However, as an indicator of how long it takes for ideas to make the rounds and result in something useful for the troops, Paul F. Braim makes the following observations about the AEF's performance during the Meuse-Argonne battle: "Medical support was weak; water was not moved forward; food did not move forward; reserves employed to fill up the line; close support weapons improperly employed; infantry attacked in waves in the open—no attempt to use cover."[16]

Although it may not have been readily apparent from the narrative, we have offered hints that the American Army at Soissons employed a similar style to that of the European armies of 1914. Recall, for instance, the admiration expressed in the narratives for the upright, dressed lines. The U.S. Army had a long distance to travel before it was really ready to win a battle at a reasonable cost in casualties.

Ironically, the officer in charge of training the AEF at the time was Brig. Gen. Harold B. Fiske. As a major and an instructor at Fort Leavenworth in January, 1917, Fiske delivered a lecture in which he sought to establish the principles of the American drill regulations. He concluded his historical introduction by describing the early British experiences in the Boer War, when in the face of Boer fire, the British so thinned their skirmish lines that they had no impetus, nor could they generate a sufficient volume of fire. He contrasted this with the Prussian experiences during the Franco-Prussian War, where the Prussians, armed with an inferior rifle, were forced to maneuver and fire by small groups to be able to come to grips with the French. At that point it was clear he understood the relationship between these two tactical actions. He then introduced the American drill regulations with the comment that they were the product of Major General Morrison and reflected his observations of the Japanese during the Russo-Japanese War without explaining exactly what those observations were. His two major points were these: "The object was to maneuver infantry forces so as best to bring infantry fire upon the opposing infantry. As rapidly as possible, the firing line was to be built up so that 'fire superiority' could be gained. Once gained, the stage was set for the ultimate act, the bayonet charge."[17] Doubtless because of his Leavenworth experience and expertise in infantry doctrine, Fiske was put in charge of all AEF training.

The Superior Board reiterated the centrality of infantry to the success of war but conceded that tactics would have to change and incorporate "a combination of position and open warfare." The Board carried one central message other than that of the continued primacy of infantry, and that was the necessity for combined-arms action. Machine-gun units, for example, needed to be incorporated into infantry units in order that the two would be compelled to learn how to operate together. In like manner, what the army later came to call "habitual association" was strongly recommended with regard to the artillery in particular, but other arms as well. Fire superiority was still considered essential to the preparation for the attack. However, "fire superiority can no longer be gained by thickening the firing line as formerly . . . the superiority must be gained by maneuvering for position so as to deliver a more effective fire and by the use of automatic and auxiliary weapons."

The term "auxiliary weapons" means tanks and airplanes as well as 37-mm infantry cannons. The report noted the need to retain a full regiment of 155-mm artillery as essential in modern war even if it would slow the division down. Then, with regard to tanks, the writers noted that "exercises of infantry accompanied by tanks should be held frequently." Some learning was going on, but the Board readily acknowledged that tank and airplane technology was still in transition and that tactics would have to be further modified as those weapons matured.

The Board evidently was stumped on how to better handle infantry-artillery control. Many lines were devoted to habitual association and the exercising of infantry and artillery soldiers to better integrate fire support with infantry maneuver, but nothing useful emerged in the way of techniques such as those learned and practiced by the British. We know well enough today that the solution was in the further development of wireless radios, but at the time the prospects for rapid developments in that regard were not so obvious.[18]

At Soissons, the artillery did not get forward soon enough, moved its rolling barrages too fast for the infantry to follow, fired only upon prearranged targets rather than attacking "targets of opportunity," had far too few observers, and failed to employ smoke or offensive gas.

There was another massive failure to move information rearward and forward, which was partially a function of higher headquarters again being too far to the rear.

Command influence during the battle was erratic and sporadic, almost entirely personality dependent. It rested partly upon the ability to move information. While it has long been and continues to be a tenet of American operations that initiative is prized above all else, when coordinated action is required, communications become the indispensable centerpiece. When communications fail and senior commanders do not move forward to take control, coordinated action does not take place.[19]

Troops in battle are always hungry and thirsty, but in both of these battles water was a particular problem. Local water was always contaminated by poison-gas residue, and provisions for forward hauling were inadequate. In like manner, all soldiers and commanders complained bitterly about the breakdown of medical services. Both these relate to the same problem: an inability to move through the rear areas. They also reflect the tendency in most armies to think of the support structure last.

Reserves were barely an issue during the Battle of Soissons. In retrospect, it seems poor planning to have held the 1st Battalion, 28th Infantry, in 1st Division reserve once the nature of the terrain was known. But that was properly the division commander's call, and Summerall seems to have committed it at about the right time—and also to have committed the remaining division reserve to buttress the final attack on Berzy-le-Sec at just the right time. On the other hand, the use of the 6th Marines on the nineteenth deserves some criticism. When the 28th Infantry made its final lunge at Berzy-le-Sec, everyone in the vicinity went forward with it. Not so in the 2d Division's 3d Brigade. Only the 6th Marines went over to the attack, although there were plenty of other soldiers and marines available to straggle along with them. It does appear that Summerall had the fragments of his division under better control at the end than did Harbord.

Where was Ely in that final attack? All the evidence points to a large cluster of headquarters at or near Beaurepaire Farm. Furthermore, no one made an effort to move to the front to see what the situation really was or attempt to coordinate the final assault—shades of Pickett's charge at Gettysburg—by twelve thousand men out of a force of some sixty-five thousand.

Where was the supporting artillery for the 6th Marines's attack? Photographs of the area make it clear that observation of the attack sector was not that hard to obtain; the ground is flat or rolling and observation should not have been a problem. Nevertheless, fire support was provided independent of the attack and the attack went in unsupported, as criminal an act as can be charged to a supporting artillery commander. And where was the command group? Everyone was at Beaurepaire Farm and so was some of the supporting artillery. Did no one notice?

What of the commanders' behavior? Summerall was evidently handicapped by personal insecurities that haunted him and distorted his behavior throughout his life. While he seems to have made more correct than bad decisions in combat, his ridiculous blathering and evident fear of any challenge to his authority made his performance as army chief of staff poor. He must be credited for twice trooping the line to gauge the truth of the frontline situation. It is evident that he had a much better appreciation of affairs by the end of his journey than at the first else he would have sent Frank Parker packing. If he had a blind spot with regard to Conrad Babcock, he had another with regard to Beaumont Buck. How much perfection can we rightly demand?

Harbord never really commanded his division. He joined it in transit and watched it do what it could with the minimum of input from him or his staff. While that was excusable on July 18, it seems to be less so on the nineteenth.

Buck has already been dissected. There is almost no information on which to base an assessment of Hines save the general success of his brigade. Ely remains something of a mystery for the nineteenth. Neville and his marines did all that was asked of them up to the limits of human endurance. What might the remnants of the 5th Marines and the 9th and 23d Infantry Regiments have done together with the 6th Marines—and with intelligent artillery support?

It has been suggested that in this battle we can see patterns that afflict the American officer corps and its leadership style throughout its history. I am of the opinion that the press of battle reduces all but the most sensitive men to an elemental level of brutality. Gerald F. Linderman's *The World Within War* provides sensitive support for this conclusion. As Gen. Freytag von Lorighoven noted in his classic *The Power of Personality in War,* some men are unsuited for combat leadership, being too sensitive to the brutality of combat, which tends to paralyze them. He does not go on to say that the naturally brutish do better but instead argues that combat leadership requires a steadiness of character possessed by relatively few men. Jonathan Shay, author of *Achilles in Vietnam,* argues vigorously that brutes are exactly the wrong men to lead. As noted earlier in the American *Field Service Regulations,* senior commanders need to be sufficiently removed from the carnage of battle to allow even the sturdiest to make objective decisions not based upon the slaughter their orders have already brought about or that will ensue.[20]

But the small-unit commander does not have that luxury. He is charged by his profession to make the bitter decisions and to participate in them in the most personal way. That is the business of officers and noncommissioned officers. Those who cannot make the hard decisions must be removed. That is the light in which Summerall apparently saw Babcock: as one unwilling to obey because of his proximity to the situation, which had apparently weakened him. The fact that that was not the case at all, and that Babcock was actually doing a first-rate job with little or no support from those who should have been out looking and verifying and searching for solutions is one of the ironies of this bit of history. Why Summerall did not ask Buck to look into the situation remains a mystery—except that Buck was seldom to be found. Buck never mentions the incident and may never have known of it. But if Summerall was especially hard on Babcock, why was he blind to the question of Buck's where-abouts?

When all is said and done, the behavior of men in battle has to be judged by different standards than we would like to apply. Everyone is tired in combat; no matter how good the information, it is never enough or sufficiently accu-rate; the best of coordination always slips to some degree or another; and the best laid plans in battle "gang" more "aft agley" than the poet Robert Burns could have imagined. Perhaps Hanson Ely, however his performance may be judged, has it more correct than all the others: Battles are indeed won by remnants.[21]

German Order of Battle

Organization of the Principal Units of Army Group Crown Prince Opposed to the American 2d Division Southwest of Soissons

Seventh Army

Ninth Army

XIII (Royal Wurttemburg) Corps [Corps Watter]

3d Reserve Division
  5th Brigade
    2d Reserve Infantry
    49th Reserve Infantry
    34th Fusilier Regiment
    3d Reserve Field Artillery
    2d Battalion, 14th Reserve Foot Artillery

14th Reserve Division
  27th Reserve Brigade
    159th Infantry
    16th Reserve Infantry
    53d Reserve Infantry
    14th Reserve Field Artillery
    1st Battalion, 16th Foot Artillery

20th Division
  40th Brigade
    77th Infantry
    79th Infantry

92d Infantry
46th Field Artillery
155th Foot Artillery

28th Division
55th Brigade
40th Fusilier Regiment
109th Body Grenadier Regiment
110th Grenadier Regiment
14th Field Artillery
55th Foot Artillery

42d Division
65th Brigade
17th Infantry
131st Infantry
138th Infantry
15th Field Artillery
2d Battalion, 15th Foot Artillery

46th Reserve Division
92d Reserve Brigade
214th Reserve Infantry
215th Reserve Infantry
216th Reserve Infantry
46th Reserve Field Artillery

47th Reserve Division
94th Reserve Brigade
218th Reserve Infantry
219th Reserve Infantry
220th Reserve Infantry
47th Reserve Field Artillery

115th Division
229th Brigade
40th Reserve Infantry
136th Infantry
171st Infantry
229th Reserve Field Artillery
94th Foot Artillery

APPENDIX 2
Tenth Army Order of Battle, July 18–22

Tenth Army
  I Corps
  XI Corps
  XVIII Corps
  XX Corps
  XXX Corps
  II Cavalry Corps

XX Corps

1st Division, AEF
  1st Brigade
      16th Infantry
      18th Infantry
      2d Brigade
      26th Infantry
      28th Infantry

1st Moroccan Division
  1st Brigade
      Regiment du Marche, Legion Etranger (RMLE)
      4th Tirailleurs
  2d Brigade
      7th Tirailleurs
      8th Zouaves

2d Division, AEF
   3d Brigade
      9th Infantry
      23d Infantry
   4th (Marine) Brigade
      5th Marine Regiment
      6th Marine Regiment

58th Division

69th Division

APPENDIX 3
Organization of an AEF Division, 1918

SQUAD: Varied sharply from time to time and according to type.[1]

PLATOON: 58 men, commanded by a lieutenant.

COMPANY: 250 men, commanded by a captain.

BATTALION: 4 infantry companies, commanded by a major (about 1,000 men).

REGIMENT: 3 battalions and a machine-gun company, commanded by a colonel (about 3,800 men).

BRIGADE: 2 regiments and a machine-gun battalion of 3 and eventually 4 companies, commanded by a brigadier general (about 8,500 men).

DIVISION[2]: Two infantry brigades, one field artillery brigade consisting of 3 regiments, one engineer regiment, one machine-gun battalion of 5 companies, one signal battalion, and the division trains, all commanded by a major general (72 artillery pieces; 260 machine guns; 17,666 rifles; 28,150 men, of whom 12,288 were in the infantry companies).

Division Sanitary Train: 3 motorized ambulance companies, 1 animal drawn; 3 motorized field hospitals, 1 animal drawn.

1 For a discussion of the various changes in basic organization, see Douglas V. Johnson II, "A Few 'Squads-Left' and Off to France: Training the A.E.F. for WWI in the United States," Ph.D. diss., Temple University, 1992; see also Center of Military History, *U.S. Army in the World War 1917–1919,* vol. 1, *Organization of the American Expeditionary Forces,* pp. 109-24.
2 TO&E on November 11, 1918.

APPENDIX 4

Tank Allocation
and Description

Allocation

Unit	Type	Number	Corps	Division
Gp 3	Schneider	27	I	153d French
Gps 11, 12	St.-Chamond	60	XX	1st American
Gp 4	Schneider	48	XX	Moroccan
Gp 1	Schneider	48	XX	2d American
Gp 10	St.-Chamond	30	XXX	38th French
1st Bn	Renault	45		
2d Bn	Renault	40	Reserve	
3d Bn	Renault	45		

Source: Ludwig Ritter von Eimannsberger, *Mechanized Warfare,* p. 30. See also John F. C. Fuller, *Tanks in the Great War, 1914–1918,* p. 191. Although Fuller concludes that the 1st Division received only 48 tanks and the French 38th Division only 24, the alignments agree.)

Description

Type	Tons	Crew	Weapons	Speed	Range
Schneider	13.5	6	75-mm gun, 2 machine guns	4 kph	60 km
St.-Chamond	23	9	75-mm gun, 4 machine guns	4 kph	60 km
Renault	7	2	37-mm gun or 1 machine gun	8 kph	60 km

Source: Eimannsberger, *Mechanized Warfare,* p. 36.

Notes

Introduction: The War to Date

1. See Gerhard Ritter's *The Schlieffen Plan: Critique of a Myth* and Dennis Showalter's *Tannenberg: Clash of Empires.*
2. There are numerous good histories of the war that lay this all out in detail. Among those with a particularly German focus is Robert B. Asprey's *The German High Command at War: Hindenburg and Ludendorff Conduct World War I.* Rod Paschall's *The Defeat of Imperial Germany, 1917–1918* is an equally useful study.
3. Paschall, *Defeat of Imperial Germany,* pp. 128–33; and David T. Zabecki, *Steel Wind: Colonel Georg Bruchmeuller and the Birth of Modern Artillery.*
4. Ludwig von Eimannsberger, *Mechanized Warfare,* pp. 31–32.
5. John Frederick Charles Fuller, *Tanks in the Great War, 1914–1918,* p. 189; Eimannsberger, *Mechanized Warfare,* pp. 30–32.
6. J. A. Porter, "The German Supply System," *Command and General Staff College Monographs,* pp. 3–5 (hereafter cited as *CGSC Monographs*). There are three different sets of monographs relating to AEF actions. The *CGSC Monographs* were all written as part of the course of instruction at the Command and General Staff College, Fort Leavenworth, Kans., in 1923. They are particularly valuable because most of the authors were participants in the actions described and cite themselves as the authority from time to time. In addition, they had easy access to official U.S. and French Army documentation, some of which is difficult to come by now. *Monograph Soissons* is a collection of monographs assembled to assist in analyzing this particular battle. They were written under the general guidance of the War Department Historical Branch, War Plans Division. They closely follow or are obvious predecessors to the *CGSC Monographs.* One photocopy is in the U.S. Army Military History Institute (hereafter cited as USAMHI) archives. *AWC Monograph* is an untitled, legal-size, mimeographed draft narrative of Soissons, edited by John Thomason while he was serving with the 2d Division Historical Association at the Army War College in 1929. Thomason sent the copy to a contributor to the study, Ludislav Janda, who was a lieutenant in Company M, 9th Infantry, at Soissons (and later a major commanding the 3d Battalion, 9th Infantry.) It came to Rolfe Hillman, along with Janda's eleven-page narrative of Soissons, from Janda's daughter, Mrs. Ned Beard, of Wilmington, Del. Janda's narrative is cited in Thomason's draft and in Spaulding and Wright's 1937 history of the 2d Division. Now in the USAMHI archives, this document contains extracts from the official records, including original French documents, and other pertinent material not elsewhere located. See also Erich F. W. Ludendorff, *Ludendorff's Own Story,* p. 307; *World War Records, First Division, A.E.F., Regular: German Documents, Aisne-Marne (Soissons)* (hereafter cited as *WWR, GE*), serial 1–10, vol. 2, pt. 1, "Extracts from War Diary, 11th

Bavarian Infantry Division, 1–8–1918"; and *WWR, GE,* Headquarters, XIII Corps (Royal Wurttemburg), "Corps Order No. 10/July, dated July 11, 1918;" and "Corps Order No. 11/July," same date. Prior intelligence that an attack was being considered had been received but deserters and prisoners apparently captured on July 10 confirmed the information. These two orders directed the necessary defensive actions.

It is worth noting that some of the actions of American units are best clarified by the German accounts. Some American claims are validated and others are thrown into question. If there is one thing about the German accounts that is remarkable, it is their objectivity and thoroughness. There is no page numbering for German documents. They are grouped by command in descending order, and chronologically in order within each unit.

7. John J. Pershing, *My Experiences in the World War,* 2:158.

8. "Instructions for the Commanding Generals, Groups of Armies of the Reserve and Group of Armies of the Center," from Headquarters, French Armies of the North and Northeast, July 12, 1918, *United States Army in the World War* (hereafter cited as *USAWW*), vol. 5, pp. 235–37; "Annex 99, HQ, Tenth Army, July 17, 1918," *World War Records, First Division, A.E.F., Regular: French Documents, May 14, 1918 to Sept. 6, 1918,* vol. 25 (hereafter cited as *WWR, FR*).

9. Marshal Henri Pétain, July 12, 1918, "Instructions for the Commanding Generals, Group of Armies of the Reserve and Group of Armies of the Center," *USAWW,* vol. 5, pp. 235–37.

10. Porter, "The German Supply System," pp. 2–3.

11. "Major General Mangin, Commanding the X Army, TO: The Commanding General, I A.C., July 17, 1918," *WWR, FR.*

12. "War Diary, Group of Armies German Crown Prince," July 18, 1918, *USAWW,* vol. 5, *Military Operations of the American Expeditionary Forces,* pp. 678–80.

13. Entry for July 18, 1918, "War Diary of the Seventh Army from July 13 to July 22, 1918"; entry for July 17, 1918, Annex 4, "Report Covering the French Attack on July 18, 1918," Headquarters, XIII (Royal Wurttemburg) Army Corps, August 6, 1918"; Annex 1, 2d Division Historical Section, *Translations, War Diaries of German Units Opposed to the Second Division (Regular) 1918,* vol. 5., pts. 1–3, *Soissons* (hereafter cited as *War Diaries*); 94th Brigade Order, July 17, 1918, "Subject: Estimate of the Situation," *War Diaries.* [These records, like the German records in the 1st Division war records, are unnumbered and arranged by command and then chronologically within commands.]

14. Second Lt. Herbert Sulzbach, *With the German Guns: Four Years on the Western Front, 1914–1918,* pp. 201–202.

15. Ibid.

16. Message, "Army Group Crown Prince to HQ, Seventh and Ninth Armies, July 11, 7:05 P.M.," entry for July 15, War Diary Seventh Army, *WWR, GE.*

17. Headquarters, Tenth Army, Maj. Gen. Mangin to the Commanding General of the Group of Armies of the Reserve, July 5, 1918, SECRET, *WWR, FR,* vol. 18; "Plan of Action," French Tenth Army, June 20, 1918, *USAWW,* vol. 5., p. 225.

18. "War Diary of the Seventh Army from July 13 to July 22, 1918," entries for July 13, 14, and 16, 1918; also Headquarters, XIII Army Corps, "Report Covering the French Attack on July 18, 1918, II. Combat Value of the Troops," *War Diaries;* "Conditions for Attack," French Tenth Army, July 13, 1918, *USAWW,* vol. 5, p. 275.

19. Col. Conrad H. Lanza, "Five Decisive Days," *Field Artillery Journal* (Jan.–Feb., 1937): p. 49. Colonel Lanza wrote without footnotes but it is clear he used official German and AEF records.

20. Headquarters, Tenth Army, July 14, 1918, "3d Section, No. 681/S," *War Diaries.*

21. "Report Concerning the French Attack on July 18, 1918," Headquarters, XIII (Royal Wurttemburg) Army Corps, August 6, 1918, *War Diaries.*

22. "SECRET Code Telegram, HQ, XX Army Corps, July 16, 1918," 12:25 A.M., *WWR, FR.*

23. Annex 1, "Report Covering the French Attack on July 18, 1918," Headquarters, XIII (Royal Wurttemburg) Army Corps, Aug. 6, 1918, *War Diaries.*

Chapter 1. The American Army in 1918

1. The best source for the condition and development of the American army in the prewar period is Russell F. Weigley, *History of the Untied States Army.* The most comprehensive single work on the U.S. Army in World War I is Edward M. Coffman, *The War to End All Wars.* Most of the replacement material is best gleaned from Leonard L. Lerwill, *The Personnel Replacement System in the United States Army.* DA Pamphlet 20–211. For a comprehensive review of training problems in the United States, see Douglas V. Johnson II, "A Few 'Squads-Left' and Off to France: Training the American Army in the United States for World War I," Ph.D. diss., Temple University, 1992. Comments about officer strengths and vacancies are found repeatedly in the Annual Reports of the War Department during the interwar period. The reports of the prewar summer maneuvers await full development. Hugh Drum wrote a report on his experiences with the Connecticut National Guard and several others exist. General Pershing's commission to create an independent American army is found in his memoir, *My Experiences in the World War.* Peyton March's role is detailed in Edward M. Coffman, *The Hilt of the Sword: The Career of Peyton C. March.* These two works contrast the deep antagonism that developed between the AEF (Pershing) and the War Department (March). Details of the internal AEF establishment to include weaponry, strengths, and other important matters are found in the *USAWW.* Allan R. Millett, *The General: Robert Lee Bullard and Officership in the United States Army, 1881–1925,* offers one of several glimpses of training the National Guard.

2. John K. Mahon, *History of the Militia and the National Guard,* pp. 125–46.

3. *Field Service Regulations, United States Army, 1914,* March 19, 1914, Corrected to July 31, 1918 (Changes 1 to 11), War Department Directive. No. 475 (hereafter cited as *FSR*), p. 3.

4. Ibid., p. 72.

5. "Memorandum to Chief of Staff, December 6, 1917, Subject: General Pershing's Request Regarding Composition of Second Corps," RG 165, File 8481-60, National Archives, Washington, D.C. (Hereafter cited as NA.) The Inspector General reports covering evaluation of the 35th Division are found in U.S. Army War College Historical Section, *The Thirty-fifth Division, 1917–1918,* pp. 8–11.

6. Coffman, *War To End All Wars,* p. 23.

7. "The General Principles Governing the Training of Units of the American Expeditionary Forces," Aug. 8, 1917, (Cable P-85-S to AGWAR), *USAWW,* vol. 14, *Reports of the Commander-in-Chief, A.E.F., Staff Sections and Services,* pp. 304–305.

8. Ibid. See also "Training, 3. Infantry, Baker Board Report," July, 1917, *USAWW,* vol. I, *Organization of the American Expeditionary Forces,* p. 77.

9. A review of the AEF training program in France can be found in *USAWW,* vol. 14, pp. 289–442. For a thorough analysis, see James W. Rainey, "Ambivalent Warfare: The Tactical Doctrine of the AEF in World War I," *Parameters,* 13 (Sept., 1983): 34–46; and Rainey, "The Training of the American Expeditionary Forces in World War I," MA thesis, Temple University, 1981.

10. Coffman, *Hilt of the Sword,* pp. 74–75, 141; and Coffman, *War to End All Wars,* p. 81. For the 86th Division see Charles H. Martin Papers, "A Brief History of the Eighty-sixth Division," Archives, USAMHI.

11. Coffman, *War to End All Wars,* p. 38.

12. Ibid., p. 84.

13. Ibid., pp. 23, 37; William G. Pagonis, *Moving Mountains: Lessons in Leadership and Logistics from the Gulf War,* 205–206.

14. For the details of this report, see "Memorandum of A Conference on Organization and Equipment, HQ, A.E.F., Paris, July 11, 1917," *USAWW,* vol. I, pp. 107–14; see also Coffman, *War to End All Wars,* p. 28.

15. Coffman, *War to End All Wars,* pp. 141, 159–67.

16. *FSR,* p. 72.

17. Robin Prior and Trevor Wilson *Passchendaele: The Untold Story.* See also Cable P-178-S, Sept. 24, 1917, p. 305; Cable 408-S, Dec. 22, 1917, p 319; and Cable 952-S, Apr. 18, 1918, p. 320, all in *USAWW,* vol. 16.

18. There are hundreds of first person stories from this war detailing how attacks were conducted. Among the best are Robert Graves, *Goodbye to All That;* Ernst Junger, *Storm of Steel;* and, albeit somewhat florid and semifictional, John Thomason, Jr., *Fix Bayonets!* Another fictional but darkly realistic account is Thomas Boyd, *Through the Wheat.* There are several new studies dealing with the details of tactical operations in this war. Among the best of these is Hubert C. Johnson, *Breakthrough!: Tactics, Technology, and the Search for Victory on the Western Front in World War I;* Paddy Griffith, *Battle Tactics of the Western Front: The British Army's Art of Attack, 1916–1918;* Paddy Griffith, ed., *British Fighting Methods in the Great War;* and a particularly useful work, Martin Samuels, *Command or Control? Command, Training and Tactics in the British and German Armies, 1888–1918.* A classic study examining the change of doctrine is Timothy T. Lupfer, *The Dynamics of Doctrine: The Changes in German Tactical Doctrine during the First World War.* Elton Mackin, *Suddenly We Didn't Want to Die: Memoirs of a World War I Marine.*

19. *FSR,* pp. 79–80.

20. Ibid., p. 82.

21. Ibid., pp. 83, 85.

22. *Infantry Drill Regulations,* p. 123.

23. John Frederick Charles Fuller, *Generalship: Its Diseases and Their Cure–A Study of the Personal Factor in Command,* p. 61.

24. An example of this multiple means setup is found in Appendix 1, "Schematic control net of the 46th Reserve Division," *WWR, GE.* Note the alternate routes available. Wherever possible this practice was followed by all armies, but in the attack its forward projection took a long time. On the role of runners, see Private (First Class) James H. McCain, "The Taking of Montfaucon," in *Americans vs. Germans: Individual Battle Experiences,* pp. 67–80. McCain's story is one of a

very few describing his period of duty as a runner. Mackin, *Suddenly We Didn't Want to Die.*

Chapter 2. Promise: July 18 — 1st Division and 1st Moroccan Division

1. American Battle Monuments Commission (hereafter cited as ABMC), *1st Division Summary of Operations in the World War,* p. 1; ABMC, *2d Division Summary of Operations in the World War,* p. 1; Center of Military History (hereafter cited as CMH), *Order of Battle of the United States Land Forces in the World War, American Expeditionary Forces: Divisions,* vol. 2, pp. 25–27; Coffman, *War to End All Wars,* pp. 48, 125–35, 174–75; Donald Smythe, *Pershing: General of the Armies,* pp. 87, 111.

2. Figures for the tanks are from Ralph E. Jones, George H. Rarey, and Robert J. Icks, *The Fighting Tanks from 1916 to 1933,* pp. 55–56, 72. A primary source showing the breakout by number and type to each division is "French XX Corps Etat Major 3d Bureau Ordre d'Operations 227, 16 July 1918." It is reprinted in full in French in John Thomason's *AWC Monograph.* See also Fuller, *Tanks in the Great War,* pp. 191–94; and Eimannsberger, *Mechanized Warfare,* pp. 36–37; and *USAWW,* vol. 5, pp. 233–34, 277–78. The American observer's remark "more than we knew were in the world" is from Maxwell Murray's address, "Soissons," to the Harvard Club in *Monograph Soissons.* Figures for tanks at Cambrai are from Richard M. Ogorkiewicz, *Armor: A History of Mechanized Forces,* p. 12.

3. "Mission of Air Division," *USAWW,* vol. 5, p. 247. The 1st Division received as attachments the French 42d Aero (Spad) Squadron — they had worked together at Cantigny — and French Balloon Company No. 83. ("Report on Operations South of Soissons, 1st Division, A.E.F., July 27, 1918," *USAWW,* vol. 5, p. 325.) The 2d Division was allocated ten French observation aircraft. ("Field Order No. 15, 2d Division, A.E.F. July 17, 1918 — 4:30 A.M.," *USAWW,* vol. 5, pp. 328–29.) For effectiveness, see "Evening Report, German Seventh Army, Aviation Commander, July 15, 1918," *USAWW,* vol. 5, p. 181.

4. "Annexe No. 75, HQ, 20th Corps d'Armée, Orde d'operations No. 227, July 16, 1918," *Les Armées Français dans la Grande Guerre,* pp. 112–15 (hereafter cited as *Les Armées*). "Annexe No. 107, July 17, 1918," *Les Armées,* pp. 155–56; "Annexe No. 108, July 17, 1918," *Les Armées,* p. 158. English translations are available only in part in the *USAWW.* Portions pertaining to the activities of the First Division are available in full English translation in *WWR, FR.*

5. "General Foch, Commander-in-Chief of the Allied Armies, To the Commander-in-Chief of the Armies of the North and Northeast, GHQ of the Allied Forces, June 14, 1918," *USAWW,* vol. 5, p. 223. Pétain forwarded this message to his subordinates on June 16 (p. 224).

6. Larry H. Addington, "Charles Pelot Summerall," in *Dictionary of American Military Biography,* ed. Roger J. Spiller, pp. 1077–80; For Summerall vice Bullard, see William A. Ganoe, *The History of the United States Army,* pp. 543, 546. Ganoe's Appendix B, "Commanders of Larger Units in World War I," is the most convenient place to check commanders of AEF corps and divisions and the dates of their tenure. Summerall's aide-de-camp for this period, 1st Lt. Alban B. Butler, maintained a simple journal of operations that is useful but by no means as de-

tailed and full of insightful observations as that kept by Pierpont Stackpole, aide
to Maj. Gen. Hunter Liggett. Millett's *The General* is the best chronicle of the 1st
Division in France up to Bullard's departure.

7. Charles E. Heller and William A. Stofft, eds., *America's First Battles, 1776–1965,*
pp. 149–85; "A fine brave fellow . . ." is from Don Robertson, *Prisoners of Twilight,*
p. 93; "Take that crossing . . ." is from Wendell Westover, *Suicide Battalions,* p.
267. "Hogwash" is from William T. Scanlon, *God Have Mercy on Us!,* p. 304.
Scanlon's book is a fictional account of his 6th Marines experience but the context makes it clear he listened to Summerall's speech to the 2d Division on Nov. 9.
"You may have paused for reorganization . . ." is from Joseph Dorst Patch, *A
Soldier's War: The First Division, A.E.F., 1917–1919,* p. 37; ". . . echeloned in depth
and attacking toward Berlin . . ." is from Mrs. Theodore Roosevelt, *Day before
Yesterday,* p. 103. "In a class by himself . . ." is Lt. Gen. Hunter Liggett's opinion
of Summerall as a division commander, recorded in P. J. Stackpole's diary entry
for 12 October. "Epitome of a military leader . . ." is from Thomas Marvin Johnson,
Without Censor: New Light on Our Greatest World War Battles, pp. 256–57.

8. Shipley Thomas, *The History of the A.E.F.,* p. 141.

9. Clarence R. Huebner, "The Operations of the 28th Infantry in the Aisne-Marne
Offensive, July 17–23, 1918," *CGSC Monographs,* pp. 428–29; for German reaction, see "War Diary and Annexes, Headquarters, 11th Bavarian Infantry Division, To the Royal Bavarian War Ministry Concerning the 18th of July 1918,"
WWR, GE, vol. 2, par. 1 and 2.

10. Millett, *The General,* pp. 310–11; *The Bridgehead Sentinel,* July, 1950, p. 30; Beaumont B. Buck, *Memories of Peace and War,* p. 149.

11. *General Cullum's Biographical Register of the Officers and Graduates of the United
States Military Academy,* vol. 7, *Supplement 1920–1930,* Sequence Number 3857, pp.
609–10; Original material taken from Babcock's typescript career summary sent
to USMA Cullum Register in April, 1919.

12. "HQ, Tenth Army to CG, 1st Corps, July 17, 1918," Tome VII, Annexe No. 99,
Les Armées, pp. 140–41.

13. *World War Records, First Division A.E.F., Regular* (hereafter cited as *WWR*), vol.
15, pt. 2, *Field Messages All Units.* This is a more or less organized collection of
messages requiring careful scrutiny because of missing dates and mixed-up order. See also Book 12, *Monograph Soissons.*

14. Clarence R. Huebner, "The Twenty-Eighth Infantry in the Aisne-Marne Offensive,
July 18–21, 1918," Book 16, *Monograph Soissons,* pp. 1–2.

15. U.S. War Department *Decorations, United States Army: 1862–1926,* p. 353.

16. For the tanks, see Barrie Pitt, *1918: The Last Act,* p. 205. See also Conrad S. Babcock,
"Report of Offensive July 18-22, 1918, 26 July 1918," and Clarence R. Huebner,
"The Twenty-eighth Infantry in the Aisne-Marne Offensive, July 18-21, 1918," in
WWR, vol. 13, pt. 2. Huebner says the tanks were destroyed before entering the
ravine.

17. *The Story of the Twenty-eighth Infantry in the Great War,* p. 23. [n.p. Copy available
in Pentagon Library, call number UX240 No. 28.] Summerall also notes this
incident in "Notes on the First Division in the Battle of Soissons, With Reference to the Employment of the Field Artillery," *Monograph Soissons,* p. 3.

18. Huebner, "The Twenty-Eighth Infantry in the Aisne-Marne Offensive, July 18–
21, 1918," Book 16, *Monograph Soissons,* p. 2.

19. Ibid.

20. Clarence R. Huebner to the ABMC, Dec. 8, 1926, File 710.1-G/AM "Summary of Operations, 1st Division, South of Soissons, (Aisne-Marne Offensive) received." RG 117, NA.

21. *WWR,* vol. 15, pt. 2, *Field Messages All Units.* Huebner, "The Twenty-Eighth Infantry in the Aisne-Marne Offensive, July 18–21, 1918," Book 16, *Monograph Soissons,* p. 3, says "twenty officers and over five hundred men"; Babcock, para 10, "Report on Operations South of Soissons. July 1918," says "Over twenty officers and some four hundred prisoners." *WWR,* vol. 13, Operations Reports, *The Story of the Twenty-Eighth Infantry in the Great War,* reports "24 officers and 580 men had been taken," p. 14. The photograph of the "Commandant" was supplied to the author by Mr. Avishai Halevy following an internet encounter. Mr. Halevy discovered this photograph in a book he purchased in a used book store. The inscription on the back notes the subject of the photo is "a German Commandant captured near Soissons July 18, 1918." Only one such capture was made that day.

22. "Field Order No. 27, 1st Division, A.E.F., July 16, 1918," *USAWW,* vol. 5, p. 313.

23. *WWR,* vol. 15, pt. 2, *Field Messages All Units.*

24. Babcock reports moving his PC forward to le Mont D'Arly at 2 P.M. and says he went forward at about 11 A.M. (See "Report of Offensive July 18-22, 1918," dated 26 July 1918, in *WWR,* vol. 13, pt. 2.) However, he does not mention moving his PC forward in his "Report of Operations South of Soissons, July 1918," dated Aug. 4, 1918 (Ibid.). Other differences include mention of another attack order in the July 26 report only, and mention of the capture of "a fortified farm" in the Aug. 4 report.

25. Huebner, "The Twenty-Eighth Infantry in the Aisne-Marne Offensive, July 18–21, 1918," Book 16, *Monograph Soissons,* pp. 1–2; Butler, "Journal of Operations."

26. *WWR,* vol. 15, pt. 2, *Field Messages, All Units.*

27. The subject of French failures to keep up with the Americans is referenced in: Jennings C. Wise, *The Turn of the Tide: American Operations at Cantigny, Chateau Thierry, and the Second Battle of the Marne,* p. 156; Book 16, *Monograph Soissons;* Robert L. Bullard, *Personalities and Reminiscences of the War,* pp. 243–44; Alden Brooks, *As I Saw It,* pp. 209–10; the "however" quote is from Wise, *Turn of the Tide,* p. 154; For General Pétain's comment, see David F. Trask, *The AEF and Coalition Warmaking, 1917–1918,* pp. 9–10.

28. "Para. 2, "HQ, Tenth Army to CG, 1st Corps, July 17, 1918," Tome VII, Annexe No. 99, *Les Armeés.*

29. "Report to the Royal Bavarian War Ministry Concerning the 18th of July 1918," Headquarters, 11th Bavarian Division, Aug. 1, 1918, *WWR, GE.*

30. Huebner, "The Twenty-Eighth Infantry in the Aisne-Marne Offensive, July 18–21, 1918," Book 16, *Monograph Soissons,* p. 2.

31. "Memorandum: Headquarters 3d Battalion, 26th Infantry, France, August 2, 1918," *WWR,* vol. 13, pt. 2. Although there are several other reports on the 26th Infantry, they are very brief and reveal only a glimpse of the action.

32. Irving B. Holley, Jr., *General John M. Palmer, Citizen, Soldiers, and the Army of a Democracy,* p. 38; *Cullum's Biographical Register,* p. 474; Edward M. Coffman, "American Command and Commanders in World War I," in *New Dimensions in Military History,* ed. Russell F. Weigley, p. 187; Louis A. Peake, "John Leonard Hines," in *Dictionary of American Military Biography,* pp. 472–75. In a letter to Colonel Hillman dated Apr. 5, 1990, Dr. Coffman wrote: "As I worked on the

WWI book [*War to End All Wars*], I was struck by the different personalities of Hines and Summerall—the former taciturn, the latter flamboyant and rhetorical. Both were very effective but I gather that Hines thought CPS [Summerall] was a bit too much at times."

33. ABMC, *1st Division Summary,* pp. 22–23; see also Benjamin H. Chastaine, *History of the U.S. Eighteenth Infantry, First Division, 1812–1919,* p. 64; For the Moroccans see "General Operation Order, 1st Moroccan Division, July 16, 1918," *WWR,* vol. 25, pt. 2, p. 115.

34. Patch, *A Soldier's War,* pp. 132.

35. Paragraph 1, "Right Division Sector, Section III. Situation Preceding the Attack on the Early Morning of July 18, 1918. Report Covering the French Attack on July 18, 1918," Headquarters, XIII (Royal Wurttemburg) Army Corps, Aug. 6, 1918, *War Diaries;* and Paragraph 2, "Corps Order No. 10/July, HQ XIII (Royal Wurttemburg) July 11, 1918," *WWR, GE.*

36. Charles Mangin, *Comment Finit la Guerre,* p. 136.

37. Tony Geraghty, *March or Die: A History of the French Foreign Legion,* pp. 132–49.

38. Headquarters, 1st Moroccan Div, "General Operations Order," July 16, 1918, in *WWR, FR,* vol. 25, pt. 2. This was supplemented the next day by another two-page order: Headquarters, 1st Moroccan Division, "Employment of Artillery," July 17, 1918.

39. Chastaine, *History of the 18th Infantry,* p. 64; ABMC, "Summaries of Comments of Officers of the 18th Infantry Regarding Chaudun and Contact With the 2d U.S. Division," RG 117, file 710.1-G/AM, NA. See also Charles D. Barrett, "Memorandum to Major X. H. Price," Feb. 24, 1928, which contains files and affidavits from participants on the subject of who captured Chaudun. The Barrett memo is in the ABMC file 710.1-G/AM, RG 117, NA; Frank M. Owens to Capt. H. F. K. Cahill, Jan. 17, 1929, ABMC file 710.1-G/AM, RG 117, NA. For the Marine account, see Edwin N. McClellan, "The Aisne-Marne Offensive," pt. 2, *Marine Corps Gazette* (June, 1921): pp. 188–227.

40. "War Diary, 110th Grenadier Regiment," entry for July 18, 1918. *War Diaries.*

41. Record of telephone call, 6:20 P.M., *WWR,* vol. 15, pt. 2, *Field Messages, All Units.*

42. 42d Division, "Brief Combat Report Concerning the Events of July 18, 1918," *War Diaries.*

43. Sulzbach, *With the German Guns,* pp. 202–203.

Chapter 3. Break-in: July 18—2d Division

1. James G. Harbord, *The American Army in France, 1917–1919,* pp. xiii, 303–16; Pershing, *My Experiences,* 1:19. For the rivalry between these two AEF divisions, see Laurence Stallings, *The Doughboys: The Story of the AEF, 1917–1918.* On attempts to quantify measures of combat effectiveness, see Braim, *Test of Battle,* pp. 148–49; Basil H. Liddell Hart, *Reputations Ten Years After,* p. 316; Rolfe Hillman "Second to None: The Indianheads," *U.S. Naval Institute Proceedings* (Nov., 1987): pp. 57–62. Critiques of Harbord's command of the Marine Brigade are in Robert Asprey, *At Belleau Wood,* and Brooks, *As I Saw It.* Neither of James G. Harbord's books—*Leaves from a War Diary* nor *The American Army in France*— gives details of his personal actions at Soissons. On the matter of Harbord writing *American Army in France* to refute Peyton March's criticisms of Pershing in

The Nation at War, see Donald Smythe, *Pershing: General of the Armies,* pp. 294–95; Donald Smythe "The Battle of the Books," *ARMY,* Sept., 1972; and Coffman, *Hilt of the Sword.* Harbord's request for brigade command is in Millett, *The General,* p. 365; Allan R. Millett, *Semper Fidelis: The History of the United States Marine Corps,* p. 304; Edwin H. Simmons, "The First Day at Soissons," *Fortudine* 23, no. 1 (Summer, 1993): p. 4; Coffman, *War to End All Wars,* p. 235–36; and Oliver L. Spaulding and John W. Wright, *The Second Division American Expeditionary Forces in France, 1917–1919.*

2. Harbord, *American Army in France,* pp. 314–17.

3. Thomason, *AWC Monograph,* pp. 50, 56–58.

4. Harbord, *American Army in France,* p. 317.

5. Allan R. Millett, "Hanson Edward Ely," in *Dictionary of American Bibliography, Supplement Six, 1956–1960,* ed. Tony A. Garraty; Coffman, *War to End All Wars,* p. 157; Millett, *The General,* p. 333; Stallings, *The Doughboys,* p. 75; Bullard, *Fighting Generals,* pp. 43–45.

6. Anne Cipriano Venzon, ed., *The United States in the First World War: An Encyclopedia,* s.v. Clark, George. 'Neville' Wendell Cushing (1870–1930).

7. Thomason, *AWC Monograph,* p. 63.

8. Ibid., p. 73.

9. *Monograph Soissons,* pp. 63, 73; Simmons, " First Day at Soissons," pp. 6–8; Pershing, *My Experiences,* 2:163–64; Thomas F. Farrell, "Memories of the Battle of Soissons," *Military Engineer* 15, no. 83 (July–Aug., 1923): pp. 327–28; Harbord, *American Army in France,* pp. 322–26.

10. "Supplement to Operations Order No. 227, French XX Army Corps, July 17, 1918," *USAWW,* vol. 5, pp. 294–95; Harbord, *American Army in France,* pp. 318–28.

11. ABMC, *2d Division Summary,* p. 26. Thomason says Neville gave it personally at 6 P.M. (*AWC Monograph,* p. 6.) See also Harbord, *American Army in France,* pp. 324–26; The best maps available are the 1:20,000 maps accompanying the ABMC's summaries of operations.

12. Spaulding and Wright, *The Second Division,* p. 114; Thomason, *AWC Monograph,* pp. 66, 88.

13. Harbord, *American Army in France,* pp. 329–30; Simmons, "First Day at Soissons," p. 8. See also Par. 5, 2d Division Field Order No.15, July 17, 1918, *USAWW,* vol. 5, p. 329; "sacrificing the fine points" is from a typescript history of the 2d Battalion 5th Marines (hereafter cited as "2d Battalion, 5th Marines" dated Dec. 1, 1938 (with a foreword later added by Lt. Col. Lemuel G. Shepherd, Jr) in the Reference Section of the U.S. Marine Corps Historical Center, Washington, D.C. (Hereafter cited as USMC Historical Center.)

14. Thomason, *AWC Monograph,* p. 76–77.

15. The map in ABMC, *American Armies and Battlefields in Europe,* p. 83, shows in color the routes of the 1st and 2d Divisions that took them into the assigned zone of the French 1st Moroccan Division from the north and south respectively. Between Chaudun and Maison Neuve Farm, the Moroccan's zone was narrowed to well less than half a mile. On this map, Chaudun itself should be marked as having been captured by Americans. The ABMC concluded that the 5th Marines captured Chaudun. Refer to Bartlett, "Memorandum to Major X. H. Price," that includes as attachments, the statements of all living, 18th Infantry witness to the action.

16. Thomason, *AWC Monograph,* pp. 93–94.
17. Ibid., pp. 90–92. See also James M. Yingling, *A Brief History of the 5th Marines,* pp. 7–8.
18. Thomason, *Fix Bayonets!,* pp. 103–106. In other passages, especially in his "Red Pants" in "*—And a Few Marines,* and in the captions accompanying his drawings, Thomason uses some of the blatantly racist terms that were common to his time. Brigadier Edmund L. Spears, the British liaison officer to the French GHQ, uses similar language in *Prelude to Victory;* John Sloan Brown, *Draftee Division,* tells of Americans fighting adjacent to a French colonial corps in Italy in World War II. Their alleged terrorization of Italians is mentioned in Barbara G. Harrison, *Italian Days.*
19. McClellan, " Aisne-Marne Offensive," pt. 2, p. 227.
20. Thomason, *—And a Few Marines,* pp. 379–80.
21. Thomason, *AWC Monograph,* pp. 53, 83.
22. Upton's reaction to his nonselection for promotion to brigadier general opens his July 22, 1918, "Dear Mouse" letter to his sister, Mrs. J. E. Miner, in Minneapolis. The letter is in the Upton papers at the Minnesota Historical Society in Saint Paul. In the same file is Upton's 1919–20 collection of testimonial letters he solicited from wartime commanders and associates. The Hanson Ely quotation is from his address, "Leadership and Morale in War," to the Army War College on Feb 3, 1938, p. 9. Ely did not name Upton, he spoke only of "a regimental commander," but the identification is made obvious by the Lewis letter. For the promotion situation, see Smythe, *Pershing,* p. 167 and references in the footnote thereto. See also Tim Travers, *The Killing Ground: The British Army, The Western Front, and the Emergence of Modern Warfare, 1900–1918,* p. 31. Travers addresses "removals" in the British Army on pp. 13–14. Letter from Brigadier E. M. Lewis to Colonel L. S. Upton, Subject: Character of Service in A.E.F., Sept. 20, 1920.,Upton Papers, Minnesota Historical Society, St. Paul, Minn. Anyone beginning a study of officers removed from a command in the AEF should go immediately to "Index and Case Files Relating to Reclassification and Reassignment of Officers," John J. Pershing Papers 1916–24 and 1931–39, RG 200, Boxes 8–12, NA.
23. Upton to Mrs. Miner, July 22, 1918.
24. Message in "Field Messages sent by the 2d Division during the Soissons Operations," Book 20, *Monograph Soissons.*
25. Thomason, *AWC Monograph,* pp. 85–86 for Bouton and Speer. For Worthington, see Ludislav T. Janda, "M Company, 9th Infantry, Second Division South of Soissons July 18, 1918," Nov. 19, 1929, Archives USAMHI, pp. 7–9.
26. For the 1st Battalion, 9th Infantry at Maison Neuve, see ABMC, *2d Division Summary,* p. 28. That account conflicts with Thomason, *AWC Monograph,* and Spaulding and Wright, *The Second Division.* There is also disagreement among the several sources as to the order of march of the battalions. Janda, "M Company," p. 2, and Spaulding and Wright, *The Second Division,* p. 117, say the order was 1st, 2d, and 3d. Thomason, *AWC Monograph,* p. 83, and ABMC, *2d Division Summary,* say it was 1st, 3d, 2d.
27. Thomason, *AWC Monograph,* pp. 101–102.
28. Harbord, in *Leaves from a War Diary,* provides the full text of Berdoulat's June 29, 1925 letter on pp. 328–29. For Harbord's additional benefit, the *Cavalry Journal*

vol. 34, no. 141 (Oct., 1925) printed Berdoulat's article, "The First and Second American Divisions In the Offensive of July [1]8, 1918." The editor's footnote to the title reads: "General Berdoulat, the author of this article, is a very distinguished French General, now retired. He was in command of the Twentieth French Corps at the Battle of Soissons on July 18th and 19th, 1819 [*sic*], and was prompted to write this article by statements made in General Bullard's memoirs regarding the action of the Second Division on that occasion—The Editor," p. 407.

29. Feland's report is in, McClellan "Aisne-Marne Offensive," pt. 1, *Marine Corps Gazette* (Mar., 1921): p. 78.

30. Extracts from Janda, "M Company." Janda prepared the manuscript in response to a request from his wartime friend Trevor Swett (also in the 9th Infantry) for use by Capt. John W. Thomason, Jr., who was compiling war records of the 2d Division. Both Swett and Thomason were assigned to the 2d Division Historical Section at the Army War College at the time. Janda kept pertinent papers and burnished the memory of his Company M and the 3d Battalion, 9th Infantry—which he also commanded as reportedly the youngest battalion commander in the AEF. In this paper, Janda says the 3d Battalion was third in the line of march, "ready to follow the 1st and 2d Bns." Thomason, *AWC Monograph*, p. 85, has the first troops reaching Beaurepaire Farm in half an hour.

31. Scanlon, *God Have Mercy on Us!*, p. 303.

32. Janda, "M Company," pp. 5–7.

33. Ibid.

34. Air support does not appear to have been a decisive or even an important factor at Soissons. The crux of the matter at Soissons seems to be that, after the first morning, the Germans had complete air superiority. See Smythe, *Pershing*, p. 157; "Xe Armeé, 17 juillet 1918, to Commandemente L'Aeronautique, Ordre pour le 18 juillet 1918," *Les Armées*, Tome VII, Annexe No. 103, pp. 144–47; *WWR, FR*, Headquarters, 1st Moroccan Division, July 17, 1918; James T. Hudson, *Hostile Skies: A Combat History of the American Air Service*, p. 100; William Mitchell, *Memoirs of World War I: From Start to Finish of Our Greatest War*, p. 224.

35. Casualty figures are from a thirteen-page categorized roster prepared under Capt. A. P. Twyman, commanding Company M, and titled, "Roll of Honor Roster of Company 'M' 9th U.S. Infantry Regulars, From 17th September 1917 to 6th February 1919." The original is in the Janda Papers, USAMHI. The ribbon-bound copy is inscribed, "To Major L. T. Janda Compliments From Your Old Command Herein Entered." Janda's position is given as being about 175.5–287.0. That location places him well beyond the east edge of Vierzy Ravine and five hundred yards short of the "Tour san toit" marked on the ABMC Aisne-Marne 1:20,000 map. If that position is correct, he would have been well east of a line drawn north from Vauxcastille, then under attack by the 23d Infantry.

36. "Dear Mouse" letters, p. 5. Upton's signature block is on a one-page typed report, "Report of the Battle of Beaurepaire Farm, July 18, 1918." It is a jumble of out-of-chronology comments and is almost worthless in reconstructing what he did. One item of interest in that report is the following paragraph: "Liaison: Only one message was received from brigade headquarters; none from division." Upton's July 22 letter to his sister is of much greater value.

37. Bullard, *Personalities and Reminiscences*, pp. 252, 266–67.

38. Hanford MacNider, *The A.E.F. of a Conscientious Subaltern*, pp. 33–38.

39. Ibid.
40. Second Division Historical Section, *Records of the Second Division (Regular)*, vol. 5, pt. 1, "Field Message, 1918."
41. Malone, Book 24, *Monograph Soissons*, pp. 20–23; Thomason, *AWC Monograph*, pp. 79–82; ABMC, *American Armies and Battlefields*, map, p. 83; For Fechet, see *Assembly*, 1965, vol. 24, no. 2, p. 104.
42. Malone, Book 24, *Monograph Soissons*, p. 22.
43. "Notes on Recent Operations: No. 3, October 12, 1918, G-5 Document 1376, GHQ AEF," in RG 120, NA, reiterates the Aug. 29, 1918, "Secret Memo to Commanders." See also Timothy Nenninger, "American Military Effectiveness in the First World War," in *Military Effectiveness*, ed. Allan R. Millett and Williamson Murray, vol. 1, The *First World War*, p. 143; Stackpole, "Diary."
44. Malone, Book 24, *Monograph Soissons*, pp. 20–23.
45. Smythe, *Pershing*, p. 154; Hansen E. Ely, "Report of Operations, Third Brigade, July 17th to 21st, in the [A]ttack of Twentieth Army Corps, 'X' French Army; Headquarters, Third Brigade, Second Division, A.E.F., July 27, 1918," Book 22, *Monograph Soissons*, p. 4; Maj. Earl Ellis, USMC, "Liaison in the World War," *Marine Corps Gazette* (June, 1920): pp. 135–41.
46. Harbord, *Leaves from a War Diary*, p. 325.
47. "Message, HQ, 3d Div. to XIII Corps, July 19, 1918." *WWR, GE*.
48. Colonel Maxwell Murray, address to the Artillery Reserve Association at the Harvard Club, New York City, Apr. 20, 1920. A copy is in the last section of *Monograph Soissons*, p. 5.
49. Paragraph 4, "Course of the Action. Report to the Royal Bavarian War Ministry Concerning: The 18th of July 1918. HQ, 11th Bavarian Division, August 1, 1918." *WWR, GE;* The reinforcement flow may be traced largely through the records of the Army Group German Crown Prince and Headquarters, XIII Royal Wurttemburg Army Corps (also referred to as Corps Watter for its commander). Both are found for the most part in *War Diaries* and *WWR, GE*.
50. ABMC, *2d Division Summary*, p. 29; Harbord, *American Army in France*, pp. 332–33; Interview with Lt. Gen. Calvin A. H. Waller, deputy commander in chief, U.S. Central Command, U.S. Army War College, Apr. 22, 1991.
51. Malone, Book 24, *Monograph Soissons*, pp. 23–24; *USAWW*, vol. 5, p. 333; Ely, *Monograph Soissons*, p. 14; Spaulding and Wright, *The Second Division*, pp. 122–23; Ely's version, including the statement that this was the first message received from division, is in his "Report of Operations, Third Brigade, July 17th to 21st, in the [A]ttack of Twentieth Army Corps, 'X' French Army; Headquarters, Third Brigade, Second Division, A.E.F., July 27, 1918," Book 22, *Monograph Soissons*. In *USAWW*, vol. 5, neither the corps nor the division order gives an hour to attack, but the brigade order states not later than 6 P.M. ("Field Order 26, Headquarters, Third Brigade, Second Division, A.E.F., July 18, 1918 [4:30 P.M.]," Book 21, *Monograph Soissons*) Harbord, in *Leaves from a War Diary*, doesn't mention meeting Ely. See also ABMC, *2d Division Summary*, pp. 29–30.
52. "Narrative Account of the July 18th Attack by the 1st and 2nd Divisions in the Aisne-Marne Offensive," Book 3, *Monograph Soissons*, p. 14.
53. Wise, *Turn of the Tide*, p. 161; Ely, "Report of Operations, Third Brigade, July 17th to 21st, in the [A]ttack of Twentieth Army Corps, 'X' French Army; Headquarters, Third Brigade, Second Division, A.E.F., July 27, 1918," Book 22, *Monograph Soissons*, p. 4.

54. "Narrative Account of the July 18th Attack by the 1st and 2nd Divisions in the Aisne-Marne Offensive," Book 3, *Monograph Soissons*, p. 20.

55. Ibid.

56. GHQ, AEF, Deputy Chief of Staff, France, Aug. 29, 1918, "Combat Instructions: Posts of Command in Open Warfare," Manuscript Division, Library of Congress.

57. "HQ, 14th Reserve Division, July 19, 1918," *WWR, GE*.

58. Janda, "M Company," p. 9.

59. Ibid.

60. Book 23, *Monograph Soissons*, p. 3.

61. Upton, Book 25, *Monograph Soissons*, pp. 9–10; Upton to Mrs. Miner, July 22, 1918, pp. 5–6. Estimate of Upton's position when this message was sent is 177.4–287.0 on the ABMC, *2d Division Summary*, 1:20,000 map.

62. McClellan "Aisne-Marne Offensive," pt. 1, pp. 188–201; Yingling, *Brief History of the 5th Marines*, p. 8; "2d Battalion, 5th Marines," p. 8; and Spaulding and Wright, *The Second Division*, p. 125. See also "Report by CO, 5th Co, 159th Inf., to Hq, 14th Res Div, 3:50 P.M. July 18, 1918," *War Diaries*.

63. Upton, Book 25, *Monograph Soissons*, p. 9.

64. Ely's Sept. 26, 1920, letter of commendation to Upton is in the Upton Papers; Hansen E. Ely, "Leadership and Morale in War," a lecture delivered at the Army War College, Feb. 3, 1938, USAWC Curricular Archives, Carlisle Barracks, Pa., pp. 9–10.

65. Letter dated Aug. 23, 1918, from the new Company M First Sergeant, Albert W. Anderson, reviewing the personnel status of the company, "Janda Matters," Box 1, Hillman Collection, Archives, USAMHI.

66. Thomason's story of premonitions of death is "Special Cases," collected in —*And a Few Marines*. His fictional "Lieutenant Edward Weeks" is based on the case of marine gunner Henry Hulbert. See Rolfe Hillman, "Henry Hulbert: From Samoa to Blanc Mont," *Leatherneck* (Nov. 1989): pp. 32–35.

67. Major Keyser's message is in Book 20, *Monograph Soissons*, p. 17. He gives coordinates as 179.3 — 266.0, which is an obvious mistake or typo in converting message to typescript. From the 1:20,000 map showing dispositions on the night of 18 July, it is very probable that he was in the trenches at about 177.0–287.5, near the division's north boundary and about a thousand meters west-southwest of Lechelle.

68. Thomas, *History of the A.E.F.*, p. 160.

69. The account is taken mainly from Thomason, *AWC Monograph*, pp. 103–105; ABMC, *2d Division Summary*, pp. 29–30; Spaulding and Wright, *The Second Division*, pp. 123–25; and Malone, Book 24, *Monograph Soissons*, pp. 23–24.

70. Ely, Book 16, *Monograph Soissons;* Thomason, *AWC Monograph*, p. 100; Malone, Book 24, *Monograph Soissons*, p. 23;

71. Simmons, "First Day at Soissons," p. 11. Spaulding and Wright, *The Second Division*, p. 124, credit the "Report of Operations. 1st Bn., 5th Marines," dated July 21, 1918.

72. Malone, Book 24, *Monograph Soissons*, p. 24; Jones, et al., *The Fighting Tanks*, pp. 72–75.

73. Ely, "Leadership and Morale in War," p. 10; Arthur P. Watson, "America's Greatest World War Battle Leader. (Major General Hanson Ely)," 1933 typescript, Archives, USAMHI, p. 8.

74. Thomason, *AWC Monograph,* p. 105.
75. Westover, *Suicide Battalions,* pp. 167; Ely's after action report of July 27, 1918 in Book 21, *Monograph Soissons;* Malone, Book 24, *Monograph Soissons,* p. 24.
76. Malone, Book 24, *Monograph Soissons,* p. 23.
77. Harbord, *American Army in France,* p. 333.
78. Janda "M Company," p. 10.
79. Harbord, *Leaves from a War Diary,* p. 327.
80. Statements of Wegener and Ludendorff are in Charles F. Horne and Walter F. Austin, eds., *The Great Events of the Great War,* vol. 6, pp. 272–74. A full and frank discussion of the great success of the first day—and the Allies's inability to exploit it—is in "War Diary of the Group of Armies German Crown Prince," entry for July 18, *USAWW,* vol. 5, pp. 678–79.
81. Horne and Austin, *The Great Events of the Great War,* p. 274.
82. Ibid.
83. "28th Div Combat Report for the Period of July 18 to July 31, 1918," entry for July 18, 1918, *War Diaries.*
84. "28th Division, Combat Report of the 1st Battalion, 2d Baden Grenadier Regiment, Kaiser Wilhelm I, 110th Grenadier Regiment for the Period of July 18 to 21, 1918," entry for July 18, 1918, *War Diaries.*

Chapter 4. Edging Forward: July 19 — 1st Division and 1st Moroccan Division

1. Sulzbach, *With the German Guns,* p. 205.
2. "XX Corps Field Orders No. 233," July 18, 1918, 11 A.M., *USAWW,* vol. 5, pp. 296–97. The original objectives are stated in "XX Corps Field Orders No. 227," p. 290. See also Butler, "Journal," entry for July 19, 1918. Pitt, *1918,* pp. 205–206, includes a graphic account of a failed attack in which men and horses were slaughtered.
3. "HQ, French Armies of North and Northeast to the General Commanding the Group of Armies of the Reserve," *USAWW,* vol. 5, pp. 233–34, 249; *Les Armées,* Tome VII, Annexe No. 1, *Deuxième patrie,* p. 75–76.
4. "Compte-redu journalier" (Journal Report to Berdolat 11:45 P.M., July 18, 1918), provided by Mr. Patrice Demanais, Jan. 22, 1992, copy in author's possession.
5. Various reports, 145th Infantry, 21st Bavarian Infantry Brigade, 11th Bavarian Division, July 18, 1918: 4 P.M. —"A whole regiment"; 4:30 P.M. —"Two squadrons"; 5:15 P.M. —"more than 100"; 5:20 P.M. —"several squadrons," *WWR, GE.* See also Regimental Chaplain, *The Story of the Sixteenth Infantry in France,* p. 34; Bullard *Personalities and Reminiscences,* p. 219.
6. "Journal of Operations, Order 301, French Tenth Army, July 18, 1918, 8 pm," *USAWW,* vol. 5, p. 280.
7. "HQ, French Tenth Army, Order No. 232, July 14, 1918," *USAWW,* vol. 5, p. 276.
8. Berdoulat, "The First and Second American Divisions," pp. 407–12. "Report on Operations south of Soissons," 1st Division, AEF,. G-3, No. 735, July 27, 1918, *USAWW,* vol. 5, pp. 323–27.
9. War Diary of Group of Armies, German Crown Prince, July 18[?], 1918, extract in *USAWW,* vol. 5, p. 679.
10. "Field Order No. 233, HQ, French XX Army Corps, July 18, 1918," *USAWW,* vol. 5, p. 296.

11. Bullard, *Personalities and Reminiscences,* pp. 243–44; Wise, *Turn of the Tide,* p. 154. The subject of French failures to keep up with the Americans at Soissons and subsequently is, even now, sensitive. Key references and selected passages are: Wise, *Turn of the Tide,* p. 156; Huebner, "The Twenty-Eighth Infantry in the Aisne-Marne Offensive, July 18–21, 1918," Book 16, *Monograph Soissons,* p. 1; and Conrad Babcock's 28th Infantry after-action report of Aug. 4, 1918, which notes the difficulties. See also Brooks, *As I Saw It,* pp. 209–10; John A. Lejeune, *The Reminiscences of a Marine;* and Watson, "America's Greatest," for the experience of the 2d Division at Blanc Mont in early October.

12. The record of Summerall's battlefield circulation from his cave command post turns out to be a key aspect of this account, but it has to be pieced together from a number of sources, some of which conflict. Summerall's own partial account, in which he primarily mentions confrontations with regimental commanders, appears in his unpublished memoir, "The Way of Duty, Honor, Country," in The Citadel archives, Charleston, S.C. Although written in 1953–54, Summerall still wouldn't name names, and he created uncertainty by erroneously referring to the Pershing/Mangin visits to 1st Division headquarters on "the second day [July 19] when it was actually the third day [July 20]. See also Pershing, *My Experiences,* vol. 2:166–67; 28th Infantry, "Report on Operations South of Soissons," July 18, 1918, par. 11, *WWR,* vol. XIII, pt. 2. The journal of Summerall's aide, Alban Butler, is disappointing because he first mentions Summerall as visiting front lines on the twentieth, whereas it appears certain that he visited the 26th Infantry, and probably other units, on the second day, the nineteenth.

13. "Field Orders No. 28, G-3, No. 717, 1st Division, A.E.F., July 19, 1918, 1:35 A.M.," *USAWW* vol. 5, p. 317. See also "Operations Journal, 2d Brigade," Book 12, *CGSC Monograph Soissons.* Babcock reported receiving the order at 3:55 A.M. in "Report of Offensive July 18–22, 1918," *WWR,* vol. XVII, pt. 2., p. 2.

14. Colonel Maxwell Murray, *CGSC Monograph,* not tabbed, in the rear, pp. 6–8. Murray notes details of artillery coverage and particularly notes the relatively light support for a major attack. See also 28th Infantry, "Report of Operations South of Soissons, July 1918," dated Aug. 4, 1918, *WWR,* vol. 13, pt. 2.

15. "HQ, 1st Division, A.E.F., Field Orders No. 28, July 19, 1918, 1:35 A.M.," *USAWW,* vol. 5, p. 317.

16. ABMC, *1st Division Summary,* p. 25,

17. 28th Infantry, "Report on Operations South of Soissons," par. 11, pp. 26–27.

18. Fuller, *Tanks in the Great War,* pp 192–93; Eimannsberger, *Mechanized Warfare,* p. 42; and Jones, et al., *The Fighting Tanks,* pp. 73–75.

19. Society of the 1st Division, AEF, *First Division Official History,* p. 123.

20. This extract is from Col. Walter C. Short, *The Employment of Machine Guns,* p. 247. It is reproduced in "Chapter XVII, Fire of Machine Guns," *Infantry in Battle,* pp. 246–48. A full-scale treatment of machine-gun employment (highly dramatized) is Westover, *Suicide Battalions.* Westover was with the 2d Division's 4th Machine Gun Battalion.

21. 28th Infantry, "Report of Operations South of Soissons, July 1918."

22. Summerall, "The Way of Duty, Honor, and Country," pp. 205–206 (pencil corrected to pp. 206–207). Summerall includes in this paragraph the disposition of Babcock for his protest. Paul L. Ransom, "Report on Machine Guns of the 1st Brigade in recent operations South of Soissons," *WWR,* vol. 12.

23. His Medal of Honor was awarded by War Department General Order No. 1,

Feb. 1, 1937. He went on to become a colonel, a distinguished officer, and a prominent citizen of Cabarrus County, N.C.

24. 28th Infantry, "Report of Operations South of Soissons, July 1918."

25. Ibid., Para. 15; Society of the 1st Division, *First Division Official History*, p. 126.

26. Personal information on George Rozelle is from the U. S Military Academy Cullum Files. The papers in Rozelle's file include a nine-page, copyedited unpublished obituary and a poignant letter to Col. Wirt Robinson at West Point on the eve of Rozelle's retirement in Dec., 1922.

27. The source of this Rozelle statement is a peculiarity in itself. It appears as a "Memo for the Regt. Adjutant" in an enclosure to Col. Conrad Babcock's July 26 after-action report, "Report of offensive July 18–22 1918." The first sentence makes it clear that Rozelle was being called upon to explain where and why he disposed of his codebook: "The code 'Carnet Reduit, Napoleon' issued to me was torn to pieces and buried by me in the woods near the crest of the ridge just west of and overlooking Berzy-le-Sec." The report then continues as quoted above.

28. The information on Rozelle's rejoining his troops is found in only one place, and an obscure one at that. Beaumont Buck somehow managed to make pencil notes on reports that had already been filed. Despite the fact that he tended to confuse dates, the notes are often valuable additions. In *WWR*, vol. 13, in a section headed "Brief Statement of Events July 17–20" inclusive, appears: "EDITOR's NOTE: The following pencil notes in the handwriting of Brigadier General, B. B. Buck were apparently made at a date subsequent to July 22, 1918."

29. Theodore Roosevelt, Jr., *Average Americans*, pp. 114–15.

30. "Parker, Samuel I.," in U.S. Department of the Army, *The Medal of Honor of the United States Army*, p. 252.

31. Regimental Adjutant. *The 26th Infantry in France*, pp. 37–39.

32. Lieutenant Col. E. S. Sayer to Chief, Visitor's Bureau, Paris, "Subject: 28th Infantry Operations," dated Feb. 20, 1919, p. 2, Hillman Papers, USAMHI.

33. ABMC, *1st Division Summary*, p. 27.

34. Eighteenth Infantry, "Report on Operations South of Soissons, July 1918," dated Aug. 9, 1918, *WWR*, vol. 13, pt. 2. Bamford's report is short and curt saying, in effect, that there was nothing really new in this battle that needed to be recorded.

35. Buck, *Memories*, pp. 187–209. His chapter on Soissons is essential for this study, and unique in its account of the taking of Berzy-le-Sec on the morning of July 21. Buck mentions by name his own staff, several battalion commanders who became casualties, makes one reference to Col. Hamilton Smith, commander of the 26th Infantry, mentions his visits to Colonels Bamford and Parker in the 1st Brigade, and mentions many junior officers at Berzy. Nowhere does he name Colonel Babcock, commander of the 28th Infantry. No informal history mentions Babcock's personal role except for Joseph D. Patch's statement that Babcock was relieved for "losing his regiment," p. 39.

36. Ibid., pp. 202–203.

37. As quoted in Mrs. Theodore Roosevelt, Jr., *Day before Yesterday*, pp. 100–101. Roosevelt was given belated top marks as a battalion commander when Major General Ely addressed the Army War College in 1938 ("Leadership and Morale in War," p. 5.)

38. Buck, *Memories*, pp. 198–99. His account of the 1st Moroccan Division is valuable, although it seems to sacrifice accuracy for color. He states, for instance,

that two companies of the Foreign Legion held the Soissons–Château-Thierry road by 2 A.M. on the July 20, a statement not seen elsewhere (pp. 333–34).

39. Headquarters, Forty-second Division, "Brief Combat Report Concerning the Events of July 19, 1918," *WWR, GE.*

40. "War Diary 28th Division, 2d Battalion 110th Grenadier Regiment; July 19, 1918, 1:00 A.M. report to 110th Grenadier Regiment," *War Diaries.* "Notes on the 20th Division" by Lt. Col. S. Sorley, Historical Section, Army War College, records that the Twentieth Division's strength on July 12 was 6,336 and that losses for July 19–31 were 2,285 men or 36 percent of the division's previous strength. A report to Headquarters, I Bavarian Corps on July 4 says the division was short 1,380 soldiers and eighty-four officers to begin with ("Selected War Diary Annexes of the 20th Division from July 4 to July 31, 1918," *War Diaries*). See also "War Diary, 20th Division, July 19, 1918," *War Diaries,* and "War Diary 28th Division, 2d Battalion, 110 Grenadier Regiment, July 19, 1918."

Chapter 5. Futile Bravery: July 19 — Attack of the 6th Marines and Relief of the 2d Division

1. "HQ, 28th Division, Combat Report for the Period of July 18 to July 31, 1918, 1st Bn 110th Gren Regt, July 20, 1918," *War Diaries;* 28th Division, "Combat Report for the Period of July 18 to July 31, 1918, 2d Bn 110th Gren Regt," *War Diaries.*

2. Stallings, *The Doughboys,* p. 177.

3. *USAWW,* vol. 5, p. 296 (XX Corps), p. 280 (Tenth Army), and p. 281 (Tenth Army Order 301). XX Corps Operations Order 227 (Supplement), dated July 17, 1918, designated the 6th Marines as general reserve (*USAWW,* vol. 5, pp. 294–95). Nevertheless, the division memorandum to the 6th Marines's commander instructs him to "follow the course of the attack." (*USAWW,* vol. 5, p. 330.)

4. Harbord, *Leaves from a War Diary,* p. 327; *USAWW,* vol. 5, p. 339. Any good history of the 20th Maine in the 1863 battle of Gettysburg covers the diversion of Vincent's Brigade to secure unoccupied Little Round Top, where the 20th Maine subsequently saved the Army of the Potomac from being flanked. Edwin B. Coddington, *Gettysburg: A Study in Command,* is a good source.

5. The messages of the 6th Marines are largely based on the excellent report, "The Military History of the Third Battalion, Sixth Regiment, U.S. Marine Corps, AEF, from June 1st to August 10th, 1918," dated Aug. 15, 1918, Book 27, *Monograph Soissons,* pp. 1–7. See also "A Brief History of the Second Battalion, Sixth Regiment, U.S. Marine Corps, during the period from July 13th to 25th, 1918." Book 26, *Monograph Soissons,* pp. 1–3.

6. Ibid.

7. Thomason, *AWC Monograph,* p. 112; "A Brief History of the Second Battalion, Sixth Regiment," pp. 1–3.

8. Upton to Mrs. Miner, July 22, 1918.

9. "A Brief History of the Second Battalion, Sixth Regiment," pp. 1–3.

10. Gunnery Sgt. Don Paradis, Manuscript PC 463, n.d., USMC Historical Center, pp. 85–87.

11. Allan R. Millett, *In Many a Strife: General Gerald C. Thomas and the U.S. Marine Corps, 1917–1956,* p. 53.

12. "History of the Third Battalion, Sixth Regiment," p. 35; Book 27, *Monograph*

Soissons, p. 2; Simmons, "The Second Day at Soissons," *Fortudine* 23, no. 2 (Fall, 1993): pp. 4–10.

13. Chastaine, *History of the 18th Infantry,* p. 66.

14. "History of the Third Battalion, Sixth Regiment," pp. 34–35; David Bellamy, "World War I Diary of David Bellamy, 1888–1960," Box 2B43, USMC Historical Center, p. 80; Gary B. Griffin, *The Directed Telescope: A Traditional Element of Effective Command.*

15. Scanlon, *God Have Mercy On Us!,* p. 7.

16. "History of the Third Battalion, Sixth Regiment," pp. 34–35; Book 27, *Monograph Soissons,* pp. 3–4. Simmons, "Second Day at Soissons," p. 8; Thomason, *AWC Monograph,* p. 117.

17. Book 27, *Monograph Soissons,* p. 4.

18. Ibid.; Field Message, "HQ, 3d Bn, 6th Mar to CO, 6th Mar," (no time specified) in "History of the Third Battalion, Sixth Regiment," p. 39.

19. Field Messages, "CO, 6th Mar to CO, 3/6th Mar," 12:15 P.M., and "CO, 3d Bn to CO, 6th Regt," in "History of the Third Battalion, Sixth Regiment," pp. 39–40; Robert I. Denig, "Diary of a Marine Officer during the World War," Personal Papers, Box, 1, USMC Historical Center, p. 210.

20. Simmons, "Second Day at Soissons," pp. 8–9.

21. Spaulding and Wright, *The Second Division,* p. 167. For time, see Denig, "Diary," p. 209.

22. Denig, "Diary," pp. 203–209.

23. Smythe, *Pershing,* p. 37; Nenninger, "American Military Effectiveness," p. 143; and, Allan R. Millett and Peter Maslowski, *For the Common Defense: A Military History of the United States of America,* p. 355.

24. Harbord, *American Army in France,* pp. 335–36.

25. Harbord, *Leaves from a War Diary,* pp 327–28. Thomason, in *AWC Monograph,* says the entire initial barrage was wasted three hours early and this is confirmed by multiple Marine reports in Book 27, *Monograph Soissons* and elsewhere, p. 115.

26. *USAWW,* vol. 5, p. 336.

27. Ibid., p. 456; McClellan " Aisne-Marne Offensive," pt. 2, pp. 214–15.

28. *USAWW,* vol. 5, p. 340; ABMC, *2d Division Summary,* p. 33.

29. "Journal of Operations, 2d Division, A.E.F., July 19, 1918," *USAWW,* pp. 338–39.

30. ABMC, *2d Division Summary,* p. 33.

31. "French Tenth Army Journal of Operations," July 19, 1918, *USAWW,* vol. 5, p. 281.

Chapter 6. Try Again: July 20 — 1st Division Continues the Attack

1. ABMC, *1st Division Summary,* p. 28; "HQ, Tenth Army, July 20, 1918," *USAWW,* vol. 5, p. 250.

2. Pitt, *1918,* pp. 206–207.

3. Butler, "Journal," entry for July 20, 1918.

4. Thomas, *History of the A.E.F.,* pp. 163–64. Thomas, having been S-2 of the 26th Infantry, includes superior terrain analysis in his battle narrative. See also Robert K. Whitson, *CGSC Monograph,* "A Study of the Operation of the 1st Division in the Soissons Offensive, 16–25 July 1918," p. 8, citing G-3 Memorandum No. 718, 1st Division, July 19, 1918.

5. ABMC, *1st Division Summary,* p. 28 cites "G-3 Memorandum #721, 1st Division, July 20." The full text of this memorandum is in Book 9, *Monograph Soissons.* As will be seen, Babcock stated he did not receive the brigade attack order until 1:15 P.M. (Babcock, "Report of Operations south of Soissons." See also Beaumont B. Buck, "Report of Action South of Soissons, July 1918," *WWR,* vol. 13; War Diary, Twentieth Division, July 20, 1918, *War Diaries;* ABMC, *1st Division Summary,* pp. 26–27; and 1st Division, "Report on the Action South of Soissons, July 27, 1918," *USAWW,* vol. 5, p. 326. The various accounts of the 16th and 18th Infantry Regiments for actions on July 20 are conflicting and confusing. This version is skimpy but logical.

6. This account of Buck's actions is taken from two sources. The first is from the 2d Brigade's "Report on action south of Soissons, July, 1918," dated Aug. 5, 1918, *WWR,* vol. 13. This report provides a detailed third-person account of the movements and actions of Buck and his staff. Indications are that Buck, and not a staff underling, wrote it. Furthermore, it was probably written in this manner because, on Aug. 4, Conrad Babcock wrote a detailed and very defensive report of his actions, probably to "show cause" why he should not be relieved of command of the 28th Infantry. In this report, Buck specifically tells of visiting the commanders of the 16th and 18th Infantry Regiments in Chazelle Ravine on July 20. In this section of the *WWR,* vol. 13, editor Paul Ransom has included several pages of handwritten pencil notes made by Buck at some later, unspecified time. (Buck had a habit of writing notes to himself on orders and messages.) In one of these, a list of "2 Brig. P.C.s", Buck notes that on July 20 he was at Missy-aux-Bois "thence (through error) with 18th and 16th Inf Adv. P.C. in North extreme of Chazelle Ravine." The second source for this section is Buck's *Memories,* p. 201. Details differ, but Buck carefully records his wanderings and trivial actions in both accounts with no apologies for circumstances. In the book version, he puts the "by error" visit to the Sixteenth and Eighteenth Infantry commanders on July 19, but he says all the visits that day were made "alone and on foot." That seems to be a case of lapsed memory after seventeen years. In trying to reconcile Buck's versions in his official report, pencil notes included in *WWR,* vol. 13, and in his book, the only importance is in showing that he was out of his own area and not tending to his own business on one of those days.

7. Ibid.

8. Babcock, "Report . . . Aug. 4, 1918," p. 4. "First Division Memorandum, Subject: Use of Telephone and Other Means of Communication, July 16, 1918," Book 9, *Monograph Soissons,* forbade the use of telephonic communication forward of brigade PCs, it being too easy to intercept.

9. "Report of Operations of 1st Division South of Soissons, July 18–24, 1918, Headquarters, 1st Division, American Expeditionary Forces, July 27, 1918," Book 11, *Monograph Soissons.*

10. 153d Division, section 2, para. 1 "General Order No. 14," Headquarters 69th Inf. Div., dated July 20, 1918, *WWR, FR,* vol. 25, pt. 2; 153d Division, section 5, "Operations Order for the Day of July 21, 1918," dated July 20, 1918, *WWR, FR,* vol. 25, pt. 2; Book 9, "Field Order No. 29," *Monograph Soissons.*

11. "Report on action south of Soissons, July, 1918," dated Aug. 5, 1918, *WWR,* vol. 13. An exception is the figure of 190 men in Rozelle's battalion, found in a transcribed pencil note elsewhere in *WWR,* vol. 13. This is the first mention of attacking by infiltration groups. Babcock states that on arrival he read the order

received by Rozelle and thought it was merely a warning order, and that "the order suggested that we use the infiltration method of attacking," para. 18, Memorandum From: Commanding Officer, 28th Infantry, To: Commanding General, First Division, "Report of Operations South of Soissons, July, 1918," dated Aug. 4, 1918.

12. Ibid.

13. "Field Orders No. 29, Headquarters, First Division, American Expeditionary Forces, July 20, 1918, Book 10, *Monograph Soissons;* "Narrative Account of the July 18th Attack by the 1st and 2nd Divisions in the Aisne-Marne Offensive," Book 3, *Monograph Soissons,* p. 19.

14. "Documents, War Diary and Annexes, 65th Infantry Brigade and Subordinate Units, July 17 to July 28, 1918," *WWR,* vol 13.

15. Murray, Soissons lecture, p. 9. From the subsequent account, we conclude that Summerall, before he went to the front lines at whatever hour it was that day, was aware that his division had the mission of taking Berzy-le-Sec.

16. Society of the 1st Division, AEF, *History of the First Division,* pp. 131–32. The original source is not given.

17. Pershing, *My Experiences,* 2:166–67. Alban Butler states specifically, "This afternoon Genl Mangin Comdg the 10th Army & later General Pershing visited the Div. P.C." (Butler, "Journal," entry for July 20, 1918.) See also Summerall, "The Way of Duty, Honor, Country," p. 203.

18. Pershing, ibid., 2:167; Butler, "Journal," entry for July 20 simply notes the visits of Mangin and later Pershing, then notes the division commander visiting and talking to elements of every regiment.

19. Pershing, ibid. Although Harbord went on to do many great things in the army and with Radio Corporation of America, he thoroughly took to heart Pershing's rating of his two days of commanding a division in combat, and he always maintained close contact with his mentor. Recent historians are less generous. One of the foremost historians of the AEF, Edward M. Coffman, addressing an Army War College audience in 1973, said of the 2d Division: "what happened to that division at Soissons under Harbord's command indicates that his talents were much better used as the logistical manager of the services of supply." (Coffman, "American Command and Commanders in World War I," p 192.) See also Hillman, "Second to None," pp. 57–62; McClellan, "Aisne-Marne Offensive," pt. 2, p. 215. Memorandum From: Commanding General, 2d Division, To: Commanding General, 3d Infantry Brigade and Commanding General 4th Brigade, dated July 20, 1918, vol. 1, pt. 1.

21. As quoted in George H. English Jr, *History of the 89th Division, USA,* pp. 168.

22. Ely, "Leadership in Peace and War," p. 13.

23. Summerall, "The Way of Duty, Honor, Country," pp. 203–204.

24. Jeremiah M. Evarts, "The 1st Division's Vermonter," in Henry Berry, *Make the Kaiser Dance,* p. 60.

25. Patch, *A Soldier's War,* p. 39.

26. Regimental Adjutant, *The Twenty-sixth Infantry in France,* p. 40.

27. Summerall, "The Way of Duty, Honor, Country," pp. 203–204.

28. Theodore Roosevelt, Jr., mentions the Summerall-Parker episode in *Average Americans,* p. 177.

29. Summerall, "The Way of Duty, Honor, Country," p. 206.

30. Buck, *Memories,* p. 203.

31. "Narrative of the Marne Operations," Book 2, *Monograph Soissons,* p. 8; ABMC, *1st Division Summary,* pp. 28–29; and Wise, *Turn of the Tide,* pp. 174–76. See the same sources for July 21. The advance and retreat of the Fifty-eighth Division is described the XX Corps report in *USAWW,* vol. 5, p. 306.

Chapter 7. Mission Accomplished: July 21 — Taking Berzy-le-Sec, Consolidation, and Relief of the 1st Division

1. Paul von Hindenburg, *Out of My Life,* pp. 271, 283.
2. Ludendorff, *Ludendorff's Own Story,* p. 314. Ludendorff erroneously cites the with-drawal as the night of July 20 although all other accounts say it was on the nine-teenth. See also Hans von Zwehl, *The Battles of the Summer of 1918 on the Western Front,* p. 21.
3. "Report of Operations South of Soissons, G-3, 1st Division, A.E.F., July 27, 1918," *USAWW,* vol. 5, pp. 326–27, records 4 A.M. as the attack hour, whereas "Field Order No. 237, French XX Army Corps, dated July 20, 1918," shows 4:45 A.M., (*USAWW,* vol. 5, p. 302). The relief of the entire 153d Division was not accomplished by the Sixty-ninth Division until the night of July 21.
4. On Summerall, see "Headquarters, A.E.F., Office of the Chief of Staff, Paris, July 11, 1918," *USAWW,* vol. 1, *Organization,* pp. 107–14. For a discussion of the French attitude toward taking casualties, see Brooks, *As I Saw It,* pp. 209–10, 221–22. See also George S. Viereck, ed., *As They Saw Us: Foch, Ludendorff and Other Leaders Write Our War History,* pp. 48, 286, 296–303; and Lee Kennett, "The A.E.F. through French Eyes," *Military Review* (Nov., 1972): pp. 3–11.
5. "Headquarters, XIII Corps to 20th Division, 8:50 A.M., Jul 20, 18," *WWR, GE.*
6. Telephone message to Forty-second, Forty-sixth Reserve, and Twentieth Divi-sions from Headquarters, XIII Corps, July 20, 1918, *WWR, GE;* "War Diary and Annexes, 20th Division, July 20, 1918," *War Diaries.*
7. "Field Order #28, 1st Division, A.E.F., July 19, 1918, 1:35 A.M.," *USAWW,* vol. 5, p. 317; "Report on Action South of Soissons, July 1918," From: Commanding General, 2d Infantry Brigade, To: Commanding General, 1st Division, A.E.F., dated Aug. 5, 1918, *WWR,* vol. 13.
8. Buck's official 2d Brigade after-action report and Babcock's two after-action re-ports (July 28 and Aug. 4), are in *WWR,* vol. 13. Special attention should be given to a series of Buck's penciled notes transcribed to type and reproduced in the 2d Brigade section of *WWR,* vol. 3. These are fragmentary and not properly dated, but, with careful reading, give some extra details.
9. Ibid.
10. Buck, *Memories,* pp. 204–206; John R. D. Cleland, Jr., Major General, U.S. Army (Retired), to Douglas V. Johnson, Mar. 11, 1995. Included are the DSC order, dated Nov. 9, 1918, and the Heubner letter, copy of commendatory letter in author's possession. The younger Cleland commanded the 8th Infantry Divi-sion (Mechanized) in Germany in the late 1970s.
11. Buck, *Memories,* pp. 204–206
12. Stallings, *The Doughboys,* p. 178. The division's official history states that every infantry battalion commander was a casualty. Major George Rozelle, commander of the 1st Battalion, was within a short distance of Buck that morning and was transferred out of the division, unscathed, on Aug. 6.

13. Evarts, "The 1st Division's Vermonter," p. 60.

14. General Order No. 44, Headquarters First Division, AEF, France, Aug. 5, 1918, *WWR*, vol. 13.

15. Babcock, "Report . . . Aug. 4, 1918." The number of soldiers roaming the rear areas is uncounted but acknowledged to be considerable. In the by-name officer accounting accompanying this report, 42 officers are listed as present, 10 killed, 26 wounded, and 23 missing, of which 21 were second lieutenants. Para. 20, Memorandum From: Commanding Officer, 28th Infantry, To: Commanding General, First Division, "Report of Operations South of Soissons, July 1918," dated Aug. 4, 1918.

16. Letter from Major George F. Rozelle, U.S. Army (Retired), "To the American Battle Monuments Commission, War and Navy Bldg, Washington D.C.," no subject, no date. Evidently followed an earlier letter of July 24, 1924. These letters are contained in ABMC file 710.1G/AM, RG 117, NA. The remainder of this account of the action is a composite drawn from Buck's *Memories,* pp. 202–206, and his Aug. 5 report.

17. "The 11th and 12th Cos. are still at the sugar factory." (Message, 11th Company, 8th Body Regiment, July 23, 1918, 8:15 A.M., *WWR, GE.*)

18. Butler, "Journal," entry for July 21, 1918. This is a sterling example of leadership; this is how trust is established and kept. For the debilitating effects of a loss of trust, see Jonathan Shay, *Achilles in Vietnam: Combat Trauma and the Destruction of Character.*

19. "Summary of operations 21 July from XX Corps Journal of Operations, July 1918," extracted in *USAWW,* vol. 5, p. 306. For a good summary of tank reconstitution efforts, see Eimannsberger, *Mechanized Warfare,* p. 42; For the German counterattack, see "Telephone message, HQ, XIII Corps to 20th and 3d Res Divs, 9:30 pm., July 20, 1918," *War Diaries,* which notes that the 9th Division counterattack had made good progress. See also Zwehl, *Battles of the Summer of 1918,* p. 21.

20. Sulzbach, *With the German Guns,* p. 206.

Chapter 8. The Reward: July 22—The Last Day

1. ABMC, *1st Division Summary,* p. 31. This account also leaves the status of the sugar factory uncertain.

2. "First Lieutenant Shipley Thomas—Sergeant George Krahnert," in Berry, *Make the Kaiser Dance,* pp. 41–42.

3. Hans Delbruck, "The Swiss," *History of the Art of War,* vol. 3, *Medieval Warfare,* pp. 545–649.

4. Sources for this section: "Guts to drive men forward" is from Stallings, *The Doughboys,* p. 12. "War a matter of wills . . . kept exerting pressure" is from Smythe, *Pershing,* p. 208. The passage on commanders in the Pershing mold is based on Millett, *The General,* p. 305. "Make men fear you . . ." is from Millett, *The General,* p. 347. "A British general . . ." is from Spears, *Prelude to Victory,* p. 432.

5. Ely, "Leadership and Morale in War," p. 2.

6. *USAWW,* vol. 15, *Field Messages, All Units.* The records from the 28th Infantry specifically including those found in vol. 17, pt. 2, *28th Regiment, 2nd Brigade, 1st Div, WWR,* and in the collection of messages in vol. 15, pt. 2, *Field Messages, All*

Units, First Division, WWR are more complete than those of any other regiment in this action. Collectively they show a commander doing what he is supposed to do.

7. "FROM: Commanding General, 3d Infantry Brigade, C. E. Kilbourne, Brigadier General, U.S. Army, TO: Adjutant General, G.H.Q., A.E.F., December 15, 1918, SUBJECT: Report on General Officers," RG 117, GHQ, AEF 20752-a41, NA.

8. Patch, *A Soldier's War,* p. 39.

9. Coffman, *War to End All Wars,* pp. 348–53; English, *History of the 89th Division,* pp. 167–68.

10. Coffman, *War to End All Wars,* pp. 330–31.

11. Message, "Estimate of the Combat Value of the Division, 46th Res Div to HQ XIII Corps, July 22, 1918," *War Diaries,* vol. 5, *Soissons.*

12. Society of the 1st Division, AEF, *History of the First Division,* p. 138.

13. Smythe, *Pershing,* pp. 158–60. See also Coffman, *War to End All Wars,* pp. 248–61 (this source includes an excellent general map). For the time-phased movements of the U.S. 3d, 4th, 26th, 28th, 32d, 42d, and 77th Divisions, see the foldout Aisne-Marne color map in ABMC, *American Armies and Battlefields.*

Conclusion

1. Smythe, *Pershing,* pp. 157–58; "General Order 318, HQ French Tenth Army, July 30, 1919," *WWR,* vol. 13, p. 355; Hindenburg, *Out of My Life,* p. 386.

2. As quoted in James G. Harbord, *The American Army in France, 1917–1919,* p. 338. Casualty statistics are a constant source of controversy. These figures are from Braim, *Test of Battle,* pp. 148–49; and Smythe, *Pershing,* pp. 160–61. According to the ABMC, *1st Division Summary,* p. 33, 1st Division casualties totaled 7,041 [1,752 killed in action or died of wounds]. ABMC, *2d Division Summary,* p. 33, lists 2d Division casualties—including marines—as being 4,392 [823 killed in action or died of wounds]. Finally, Albert G. Love, *The Medical Department of the United States Army in the World War,* vol. 15, *Statistics,* pt. 2, *Medical and Casualty Statistics,* computes 1st Division losses for the period July 18–22 as 6,825 killed or wounded, of which 1,210 were killed. Second Division figures do not include the Marines and total 3,061, of which 535 were killed. Part of the explanation for these discrepancies is who counted those dying of wounds after being evacuated, the classification of the missing, and—it is obvious from the account of this battle that a soldier wounded to the point of speechlessness could have been counted against almost any regiment of either division—those presumed dead but who later recovered. Robert Graves, author of the World War I classic *Goodbye to All That,* is a case in point.

3. Carl von Clausewitz, *On War,* ed. and trans. Michael Howard and Peter Paret, p. 88.

4. Johnson, "A Few 'Squads-Left' and Off to France," pp. 138–71.

5. Martin Middlebrook, *First Day on the Somme: 1 July 1916.*

6. Headquarters, AEF, *Infantry Drill Regulations, 1919 (Provisional).*

7. *Infantry in Battle.* Washington: The Infantry School Press, 1934.

8. Kenneth E. Hamberger, *Learning Lessons in the American Expeditionary Forces,* p. 23.

9. *Notes on Recent Operations,* no. 3, Aug., 1919, "Report on Operations of Engineer Regiment During Recent Attack," Memorandum From: Captain Thomas F. Farrell, To: Commanding Officer, 1st U.S. Engineers, A.E.F., dated July 26, 1918.

10. "Final Report of Assistant Chief of Staff, G-5," *USAWW,* vol. 14, p. 310.

11. "Report on Operations of Engineer Regiment During Recent Attack," *WWR,* vol. 15, pt. 1.

12. "Report of Offensive July 18–22, 1918," dated Aug. 4, 1918, *WWR,* vol. 17, pt. 2.

13. Colonel L. R. Holbrook, "War Diaries, 1st FA Brigade, 5th FA Regiment," *WWR,* vol. 18, pt. 1; "Observations," Memorandum From: Commanding Officer, 1st F.A. Brigade, To: Commanding General 1st Division, American E.F., Subject: "Report of Operations South of Soissons, July 18–24," dated Aug. 4, 1918, *WWR,* vol. 14, pt. 1.

14. Lieutenant Col. Maxwell Murray, "Field Orders, 1st, 2d, 3d MG Bns; 5th, 6th, 7th FA Regiments,; 1st Engineer Regiment," *WWR,* vol. 11, pt. 1. Memorandum From: Commanding Officer, 5th F. A., To: Commanding General, 1st Division, A.E.F. "Subject: Operations South of Soissons, July 1918," dated Aug. 1, 1918, *WWR,* vol. 14, pt. 1.

15. Lieutenant Col. Courtland Parker, "Conclusions," Memorandum From: Commanding Officer, 6th Field Artillery, To: Commanding Officer, 1st Field Artillery Brigade, "Subject: Report of Operations South of Soissons," dated Aug. 1, 1918, *WWR,* vol. 14, pt. 2.

16. Braim, *Test of Battle,* pp. 153–66.

17. Harold B. Fiske, "Notes on Infantry," lecture delivered to a Class of Provisional Second Lieutenants at U.S. Army Command and General Staff School (later College), Ft. Leavenworth, Kans., January 29, 1917.

18. American Expeditionary Forces, *Superior Board on Organization and Tactics,* pp. 18, 19, 21, 25, 31, 36–39.

19. Ibid., pp. 154–55.

20. Gerald F. Linderman, "Battle: Expectation, Encounter, Reaction," in *The World Within War,* pp. 3–47; Freytag von Lorighoven, "Only a Strong Mind Can Resist the Impressions of War," in *The Power of Personality in War,* pp. 129–43; von Lorighoven, "Leaders With Strong Feelings Must Have Strength of Character," *The Power of Personality in War,* p. 153; Shay, "Berserk," in *Achilles in Vietnam,* pp. 77–99.

21. Ely, "Leadership and Morale in War," p. 8.

Bibliography

Official Documents

American Expeditionary Forces. *Superior Board on Organization and Tactics.* n.p., 1920. U.S. Army Military History Institute, Carlisle Barracks, Pa. (Hereafter cited as USAMHI.)

American Expeditionary Forces, General Headquarters, Office of the Chief of Staff. *Combat Instructions 57, Posts of Command in Open Warfare.* August 29, 1918. Manuscript Division, Library of Congress.

Mattfeldt, Cylburn O., comp. *Records of the Second Division (Regular). Field Messages, 1918.* Vol. 4, pt. 2. Washington, D.C.: Army War College, 1927.

——. *Field Orders, 1918.* Vol. 3. Washington, D.C.: Army War College, 1927.

——. *Field Messages, 1918.* Vol. 4, pt. 1. Washington, D.C.: Army War College, 1927.

——. *Field Messages, 1918.* Vol. 5, pts. 1 and 2. Washington, D.C.: Army War College, 1927.

——. *Operations Reports, War Diaries, Journals of Operations, 1918.* Vol. 7, pts. 1 and 2. Washington, D.C.: Army War College, 1927.

——. *Operations Reports, War Diaries.* Washington, D.C.: Army War College, 1927.

Twenty-Eighth Infantry Regiment. "Regimental Return, August 31, 1918." Record Group (RG) 407. Stack 14W3. National Archives and Records Administration, Washington, D.C. (Hereafter cited as NA.)

World War Records, First Division A.E.F., Regular: German Documents, Aisne-Marne (Soissons). Serial 1–10, Vol. 2, pt. 1. Washington, D.C.: n.p., 1930?–33.

——. *German Documents, Aisne-Marne (Soissons).* Serial 11–14, Vol. 2, pt. 2. Washington, D.C.: n.p., 1930?–33.

——. *German Documents, Aisne-Marne (Soissons).* Serial 15–19, Vol. 2, pt. 3. Washington, D.C.: n.p., 1930?–33.

——. *German Documents, War Diaries & Annexes, 11th Bavarian Division, July 17 to July 21, 1918.* Vol. 2, pt. 1. Washington, D.C.: n.p., 1930?–33.

——. *German Documents, 11th Bavarian Infantry to Royal Wurtemburg War Ministry Concerning the 18th of July 1918.* Serial 10. Washington, D.C.: n.p., 1930?–33.

——. *French Documents, May 14, 1918 to Sept. 6, 1918.* Vol. 25, pt. 2. Washington, D.C.: n.p., 1930?–33.

——. *Field Orders, First Division, June 1, 1918 to July 21, 1918.* Vol. 2, pt. 1. Washington, D.C.: n.p., 1930?–33.

——. *Operations Reports, First Division, May 8, 1918 to Sept. 11, 1918.* Vol. 12, pt. 2. Washington, D.C.: n.p., 1930?–33.

——. *Operations Reports, 1st FA Brigade, 4th FA Regiment.* Vol. 14, pt. 1. Washington, D.C.: n.p., 1930?–33.

——. *Operations Reports, 6th and 7th FA Regiments, 1st Trench Mortar Battery, 1st Am-*

munition Train, 1st Engineer Regiment. Vol. 14, pt. 2. Washington, D.C.: n.p., 1930?–33.

——. *Field Messages, All Units, First Division*. Vol. 15, pt. 2. Washington, D.C.: n.p., 1930?–33.

——. *War Diaries, HQ First Division, 1st Infantry Brigade, 16th Inf. Regiment*. Vol. 16, pt. 1. Washington, D.C.: n.p., 1930?–1933.

——. *War Diaries, 18th Inf. Regiment*. Vol. 16, pt. 2. Washington, D.C.: n.p., 1930?–33.

——. *War Diaries, 2d Inf. Brigade, 26th Inf. Regiment*. Vol. 17, pt. 1. Washington, D.C.: n.p., 1930?–33.

——. *War Diaries, 28th Inf. Regiment*. Vol. 17, pt. 2. Washington, D.C.: n.p., 1930?–33.

——. *War Diaries, 1st FA Regiment, 5th FA Regiment*. Vol. 18, pt. 1. Washington, D.C.: n.p., 1930?–33.

——. *War Diaries, 6th and 7th FA Regiments, 1st Trench Mortar Battery, 1st MG Battalion, Miscellaneous Units*. Vol. 18, pt. 2. Washington, D.C.: n.p., 1930?–33.

Manuscript Collections

Bellamy, David. Personal Papers. U.S. Marine Corps Historical Center, Washington, D.C. (Hereafter cited as USMC Historical Center.)

Cates, Clifton. Personal Papers. USMC Historical Center.

Cullum Files. United States Military Academy, West Point, N.Y.

Denig, Robert L. Personal Papers. USMC Historical Center.

Hines, John L. Personal Papers. Manuscripts Division. Reference Department. Library of Congress, Washington, D.C.

Hillman, Rolfe L. Personal Papers. Archives, USAMHI.

Martin, Charles H. Personal Papers. Archives, USAMHI.

Pershing, John J. Personal Papers. RG 200, NA.

Stackpole, Pierpont L. Diaries while Aide-de-Camp to Hunter Liggett. George C. Marshall Library, Lexington, Va.

Summerall, Charles P. Personal Papers. Manuscripts Division. Reference Department. Library of Congress, Washington, D.C.

Thomas, Gerald C. "Personal Papers of Gerald C. Thomas, USMC." Box 6A23. USMC Historical Center.

Upton, LaRoy S. Personal Papers. Minnesota Historical Society, Saint Paul, Minn.

Articles, Monographs, Speeches, and Unpublished Manuscripts

Berdoulat, Pierre Emile. "The First and Second American Divisions In the Offensive of July [18], 1918," *The Cavalry Journal* 34 (October, 1925): pp. 407–12.

Burress, Withers A. "The Operations of the 23d Infantry in the Soissons Offensive, July 16–25, 1918," Company Officers Course 1924–25. The Infantry School, Fort Benning, Ga. USAMHI.

Butler, Alban B. "Journal of Operations, December 23, 1917 through October 12, 1918." Cantigny/First Division Museum, Wheaton, Ill.

Cooke, Elliot D. "Statement of HQ 2d Bn., 9th Infantry, Dierdorf, Germany, July 2, 1919." RG 120. AEF AG File 21510-A-26. Entry G. NA.

CGSC Monographs. Fort Leavenworth, Kans.: U.S. Army Command and General StaV College, 1928.

"C.S.B., Jr." "Conrad Stanton Babcock." *Assembly* (July, 1951): p. 49.

Ellis, Earl. "Liaison in the World War." *Marine Corps Gazette* (June, 1920): pp. 135–41.

Ely, Hanson E. "Leadership and Morale in War." Lecture to the U.S. Army War College (hereafter cited as USAWC), February 3, 1938. USAMHI.

——. "Liaison in the World War." Lecture at the USAWC, February 3, 1938. USAWC Curricular Archives, USAMHI.

Farrell, Thomas F. "Memories of the Battle of Soissons." *Military Engineer* 15, no. 83, (July–August, 1923): pp. 327–31.

Fechet, d'Alary. "Operations of the Second Battalion, Twenty-third Infantry, Second Division, U.S.A., in the Soissons Offensive." Advanced Officers Course, 1925–26. The Infantry School, Fort Benning, Ga. USAMHI.

Fiske, Harold B. "Notes on Infantry." Lecture to a Class of Provisional Second Lieutenants at U.S. Army Command and General StaV School (later College), Ft. Leavenworth, Kans., January 29, 1917.

Fleming, Thomas. "The Iron General." *MHQ* 7, no. 2, (Winter, 1994): pp. 58–73.

——. "Day of the Storm Trooper." *Military History* (August, 1992): pp. 34–41.

"George F. Rozelle." *Assembly* 24, no. 2 (Spring 1965).

Goebert, Elmer C. "Operations of the 1st Division (U.S.) in the Soissons Offensive, July 16th to 25th, 1918" in *Monographs of the World War*. Ft. Benning, Ga: The Infantry School, 1923.

Gudmestad, Tom. "God Was Good to Me That Day!" *Over There* (Winter, 1990): pp. 7–9.

Hillman, Rolfe L. "Fighters and Writers." *Marine Corps Gazette* (November, 1988): pp. 90–98.

——. "Henry Hulbert: From Samoa to Blanc Mont." *Leatherneck* 72, no. 11 (November, 1989): 32–34.

——. "Second to None: The Indianheads." *U.S. Naval Institute Proceedings* (November, 1987): pp. 57–62.

——. "Crossing the Meuse." *Marine Corps Gazette* (November,1988): pp. 68–73.

——. "Manliness, Precision, Sheer Power." *ARMY* 40, no. 5 (May, 1990): p. 57.

——. "Flaming Sword before the Portals." *Over There* (Fall, 1989): pp. 3–5.

Huebner, Clarence R. "The Operations of the 28th Infantry in the Aisne-Marne OVensive, July 17–23, 1918" in *CGSC Monographs*. Ft. Benning, Ga: The Infantry School, 1923.

Janda, Ludislav T. "M Company, 9th Infantry, Second Division South of Soissons July 18, 1918." Unpublished typescript dated November 19, 1929. USAMHI Archives.

Johnson, Douglas V. II. "A Few 'Squads-Left' and Off to France: Training the American Army in the United States for World War I." Ph.D. diss., Temple University, 1992. Order no. DA9227482.

Johnston, E. S. "A Study of the nature of the United States infantry tactics for open warfare on July 18, 1918, and of the points of diVerence as contrasted with the United States Army tactics as taught in 1914" in *CGSC Monographs*. Ft. Leavenworth, Kans.: U.S. Army Command and General StaV College, 1931. USAMHI.

Kennett, Lee. "The A.E.F. through French Eyes." *Military Review* 52, no. 11 (November, 1972): pp. 3–11.

Lamont, Robert W. "Over There: Key Battles of the 2d Infantry Division." *Marine Corps Gazette* (June, 1993): pp. 76–83.

Lanza, Conrad H. "Five Decisive Days." *Field Artillery Journal* (Jan.–Feb., 1937): pp. 37–66.

Lee, John C. H. "Service Reminiscences." Unpublished manuscript, n.d. Library, Hoover Institution on War, Revolution, and Peace, Stanford, Calif.

McClellan, Edwin N. "The Aisne-Marne Offensive." Pt. 1. *Marine Corps Gazette* (March, 1921): pp. 68–84.

——. "The Aisne-Marne Offensive." Pt. 2. *Marine Corps Gazette* (June, 1921): pp. 188–227.

McCullough, William A. "The Aisne-Marne OVensive, 18th July–4th August 1918" in *Monographs of the World War*. Ft. Benning, Ga: The Infantry School, 1923.

Millett, Allan R. "Army General Commands Marine Corps Brigade?" *Naval History* (Summer, 1988).

Mitchell, William A. "Theory and Practice with 2d Engineers." *Military Engineer* (January–February, 1926): pp. 1–5.

Monograph Soissons. USAWC Historical Section, 1920–22. A collection of monographs, extracts, messages, maps, and orders in the USAMHI Archives.

Murray, Maxwell. "Soissons." Address to the Harvard Club, April 20, 1920. *Monograph Soissons*. USAMHI.

Nenninger, Timothy K. "Tactical Dysfunction in the AEF, 1917–1918." *Military Affairs* (October, 1987): pp. 177–81.

Peake, Louis A. "West Virginia's Best Known General since 'Stonewall Jackson': John L. Hines." *West Virginia History* 38, no. 3 (April, 1977): pp. 226–35.

Paradis, Don. Manuscript PC 463, n.d. USMC Historical Center.

Pierce, Palmer E. "LaRoy Sunderland Upton." *Assembly* (June, 1927): p. 137.

Pantozzi, Vincent. "Sgt. Vincent Pantozzi, Company B, 9th Infantry Regiment, 2d (Indian Head) Division AEF, France, War Record, 1917–1919." Typescript from manuscript by Vince Pantozzi Jr., 1989.

Pigman, M. K. "Operations of the 2d Division (U.S.) in the Soissons Offensive, July 16th to 25th, 1918" in *Monographs of the World War*. Ft. Benning, Ga: The Infantry School, 1923.

Porter, J. A. "The German Supply System" in *CGSC Monographs*. Ft. Leavenworth, Kans.: U.S. Army Command and General Staff College, 1923.

Rainey, James W. "The Training of the American Expeditionary Forces in World War I." MA thesis, Temple University, 1981.

——. "Ambivalent Warfare: The Tactical Doctrine of the AEF in World War I." *Parameters* 13, no. 3 (September 1983): pp. 34–45.

——. "The Questionable Training of the AEF In World War I." Parameters (Winter, 1992–93): pp. 89–102.

Raugh, Harold E. Jr. "Combat Command on the Western Front: Perspectives of American Officers." Stand To! 18 (December, 1986): pp. 12–14.

Simmons, Edwin H. "The First Day At Soissons." *Fortudine* 23, no. 1 (Summer, 1993): pp. 3–11.

——. "The Second Day at Soissons." *Fortudine* 23, no. 2 (Fall, 1993): pp. 3–10.

——. "Marines in the Meuse-Argonne, Part I: Reaching the Meuse." Fortudine 23, no. 3 (Winter, 1993–94): pp. 3–10.

Smythe, Donald. "St. Mihiel: The Birth of the American Army." *Parameters* 13, no. 2 (June 1983): pp. 47–57.

Stokesbury, James L. "The Aisne-Marne Offensive." *American History Illustrated* (July, 1980).

Summerall, Charles P. "Notes on the First Division in the Battle of Soissons, with Reference to the Employment of Artillery." Lecture to the Field Artillery Officers's Reserve Section, April, 1920. USAMHI Archives.

———. "Notes on the First Division in the Battle of Soissons, with Special Reference to the Employment of Field Artillery." *Field Artillery Journal* 10, no. 4 (July–August, 1920): pp. 331–64.

———. "The Way of Duty, Honor, Country." Unpublished typescript memoir. Archives/Museum, The Citadel, Charleston, S.C., n.d.

Thomason, John. USAWC Monograph "Soissons." Rolfe L. Hillman Papers, Box 1, USAMHI Archives.

Travers, Tim. "The Evolution of British Strategy and Tactics on the Western Front in 1918: GHQ, Manpower, and Technology." *Journal of Military History* 54, no. 2 (April, 1990): pp. 173–200.

Waller, Lt. Gen. Calvin. USAWC Senior OYcer Interviews, "Operation DESERT SHIELD/DESERT STORM." April 22, 1991. USAMHI Oral History Archives.

Waller, L. W. T. Jr. "Machine guns of the Fourth Brigade." *Marine Corps Gazette* 1 (March, 1920): pp. 1–31.

Watson, Arthur P. "America's Greatest World War Battle Leader (Major General Hanson E. Ely)." 1933 typescript. USAMHI Archives.

Williamson, S. T. "The Night March: An Untold Story. Headlong Audacity Took the Ninth Infantry, Under Cover of Darkness, Five Miles Within the German Lines." *The New York Times Magazine,* November 4, 1928.

Books

American Battle Monuments Commission. *American Armies and Battlefields in Europe: A History, Guide, and Reference Book.* Washington, D.C.: GPO, 1938.

———. *1st Division Summary of Operations in the World War.* Washington, D.C.: GPO, 1944.

———. *2d Division Summary of Operations in the World War.* Washington, D.C.: GPO, 1944.

———. *Terrain Photographs, 1st Division.* Vol. 3, *Aisne-Marne.* Washington, D.C.: GPO, 1923.

———. *Terrain Photographs, 2d Division.* Vol. 2, *Aisne-Marne.* Washington, D.C.: GPO, 1923.

Asprey, Robert B. *At Belleau Wood.* New York: G. P. Putnam's Sons, 1965.

———. *The German High Command at War: Hindenburg and Ludendorff Conduct World War I.* New York: William Morrow and Company, Inc., 1991.

Balesi, Charles John. *From Adversaries to Comrades in Arms: West Africans and the French Military, 1885–1918.* n.p.: Crossroads, 1979.

Berry, Henry. *Make the Kaiser Dance.* Garden City, N.Y.: Doubleday, 1978.

Blumenson, Martin, and James L. Stokesbury. *Masters of the Art of Command.* Boston: Houghton-Mifflin, 1975.

Boyd, Thomas. *Through the Wheat.* New York: Charles Scribner's Sons, 1923.

Braim, Paul. *The Test of Battle: The American Expeditionary Forces in the Meuse-Argonne Campaign.* Newark: University of Delaware Press, 1987.

Brooks, Alden. *As I Saw It.* New York: Knopf, 1930.

Brown, John Sloane. *Draftee Division.* Lexington: University Press of Kentucky, 1986.

Buck, Beaumont B. *Memories of Peace and War.* San Antonio: Naylor, 1935.

Bugnet, Charles. *Mangin.* Paris: Libraire Plon, 1934.

———. *Foch Speaks.* Translated by Russell Green. New York: Dial, 1929.

Bullard, Robert L. *Personalities and Reminiscences of the War.* Garden City: Doubleday, Page, 1925.

———. *American Soldiers also Fought.* New York: Longmans, Green, 1936.

———. *Fighting Generals: Illustrated Biographical Sketches of Seven Major Generals in World War I.* Ann Arbor, Mich.: J. W. Edwards, 1944.

Butler, Alban B., Jr. *Happy Days.* New York: Coward-McCann, 1928.

Center for Military History, United States Army. *Order of Battle of the United States Land Forces in the World War, American Expeditionary Forces: Divisions.* Vol. 2. Washington, D.C.: GPO, 1988.

Chastaine, Benjamin H. *History of the U.S. Eighteenth Infantry, First Division, 1812–1919.* New York: Hymans Company, 1920.

Clayton, Anthony. *France, Soldiers, and Africa.* London: Brassey's, 1988.

Clausewitz, Carl von. *On War.* Edited and translated by Michael Howard and Peter Paret. Princeton, N.J.: Princeton University Press, 1976.

Coddington, Edwin B. *The Gettysburg Campaign: A Study in Command.* New York: Charles Scribner's Sons, 1984.

Coffman, Edward M. *The Hilt of the Sword: The Career of Peyton C. March.* Madison: The University of Wisconsin Press, 1966.

———. *The War to End All Wars: The American Military Experience in World War I.* Madison: The University of Wisconsin Press, 1968.

———. "American Command and Commanders in World War I" in *New Dimensions in Military History: An Anthology.* Edited by Russell F. Weigley. San Rafael, Calif.: Presidio, 1975.

Delbruck, Hans. "The Swiss," in *History of the Art of War.* Vol. 3, *Medieval Warfare.* Translated by Walter J. Renfroe, Jr. Originally Geschichte Der Kriegskunst Im Rahmen Der Politischen Geschichte. Lincoln, Nebr.: University of Nebraska Press, 1985.

Eimannsberger, Ludwig Ritter von. *Mechanized Warfare.* Translated by USAWC. Munich: J. F. Lehmanns, 1934.

English, George H. Jr. *History of the 89th Division, USA.* Denver: Smith-Brooks, 1920.

Ferro, Marc. *The Great War 1914–1918.* Translated by Nicole Stone. Boston: Routledge and Kegan Paul, 1973.

Foch, Ferdinand. *The Memoirs of Marshal Foch.* Translated by T. Bentley Mott. Garden City, N.Y.: Doubleday, Doran, 1931.

Fuller, John Frederick Charles. *Generalship: Its Diseases and Their Cure—A Study of the Personal Factor in Command.* Harrisburg, Pa.: Military Service Publishing Company, 1936; Ft. Leavenworth: Command and General Staff College, 1984.

———. *Tanks in the Great War, 1914–1918.* London: John Murray, 1920.

Ganoe, William A. *The History of the United States Army.* New York: D. Appleton–Century, 1943.

General Cullum's Biographical Register of the Officers and Graduates of the United States Military Academy, vol. 7, *Supplement 1920–1930.* Saginaw, Mich.: Seeman and Peters, 1930.

Gazin, F. *La Cavalerie Français dans la Guerre Mondiale, 1914–1918.* Paris: Payot, 1930.

Geraghty, Tony. *March or Die: A History of the French Foreign Legion.* New York: Facts on File, 1986.

German Reichsarchives. *Schlachten des Weltkrieges: Band 35, Schicksalswende, von der Marne bis zur Vesle, 1918.* Oldenburg i.D./Berlin: Gerhard Stalling, 1930.

Gibbons, Floyd. *And They Thought We Wouldn't Fight.* New York: Doran, 1918.

Goode, James M. *The Outdoor Sculpture of Washington, D.C.* Washington, D.C.: Smithsonian Institution, 1974.

Graves, Robert *Goodbye to All That: An Autobiography.* Cassell, 1929. Reprint, London: Penguin, 1960.

Griffin, Gary B. *The Directed Telescope: A Traditional Element of Effective Command.* Fort Leavenworth, Kans.: Combat Studies Institute, 1991.

Griffith, Paddy. *Battle Tactics of the Western Front: The British Army's Art of Attack, 1916–1918.* New Haven: Yale University Press, 1994.

———, ed. *British Fighting Methods in the Great War.* London: Frank Cass, 1996.

Griffiths, Richard M. *Pétain: A Biography of Marshal Philippe Pétain of Vichy.* Garden City, N.Y.: Doubleday, 1972.

Hamberger, Kenneth E. *Learning Lessons in the American Expeditionary Forces.* Center of Military History Publication 24-1. Washington, D.C.: Center of Military History, 1997.

Harbord, James G. *Leaves from a War Diary.* New York: Dodd, Mead, 1925.

———. *The American Expeditionary Forces, Its Organization and Accomplishments.* Evanston, Ill.: Evanston, 1929.

———. *The American Army in France, 1917–1919.* Boston: Little, Brown, 1936.

Harrison, Barbara G. *Italian Days.* Boston: Houghton-Mifflin, 1975, 1989.

Heller, Charles E., and William A. Stofft, eds. *America's First Battles, 1776–1965.* Modern War Studies. Lawrence, Kans.: University Press of Kansas, 1986.

Hindenburg, Paul von. *Out of My Life.* New York: Harper and Brothers, ca. 1921.

Holley, Irving B., Jr. *General John M. Palmer, Citizen, Soldiers, and the Army of a Democracy.* Contributions in Military History, no. 28. Westport, Conn.: Greenwood Press, 1982.

Holmes, Richard. *The World Atlas of Warfare: Military Innovations that Changed the Course of History.* New York: Viking Studio Books, 1988.

Horne, Charles F., and Walter F. Austin, eds. *The Great Events of the Great War.* 7 vols. n.p.: National Alumni, 1923.

Horne, Alistair. *The Price of Glory: Verdun, 1916.* New York: St. Martin's, 1962.

Hudson, James T. *Hostile Skies: A Combat History of the American Air Service.* Syracuse, N.Y.: Syracuse University Press, 1968.

Hure, R., ed. *L'Armée d'Afrique, 1830–1916.* Paris: Henri Charles-Lavauzelle, 1920.

Infantry in Battle. Washington, D.C.: The Infantry School Press, 1934.

Johnson, Thomas Marvin. *Without Censor: New Light on Our Greatest World War Battles.* Indianapolis: Bobbs-Merrill, 1928.

Johnson, Hubert C. *Breakthrough!: Tactics, Technology, and the Search for Victory on the Western Front in World War I.* Novato, Calif.: Presidio, 1994.

Jones, Ralph E.; George H. Rarey; and Robert J. Icks. *The Fighting Tanks since 1916.* Washington, D.C.: National Service, 1933.

———. *The Fighting Tanks from 1916 to 1933.* Old Greenwich, Conn.: We, 1969.

Jones, William K. *A Brief History of the 6th Marines.* Washington, D.C.: History and Museums Division, Headquarters, U.S. Marine Corps, 1987.

Junger, Ernst. *The Storm of Steel*. London: Chatto and Windus, 1929.

Laffitte, R. *The French Tank Corps from 1916 to 1918*. Translated by F. G. Dumont. Paris: Henri Charles-Lavauzelle, 1921. Reprint, Fort Benning, Ga.: The Infantry School, 1936.

Lejeune, John A. *The Reminiscences of a Marine*. Philadelphia: Dorrance and Company, 1930.

Lerwill, Leonard L. *The Personnel Replacement System in the United States Army*. CMH Pam 104–9. Facsimile Edition of 1954 DA Pam 20–211. Washington, D.C.: GPO, 1988.

Liddell Hart, Basil H. *Reputations Ten Years After*. Boston: Little, Brown, 1928.

Linderman, Gerald F. *The World Within War: America's Combat Experience in World War II*. New York: Free Press, 1997.

Lorighoven, Freytag von. *The Power of Personality in War*. Harrisburg: Military Service, 1955.

Love, Albert G. *The Medical Department of the United States Army in the World War*. Vol. 15, *Statistics,* pt. 2, *Medical and Casualty Statistics*. Washington, D.C.: GPO, 1925.

Ludendorff, Erich F. W. *Ludendorff's Own Story, August 1914–November 1918: The Great War from the Siege of Liege to the Signing of the Armistice as Viewed from the Grand Headquarters of the German Army*. 2 vols. New York: Harper, 1919.

Lupfer, Timothy T. *The Dynamics of Doctrine: The Changes in German Tactical Doctrine during the First world War*. Leavenworth Paper no. 4. Ft. Leavenworth, Kans.: U.S. Army Command and General Staff College, 1981.

Mackin, Elton. *Suddenly We Didn't Want to Die: Memoirs of a World War I Marine*. Novato, Calif.: Presidio, 1993.

MacNider, Hanford. *The A.E.F. of a Conscientious Subaltern*. Mason City, Iowa: KLIPTO, n.d.

McCain, James H. "The Taking of Montfaucon." In *Americans vs. Germans: Individual Battle Experiences*. New York: Penguin Books, 1942.

McClellan, Edwin N. *The United States Marine Corps in the World War*. Washington, D.C.: Historical Branch, G-3 Division, Headquarters, U.S. Marine Corps, 1920. Facsimile reprint, 1968.

McCormick, Robert R. *The Army of 1918*. New York: Harcourt, Brace, and Howe, 1920.

McDonnald, Muckleroy. *A Charmed Life: An Enlisted Man's Experience in World War I*. San Antonio: M. McDonnald, 1975.

McEntee, Girard L. *Military History of the World War*. New York: Charles Scribner's Sons, 1943.

Mahon, John K. *History of the Militia and the National Guard*. The Macmillan War of the United States. Edited by Louis Morton. New York: Macmillan, 1983.

Mangin, Charles Marie Emmanuel. *Comment Finit la Guerre*. Paris: Plon-Nourrit, 1920. Reprinted as *How the War Ended*. Fort Leavenworth, Kans.: General Service Schools, 1924.

——. *Lettres de Guerre, 1914–1918*. Paris: Libraire Artheme Fayard, 1950. Reprint edition.

March, Peyton C. *The Nation at War*. Garden City, N.Y.: Doubleday, Doran, 1932.

March, William. *Company K*. 1933. Reprint, New York: Arbor House, 1984.

Messenger, Charles. *The Blitzkrieg Story* New York: Charles Scribner's Sons, 1976.

Michel, Marc. *L'Appel a l'Afrique: Contributions et reactiones a l'effort de guerre en A.O.F., 1914–1919*. Paris: Publications de la Sorbonne, 1982.

Middlebrook, Martin. *First Day on the Somme: 1 July 1916*. London: Penguin, 1978.
Millett, Allan R. *The General: Robert Lee Bullard and Officership in the United States Army, 1881–1925*. Contributions in Military History, no. 10. Westport, Conn.: Greenwood, 1975.

——. *Semper Fidelis: The History of the United States Marine Corps*. New York: Free Press, 1980.

——. *In Many a Strife: General Gerald C. Thomas and the U.S. Marine Corps, 1917–1956*. Annapolis, Md.: Naval Institute, 1993.

——. "Hanson Edward Ely" in *Dictionary of American Biography, Supplement Six, 1956–1960*. Edited by Tony A. Garraty. New York: Scribner's Sons, 1980.

——. "Cantigny" in *America's First Battles, 1776–1965*. Edited by William A. Stofft and Charles E. Heller. Lawrence: University Press of Kansas, 1986.

——, and Peter Maslowski. *For the Common Defense: A Military History of the United States of America*. New York: Free Press, 1984, 1994.

——, and Williamson Murray, eds. *Military Effectiveness*. Vol. 1, *The First World War*. Boston: Allen and Unwin, 1988.

Ministere de La Guerre. *Les Armées Français dans la Grande Guerre*. Tome VII, La Campagne Offensive de 1918 et la Marche au Rhin, 18 Juillet 1918–28 Juin 1919, pt. 1, 18 Juillet 1918–25 Septembre 1918. Paris: Imprimerie Nationale, 1938.

Mitchell, William. *Memoirs of World War I: From Start to Finish of Our Greatest War*. New York: Random House, 1928.

Mitchell, William A. *The Official History of the Second Engineers in the World War*. San Antonio: San Antonio, 1920.

Nelson, Keith. *Victors Divided: America and the Allies in Germany, 1918–1923*. Berkeley: University of California Press, 1975.

Ney, Virgil. *The Evolution of Military Unit Control, 500BC–1985AD*. Combat Operations Research Group Memorandum 217. Washington, D.C.: Combat Operations Research Group Technical Operations, 1965.

Ogorkiewicz, Richard M. *Armor: A History of Mechanized Forces*. New York: Frederick A. Praeger, 1960.

Otto, Ernst. *The Battle at Blanc Mont*. Annapolis, Md.: Naval Institute, 1930.

Page, Arthur W. *Our 110 Days' Fighting*. Garden City, N.Y.: Doubleday, Page, 1920.

Pagonis, William G. *Moving Mountains: Lessons of Leadership and Logistics from the Gulf War*. Cambridge, Mass.: Harvard University Press, 1992.

Palmer, Frederick. *America in France*. Westport, Conn.: Greenwood, 1975.

Paschall, Rod. *The Defeat of Imperial Germany, 1917–1918*. Major Battles and Campaigns, ed. John S. D. Eisenhower. Chapel Hill, N.C.: Algonquin, 1989.

Patch, Joseph Dorst. *A Soldier's War: The First Division, A.E.F., 1917–1919*. Corpus Christi, Tex.: Mission, 1966.

Pershing, John J. *My Experiences in the World War*. 2 vols. New York: Frederick A. Stokes, 1931.

Pitt, Barrie. *1918: The Last Act*. New York: Ballentine, 1963.

Porch, Douglas. *The March to the Rhine: The French Army, 1871–1914*. Cambridge, England: Cambridge University Press, 1981.

Pratt, Fletcher. *Eleven Generals: Studies in American Command*. New York: William Sloane, 1949.

——. "The French Army in the First World War" in *Military Effectiveness*. Vol. 1, *The First World War*. Edited by Allan R. Millett and Williamson Murray. Boston: Allen and Unwin, 1988.

Prior, Robin, and Trevor Wilson. *Passchendaele: The Untold Story*. New Haven: Yale University Press, 1996.

Regimental Adjutant. *The Story of the Twenty-sixth Infantry in France*. Montabaur-Frankfurt, Germany: Martin Flock, 1919.

Regimental Chaplain. *The Story of the Twenty-sixth Infantry in France*. Montabaur-Frankfurt, Germany: Martin Flock, 1919.

Ritter, Gerhard. *The Schlieffen Plan: Critique of a Myth*. London: Oswald Wolff (Publishers) Limited, 1958.

Robertson, Don. *Prisoners of Twilight*. New York: Crown, 1989.

Rockwell, Paul Ayers. *American Fighters in the Foreign Legion, 1914–1918*. Boston: Houghton-Mifflin, 1930.

Roosevelt, Mrs. Theodore. *Day before Yesterday*. Garden City, N.Y.: Doubleday, 1959.

Roosevelt, Theodore, Jr. *Average Americans*. New York: G. P. Putnam's Sons, 1919.

Samuels, Martin. *Command or Control? Command, Training and Tactics in the British and German Armies, 1888–1918*. London: Frank Cass, 1995.

Scanlon, William T. *God Have Mercy on Us!* Boston: Houghton-Mifflin, 1929.

Second Division Historical Section. *Translations, War Diaries of German Units Opposed to the Second Division (Regular), 1918*. Vol. 5, pts. 1, 2, and 3, *Soissons*. Washington, D.C.: 2d Division Historical Section, USAWC, 1933.

Shay, Jonathan. *Achilles in Vietnam: Combat Trauma and the Undoing of Character*. New York: Touchstone, 1994.

Short, Walter Campbell. *The Employment of Machine Guns*. Washington, D.C.: U.S. Infantry Association, 1922.

Showalter, Dennis. *Tannenberg: Clash of Empires*. Hamden, Conn.: The Shoestring Press, Inc., 1991.

Smith, John. *Leadership in Battle, 1914–1918*. New York: Hippocrene, 1967.

Smythe, Donald. *Pershing: General of the Armies*. Bloomington: Indiana University Press, 1986.

Spaulding, Oliver L., and John W. Wright. *The Second Division, American Expeditionary Forces in France, 1917–1919*. New York: Hillman, 1937. Reprint, Nashville: Battery, 1990.

Spiller, Roger J., ed. *Dictionary of American Military Biography*. Westport, Conn.: Greenwood Press, 1984.

Society of the First Division, AEF. *History of the First Division A.E.F. during the World War, 1917–1919*. Philadelphia: John C. Winston, 1922.

Spears, Edmund L. *Prelude to Victory*. London: Jonathan Cape, 1939.

Stallings, Laurence. *The Doughboys: The Story of the AEF, 1917–1918*. New York: Harper and Row, 1963.

Sulzbach, Herbert. *With the German Guns: Four Years on the Western Front, 1914–1918*. Translated by Richard Thonger. London: Leo Conger, Ltd., 1973; London: Fredrick Warne Publishers, Ltd., 1981.

The Thirty-Fifth Division, 1917–1918. Washington, D.C.: The Army War College, 1921–22. U.S. Army War College Historical Section, USAMHI.

Thomas, Shipley. *The History of the A.E.F.* New York: George H. Moran, 1920.

———. *S-2 in Action*. Harrisburg: Military, 1940.

Thomason, John W. Jr. *Fix Bayonets!* New York: Charles Scribner's Sons, 1926.

———. *—And a Few Marines*. New York: Charles Scribner's Sons, 1943.

———. *Combat: World War I*. Edited by Don Congdon. New York: Dell, 1964.

Trask, David F. *The AEF and Coalition Warmaking, 1917–1918*. Modern War Studies, ed. Theodore A. Wilson. Lawrence: University Press of Kansas, 1993.

Travers, Tim. *The Killing Ground: The British Army, The Western Front, and the Emergence of Modern Warfare, 1900–1918.* London: Unwin Hyman, 1987.

United States Army in the World War, 1917–1919. 17 vols. Washington, D.C.: Center of Military History, 1948. Reprint, Washington, D.C.: GPO, 1988.U.S. War Department General Staff. *Two Hundred and Fifty-one Divisions of the German Army which Participated in the War 1914–1918.* Washington, D.C.: GPO, 1920.

U.S. Department of the Army. *The Medal of Honor of the United States Army.* Washington, D.C.: GPO, 1948.

U.S. War Department Document No. 394, *Infantry Drill Regulations, United States Army, 1911.* Washington, D.C.: GPO, 1911.

——. *Infantry Drill Regulations, (Provisional), 1919.* Washington, D.C.: GPO, 1919.

——. *Decorations, United States Army: 1862–1926.* Washington, D.C.: GPO, n.d.

Venzon, Anne Cipriano, ed. *The United States in the First World War: An Encyclopedia.* Military History of the United States, vol. 3; Garland Reference Libraries of the Humanities, vol. 1205. New York: Garland Pub., 1995.

Viereck, George Sylvester, ed. *As They Saw Us: Foch, Ludendorff, and Other Leaders Write Our War History.* Garden City, N.Y.: Doubleday, Doran, 1927.

War Department Directive No. 475: *Field Service Regulations United States Army 1914,* March 19, 1914, Corrected to July 31, 1918. (Changes 1 to 11). Washington: GPO, 1918.

Weigley, Russell Frank. *History of the United States Army.* The Macmillan War of the United States. Edited by Louis Morton. New York: Macmillan, 1967.

Weintraub, Stanley. *A Stillness Heard Round the World.* New York: Dutton, 1985.

Westover, Wendell. *Suicide Battalions.* New York: G. P. Putnam's Sons, 1929.

Wilson, Dale E. *Treat 'Em Rough!: The Birth of American Armor, 1917–20.* Novato, Calif.: Presidio, 1989.

Winter, J. M. *The Experience of World War I.* New York: Oxford University Press, 1989.

Wise, Frederick M. *A Marine Tells It to You.* New York: J. H. Sears, 1929.

Wise, Jennings C. *The Turn of the Tide: American Operations at Cantigny, Chateau Thierry, and the Second Battle of the Marne.* New York: Henry Holt, 1920.

Yingling, James M. *A Brief History of the 5th Marines.* Washington, D.C.: Historical Branch, G-3 Division, Headquarters, U.S. Marine Corps, 1963, 1968.

Young, Hugh H. *Hugh Young: Surgeon's Biography.* New York: Harcourt, Brace, 1940.

Zabecki, David T. *Steel Wind: Colonel Georg Bruchmueller and the Birth of Modern Artillery.* The Military Profession, ed. Bruce Gudmudson. Westport, Conn.: Praeger, 1994.

Zwehl, Hans von. *Die Schlachten im Sommer 1918 an der Westfront. [The Battles of the Summer of 1918 on the Western Front.]* Berlin: E. S. Mittler and Sons, 1921. Typescript translation by Headquarters, American Forces in Germany, Intelligence Section, General Staff. USAMHI.

Index

Note: Maps are indicated in italic.

France, 3; late-war strategy of, 7; and Mangin deception, 17, 85; Ninth Army, 15, 64; 111th Infantry Regiment, 9; 115th Division, 16, 75; orders of battle for, 159–60; Soissons' importance to, 10; spring 1918 offensive summary, 7–9; submarine campaign, 6; surrender at Vauxcastille, 82; 3rd Division, 75; XIII Corps, 17, 50; views of day one actions, 91; withdrawal of, 128. *See also* defense, German

Gettysburg, Battle of, 81–82

Glaux Farm, 53

Group of Armies of the Center, 11

Group of Armies of the Reserve, 10–11

guns to the rear technique, 17

Haig, Field Marshal Sir Douglas, 6, 29, 30

Hamburger, Kenneth, 151

Harbord, Maj. Gen. James Guthrie: assessment of, 156, 186*n* 19; assignment to 2nd Division, 58–59; and command and control glitches, 76–78; on first day's action, 85; on makeshift medical facility, 84; Pershing's view of, 122; on promotion passover, 67; request for division relief, 112–13; on troop dislocations, 69

Hemingway, Ernest, 4

Hendricks, Capt. Pierre H., 131–32

heroism, 31, 46–47

Hindenburg, Field Marshal Paul von, 144

Hines, Brig. Gen. Leonard, 51, 101

Holbrook, Col. L. R., 152

Holcomb, Maj. Thomas, 105

horror of war: casualties, 66–67, 72, 99, 106–107, 108–109, 111, 120; makeshift medical facilities, 84; and need for leadership, xv

housing for soldiers, 27

Huebner, Maj. Clarence, 46–47, 49, 97, 101

Hughes, Maj. John A., 105

infantry: AEF structure for, 26–27, 111–12; procedures of attack for, 30–31; U.S. doctrine/tactics, 22, 23, 28–30, 150. *See also specific units*

Infantry Drill Regulations, 23, 28, 29

Infantry in Battle (Marshall), 150

infiltration tactics, 7

infrastructure issues, U.S. Army adjustment to large-scale conflict, 27–28

intelligence issues, 5, 14, 15, 17–18

Iraq, 4

Italy, 4

Jacques, Elliot, xv

Janda, Lt. Ludislav, 69–71, 79–80, 84–85

Johnson, Doug, 150

Joint Readiness and National Training Centers, 151

Keyser, Maj. Ralph S., 63, 82

King, Col. Campbell, 92, 121

Kocak, Sgt. Matej, 66

Lauer, Sgt. Andy, 69

leadership: Allied commitment to single commander, 7; Buck's handling of, 100–101, 102, 117–20, 130–35, 139, 185*n* 6; burden of offense for, 20; character of, 73; critique of, 155; Ely on, 138–39; flaws in French, 5–6; and German wishful thinking, 14; inexperience of American, xvi, 104, 144–57; initiative among American officers, 94–95; lessons learned, 151; management of U.S. forces, xv, 25–28; Pershing's philosophy, 138, 151; pre-WWI failures of, 3–4; promotion list irregularities, 67–68; Rozelle's actions for 28th Infantry, 97–98; 2nd Brigade (1st Div), 44, 45–46, 117–27; 2nd Infantry Division (AEF), 58–59; and straggler problem, 72; Summerall's handling of, 41–42, 122–27, 139–40, 155–57; Upton's failure of, 106; and U.S.

leadership (*cont.*)
   training in France, 22–23. *See also*
      officers
Leavenworth education, 28
Lee, Lt. Col. Harry, 103–104, 109
Lenin, Vladimir, 6
Leonard, Lt. Melvin, 68
lessons learned from Soissons, 143–57
Lewis, Brig. Gen. Edward M., 67
liaison capabilities and limitations, 40,
   59, 74, 84, 103–104
Liggett, Maj. Gen. Hunter, 113
Linderman, Gerald F., 156
lines of communication, 10, 12–13, 40,
   42, 103. *See also* communication,
   battlefield
logistics: disconnection with supply
   lines, 8–9, 60–61, 155; German
   difficulties, 86; inadequacy of U.S.,
   22, 24–25, 32, 73, 78; plans for attacking German, 12; tank delays, 68;
   traffic congestion problems, 42, 78,
   88–89
Lorighoven, Gen. Freytag von, 156
Ludendorff, Quartermaster General
   Erich, 10, 86, 128

machine guns: attack employment of,
   95–96; effectiveness from entrenched
   positions, 50; tactical challenge of,
   20, 85, 95; and tanks, 45, 80, 106
Mackensen, Gen. August von, 5
MacNider, Capt. Hanford, 72–73
Maison Neuve Farm, 64, 68
Make the Kaiser Dance (Berry), 124
Malone, Col. Paul B., 67–68, 73, 74–75,
   83, 84
management, battle: and AEF's plans
   for unit structure, 111–12; and dislocation of troops, 69; initial day lack
   of, 71; and misuse of 6th Marines,
   107–108; piecemeal commitment of
   troops, 65, 74, 107. *See also* command
   and control

management, military: U.S. Army, 25–
   28; War Department ineptitude, 21
Mangin, Gen. Charles M. E.: anticipa-
   tion of relief request, 114; commendation for Americans, 144; focusing
   of I Corps efforts, 50; insistence on
   Berzy capture, 121; on Moroccan
   Division, 53; and Nivelle offensive,
   5–6; plan of action, 15; and ravine
   problem, 13; role in Tenth Army's
   counterattack, 11; surprise plans, 16–
   18, 42, 75–76
manning issues, U.S. Army, 23–24
March, Peyton C., 19
Marine Brigade. *See* 5th Marine Regiment (2nd Div); 6th Marine Regiment (2nd Div)
marksmanship, 29
Marshall, Col. George C., 150
massive firepower, 5, 29–30
medical support, 67, 84–85, 109
messengers (runners), 49, 75
Meuse-Argonne campaign, 30, 96
Mexico, American punitive expedition
   to, xvi
Middlebrook, Martin, 150
Missy-aux-Bois, 46
Missy Ravine: day one attack, 40, 44,
   46–47, 50–51, 75; day two actions,
   89–90
Mitchell, Brig. Gen. William "Billy," 71,
   153
M1903 Springfield rifle, 22, 24
Mont d'Arly, 46
morale: during assault, 31; battle fa-
   tigue, 62, 82, 85, 87; and forward
   placement of officers, 100; and
   French preliminary counterattacks,
   16
Moroccan Division. *See* 1st Moroccan
   Division (French)
Morrison, Maj. Gen., 153
Murray, Lt. Col. Maxwell, 93, 121, 152
musketry, 29

National Army divisions, 21
National Guard, vs. Regular Army, 20–21
NCOs (non-commissioned officers), as on-the-job trainers, 22
Neville, Brig. Gen. Wendell C., 60, 62, 83
1902 model 3-inch field gun, 24
Ninth Army (German), 15, 64
9th Infantry Division (German), 14, 57
9th Infantry Regiment (2nd Div), 67, 68–73, 80–82, 83
Nivelle, Gen. Robert, 5–6
non-commissioned officers (NCOs), as on-the-job trainers, 22

objectives: final reaching of, 136; mismatched, 52; reorganizing on, 31; status of, 83–84, 90, 115
offense, perceived strength of aggressive, 20–21, 143
offensive: and disorganization during attack, 30–31; vulnerability of shoulders in, 10. *See also* attack
officers: autonomy of senior, 28–29; casualties among, 30–31, 47, 52, 68, 73, 81, 85, 97; education of, 25–26, 28; European training of American, 27; inability to survey battlefield, 63, 64; stress on, 125–26; as training program leaders, 22–23. *See also* forward vs. rearward location of officers; leadership
111th Infantry Regiment (German), 9
115th Division (German), 16, 75
153rd Infantry Division (French), 13–14, 49–50, 75, 91, 94
106th Infantry Division (U.S.), 23
110th Grenadier Infantry (German), 54–55
on-the-job training, as standard for pre-WWI U.S. Army, 22
open warfare: and machine gun use in attack, 95–96; need for balance with position warfare, 153–54; Pershing's doctrine of, 31–32; Soissons as set up for, 39, 85; vs. trench warfare, 145–46
orders of battle: American, 161–62; German, 159–60; initial attack formations, *43, 53, 63*

Palestine, 4
Paradis, Sgt. Don, 106
Paris-Soissons Road, 55–56, 93–94, 95, 100
Parker, Brig. Gen. Frank, 125, 126
Parker, 2nd Lt. Samuel I., 97, 99
Passchendaele campaign, 6, 30
Patch, Maj. Joseph Dorst, 52, 124, 140
Pearce, Lt. Percy R., 118, 131–32
Pershing, Gen. John J.: flexibility of, 148; and Harbord, 58; infrastructure for AEF, 26; insistence on Berzy capture, 121; leadership philosophy, 138, 151; on location of officers in battle, 79; loss of initiative and maneuver in Europe, 31; on musketry, 29; myopic view of European war, 145–46; on National Guard unreadiness, 21; training plan of, 22
personnel issues, U.S. Army, 23–24
Pétain, Gen. Henri Philippe, 5–6, 16–17, 29–30, 49, 89
Philippine Insurrection, xvi, 20
piecemeal commitment of troops, 65, 74, 107
pistols, 22
planning, allied attack, 10–18, 37–40, 42, 103–105
Ploisy, 99
Ploisy Ravine, 40, 93
poilus, 6, 16–17, 29–30
position warfare. *See* trench warfare
post of command (PC), and command and control, 35
Power of Personality in War, The, (Lorighoven), 156
prisoners of war, 48, 130

Taylor, Capt. John L., 68

tear gas, 70

Tenth Army (French), 11–12, 16–18, 39. *See also* French Army

terrain: and attack planning, 40–41; Berzy-le-Sec area, 116–17; caves and quarries, 47–48; effect on troop movements, 51; ravine obstacles, 12–14, 40, 46–47, 93; for 6th Marines on day two, 105; Soissons area, 12–14; and tank deployment, 15

III Corps, 11

3rd Battalion (9th Infantry), 69–70

3rd Battalion (28th Infantry), 47, 94

3rd Battalion (6th Marines), 105

3rd Brigade (2nd Div): 9th Infantry Regiment, 67, 68–73, 80–82, 83; 23rd Infantry Regiment, 61–62, 67–68, 73–75, 82–87

3rd Division (German), 75

XIII Royal Wurtemburg Army Corps, 17, 50

38th Division (French), 15, 83, 103

Thomason, 2nd Lt. John W., Jr., 64, 66, 81

Tigny, 103, 109

training: of Americans in France, 22–23, 27, 37; casualty cost of inadequate, 95; and lack of machine gun use in attack, 96; lack of U.S., 7, 28–29; lessons learned, 140–41, 143–57; losses due to replacement system, 23–24; staff, 33, 35; U.S. Army, 19–23, 37

trench warfare, 30–32, 50, 145–46

Turkey, 4

Turrill, Maj. Julius S., 63, 83

20th Division (German), 102

XX Corps (French): 58th Colonial Division, 114, 126, 136; geographical position of, 13–14; plan for Allied counterattack, 12, 37–40; 69th Division, 119, 129; tanks in, 10. *See also* 1st Infantry Division (AEF); 1st Moroccan Division (French); 2nd Infantry Division (AEF)

28th Infantry Regiment (1st Div): Babcock-Summerall flap, 96–97; Berzy-le-Sec capture, 130, 131–33, 137; day three initial position, 115; day two actions, 91, 94–95; effects of artillery lack of support, 148; initial attack actions, 42, 44–50, 55–56

26th Infantry Regiment (1st Div): Berzy-le-Sec capture, 120, 124, 130, 135; day three initial position, 115; day two actions, 99, 100; initial attack actions, 42, 44, 50–51; relief of, 137–38; stagnation after initial assault, 56

23rd Infantry Regiment (2nd Div), 61–62, 67–68, 73–75, 82–87

uniforms, American lack of, 24–25

Upton, Col. LaRoy, 67, 68, 71–72, 80–82, 106, 176*n* 22

U.S. Army: amateur status of, xvi, 6–7, 104; command and control, 32–35; doctrine and tactics of, 22, 23, 28–32, 150–51, 153–54; equipping of, 24–25, 32, 73; lack of preparation for European warfare, 35–36; management of, xv, 25–28, 78; manning of, 23–24; 106th Division, 23; reluctance to learn from past, 24; training of, 19–23, 27, 37. *See also* American Expeditionary Forces (AEF)

Vauxbuin Position, 50, 93, 99

Vauxcastille, 65, 73, 82

Verdun, Battle of, 5

Verte Feuille Farm, 68

Vierzy, 82–83, 84, 109, 111

Vierzy Ravine, 40, 66–67, 69, 70, 75

Vietnamese people, as truck drivers, 60–61, 65–66

Villemontoire, 102

Viller-Cotterêts forest, 9